CW01151385

LIBRARY OF NEW TESTAMENT STUDIES
479

Formerly Journal for the Study of the New Testament Supplement Series

Editor
Mark Goodacre

Editorial Board
John M. G. Barclay, Craig Blomberg,
R. Alan Culpepper, James D. G. Dunn, Craig A. Evans, Stephen Fowl,
Robert Fowler, Simon J. Gathercole, John S. Kloppenborg, Michael Labahn,
Robert Wall, Steve Walton, Robert L. Webb, Catrin H. Williams

PLAYING THE TEXTS
13

Series Editor
George Aichele, Adrian College, Michigan

JESSE'S LINEAGE

The Legendary Lives of David, Jesus and Jesse James

Robert Paul Seesengood

and

Jennifer L. Koosed

BLOOMSBURY
NEW YORK · LONDON · NEW DELHI · SYDNEY

Bloomsbury T&T Clark
An imprint of Bloomsbury Publishing Plc

175 Fifth Avenue	50 Bedford Square
New York	London
NY 10010	WC1B 3DP
USA	UK

www.bloomsbury.com

First published 2013

© Robert Paul Seesengood and Jennifer L. Koosed, 2013

All rights reserved. No part of this publication may be reproduced or transmitted in any form or by any means, electronic or mechanical, including photocopying, recording, or any information storage or retrieval system, without prior permission in writing from the publishers.

No responsibility for loss caused to any individual or organization acting on or refraining from action as a result of the material in this publication can be accepted by Bloomsbury Academic or the authors.

Library of Congress Cataloging-in-Publication Data
A catalog record for this book is available from the Library of Congress.

ISBN: HB: 978-0-567-02094-9

Typeset by Forthcoming Publications Ltd (www.forthpub.com)
Printed and bound in the United States of America

And in that day there shall be a root of Jesse, which shall stand as an ensign of the people; the nations shall seek him out, and his end shall be glorious.

—Isaiah 11:10

Contents

Acknowledgments ix

INTRODUCTION: 1318 LAFAYETTE
AND OTHER PILGRIMAGE SITES 1
   The Plan of This Work 9

Chapter 1
BANDITS, MARTYRS AND MESSIAHS 13
   What Has Kansas City to Do with Jerusalem? 13
   Cultural Studies and Biblical Studies 16
   Bandit-ridden Frontiers of Judea, the Galilee and Missouri:
      The Wild, Wild South, North and West 21
   Social Banditry, Martyrs, Messiahs and the History of Memory 29
   Bandits, Messiahs and Martyrs 39

Chapter 2
DAVID, THE BANDIT 42
   King of the Wild Frontier 42
   David Goes West 53
   Land and Character 59

Chapter 3
CROSSING OUTLAWS: THE LIFE AND TIMES OF
JESSE JAMES AND JESUS OF NAZARETH 61
   The Betrayal of a Bandit 61
   Jesse James 62
   Jesus of Nazareth 75
   Crossing Outlaws 84

Chapter 4
10¢ GOSPELS: THE QUEST(S) FOR THE HISTORICAL
JESSE JAMES AND JESUS OF NAZARETH 88
   Sinners and Saints 88
   Writing the Biography of a Bandit 96

Chapter 5
BANDITS BEYOND THE SUNSET 114
   To Bury a Bandit 114
   The Resurrection of a Bandit 115
   In Jesse's Steps 122
   Literary Afterlives 132

Conclusion
ON DEATH AND BIRTH AND JESSE'S LINEAGE
   On Genealogy 145
   Resurrection of the Dead, Messianic and Monstrous 148
   Narratives of Lineage 153

Bibliography 158
Index of References 165
Index of Authors 167

Acknowledgments

The ideas in this book were conceived during an idle conversation about memories of a grandparent's stories. They were nurtured through a mutual love of Wild West books and movies. In time, we shared our infant idea, toddling forward (creative, playful, curious, but a danger to itself) at regional academic conferences. Nurtured and supported by caring friends, it grew. Yet, at times, this book seemed like it would never be completed. To write it required us to learn more than we would have imagined about Missouri and Jesse James. For more than five years, it has been our chronically "back burner" project.

Now brought to the public, grown and (we hope) equipped for an independent life, our little book has grown through the care of numerous hands. We would like to thank the following, gracious and patient readers and listeners, among our colleagues at Albright: Fouad Kalouche, Ian Rhile, Christian Hamann, Elizabeth Kiddy, Kristen Woodward, Gerry Ronning, John Pankratz, and others who commented on portions of this manuscript, presented at colloquia and scholar sessions. Thanks are also due to our colleagues in Religious Studies and Classical Languages, William King, Victor Forte and Sarel Fuchs. We want, in particular, to thank Albright for its generous working context (paid for by the Sloan foundation) and forward thinking employment strategies (such as family leave and shared faculty positions). These policies most certainly enabled this book. Even more, Albright directly enabled our writing and traveling by a generous research grant from the Professional Council for the summer of 2010 which allowed us to visit several Jesse James related locations and archives in Missouri. Robert worked on the annotation and bibliography during the summer of 2011 with (yet another) summer research grant from Albright.

Beyond the lovely Rand Gate of Albright College, thanks are due to Roberta Sabbath, Stephen D. Moore, Merrill Miller and Jeff Geller who read and commented on early essays exploring the connections between Jesse James and Jesus. Thanks are due to the welcome auditors (for their penetrating questions) at the 2006 meeting of the American Comparative Literature Association meeting in Princeton, New Jersey, and at the 2006 and the 2007 meetings of the Mid-Atlantic Society of Biblical Literature in Baltimore, Maryland. Jennifer worked on "David the Bandit" during the summer of 2006 with a summer research fellowship from the Wabash Center for Teaching and Learning. We also need to say "Thank you" for the interest, moral support and for travel tips given by Michael Willet Newheart, both a New Testament scholar and a distant family member of Jesse James. Thank you, as well, to the anonymous docents and fellow pilgrims at the Jesse James Family Farm and the Patee House Museum for their gracious help and patience. On the subject of patience, our gratitude, as always, goes to George Aichele, always a generous (and prompt) reader, Duncan Burns (an able copy-editor), and to everyone at Bloomsbury T&T Clark.

Introduction:
1318 Lafayette and Other Pilgrimage Sites

St. Joseph, Missouri isn't somewhere many people plan as their final destination. The town sits on US 29, gazing out at the miles of flat and empty expanse of prairies, very near the extreme northern corner of the Missouri–Kansas border. Clinging a bit desperately to the Missouri River, poised between Southwestern Iowa and Eastern Nebraska and Kansas, St. Joe is a popular stop for travelers on their way to or from somewhere else. The town is, as it has been for over a century, a good way-station but not many travelers' ultimate goal.

We've stopped here, at least for a day. We've been traveling for three days, stopping in St. Louis, Centralia, Sedalia, as we traveled west along the Missouri river, towing along a teen and a baby. Our plan is to spend today in St. Joseph, then turn south toward Kearny and Liberty before bearing west and stopping for the night in Kansas City. Our hotel is on the east side of town, just off the highway, the best rated hotel in town at two stars. The rating is generous. The hotel, like the town, is not unfairly described as "seedy." The carpet and furnishings, cheap when new, are worn and reek of cleaning products generously applied to drown out the smell of stale cigarette smoke. Breakfast is packaged cereal, tasteless fruit, or micro-waved egg-and-biscuit sandwiches. We take some fruit and coffee, gas up the car, and proceed into St. Joseph, using a bad map of the city found on a brochure of the town's "tourist attractions," assuring us that St. Joseph was "where the west started getting wild."

As a town and region which has seen better days, it seems appropriate that St. Joseph would stress its history, and, for aficionados of the folklore and history of the American West, it actually is a fairly rich region. St. Joseph is home to the Patee House Museum.[1] Originally a luxury hotel built by John Patee in 1858 (St. Joseph has been a traveler's town for a long time), the Patee House has been, since 1965, one of the more ambitious museums of the American West, chock full of

---

1. For history and description of the Patee House Museum, see its official website: www.ponyexpressjessejames.com. See also www.stjomo.com.

transportation history (wagons, rail cars, engines), curiosities (an exhibit for Robert Wadlow, the "world's tallest man"), a macabre collection of items associated with St. Joseph area murders and an indoor re-creation of a typical St. Joseph street from the 1860s.[2]

In addition, the former hotel has two premium attractions. St. Joseph was the easternmost stop on Pony Express in the early 1860s. Indeed, William H. Russell, Alexander Majors and William B. Waddell organized and began the private overland mail service in the lobby of the Patee (then known as the "Liberty Hotel") on April 3, 1860. April 3 has been a significant day for St. Joseph's "Wild West" history. The notorious gunman and bandit Jesse Woodson James was shot in the back of the head while unarmed by a .45 caliber Colt Navy revolver wielded by Robert Newton "Bob" Ford, on April 3, 1882 in his home at 1318 Lafayette Street, just a few blocks away from the Patee House. In fact, James' mother, Zerelda, stayed in the hotel as she attended to Jesse's final internment.

Born on September 5, 1847 in western Missouri to Robert James, a Georgetown College divinity school alum and frontier Baptist preacher, and to Zerelda Cole James, a former Lexington, Kentucky convent student, Jesse Woodson James should, by most expectations, have lived a markedly different life during his 34 years. By the time of his death, Jesse James was not famous as clergy or scholar but as the most notorious gunman and bandit on the post-Bellum Missouri frontier, a reputation he embraced and fostered. Highlighting his fame and his own promotion of it through one common anecdote, a man once approached Samuel Clemens in a grocery, asking if he were, in fact, the writer Mark Twain. To Clemens' affirmative, the stranger repeatedly expressed pleasure at Twain's work and said "Guess you and I are about the greatest in our line." Clemens, taken aback, thanked him for the compliment but regretted that he did not recognize the gentleman. The man paused from

---

2. The array of trains, wagons, bicycles and early autos—most of which are accessible for patrons to climb into and atop—is in many ways the most entertaining part of the museum. In stark contrast, the ghastly collection on law and crime in St. Joseph is the most grotesquely compelling. A mixture of "true crime" and "Ripley's Believe It or Not," the macabre exhibit includes, for example, the electric drill and ball peen hammer used by 16-year-old Stuart B. Allen to torture and kill John Frank (a 59-year-old local church sexton) on April 1, 1947. Along with an assortment of other tools used in various murders of passion, one finds the rope and noose used to lynch Lloyd Warner in April of 1933. According to the exhibit, he "paid the penalty for attacking a white woman." One is left with the impression that life in St. Joseph's has been both somewhat grisly and surprisingly documented (and that April would be a good time to be out-of-town).

collecting his packages, and introduced himself as Jesse James.[3] The gunman had spent the last few years before his death living in St. Joseph, along with his wife and two children, under the alias of "Thomas Howard." Bob, and his older brother Charlie Ford, had recently been added to James' gang of bandits. Planning a new caper, both Ford brothers were staying with Jesse in his home in St. Joseph, Missouri along with Jesse's wife Zee and two young children. When shot, James was standing on a chair in his living room, dusting a wall hanging; the Fords were standing in the middle of the room. Jesse's wife was in the adjoining kitchen, cleaning the breakfast dishes; his children were playing outside.

The actual, entire "Jesse James Death House," the very small, white, four-room clapboard house where Jesse was shot by Ford, has been incorporated into the Patee House exhibits. Sitting just outside the main hotel and charging a separate admission fee, the house squats atop what little lawn was left to the nearly block-long hotel, bulging out from the hillside and facing the river about two miles to the north and west. The simple, one-story square white house has been moved, twice, from its original Lafayette Street location, both times by entrepreneurs who charged admission to tourists. The house has a somewhat meta-critical exhibit on its own history as a tourist attraction. According to that display, it was purchased and moved out to "Belt Highway" in 1939 in order to attract more tourist traffic—sparing the curious the need to travel all the way into the inner city of St. Joseph. In the name of "authenticity," it (and its fence, yet not a rear addition) was moved to the Patee on May 8, 1977 after a campaign to raise the funds for the house's purchase and relocation. This campaign to restore the house to its "authentic" location resulted in the house's present location, some couple of blocks from its original site (and missing a portion of its footage). The exhibit has several photos of the large trucks needed to haul the bi-sectioned house into town. The history of architectural preservation also attests to Jesse's enduring popularity. According to Ted Yeatman, "More older buildings have been saved in the United States because of a connection to Jesse James than to any other person in American History, with the exceptions of George Washington and Abraham Lincoln."[4]

Most of the house furnishings from the period as well as James' personal items have remained in family possession, many residing at the premiere James attractions in Kearny and Liberty, Missouri, about 30

---

3. Opie Read, *Mark Twain and I* (Chicago: Reilly & Lee, 1940), 11.
4. Ted P. Yeatman, *Frank and Jesse James: The Story Behind the Legend* (Naperville, Ill.: Cumberland House, 2000), 220 (photo caption).

miles to the southeast of St. Joseph. Instead, the "Death House" now houses paintings of James, period furniture and a few random daily items (including a piece of one of the household's chairs—perhaps the one Jesse was standing on when shot), and a few of James' minor personal items (his shaving mug, for example). The balance of the exhibit is about the history of the house, the newspaper reports of the shooting and the exhumation of James in the 1990s.

Many of these exhibits address the questions that circulate about the circumstances surrounding, including even the verity of, Jesse's murder. Nearly from the day of his death, popular reports began to circulate that the man who had been shot by Bob Ford on Lafayette Street was not, in fact, Jesse James. To settle the matter, in 1995, the family had the body exhumed and subjected to DNA testing, where mitochondrial DNA samples from the remains were compared with known descendants. An entire room is dedicated to an exhibit on the disinterment and testing of Jesse. The body was exhumed in July of 1995 and re-interred in October. In the subsequent months, it was held at William Jewell College in Liberty (Jesse's father, Robert, had been a founding trustee of the college). The exhibit also contains the program from Jesse's (most recent) funeral, presided over by Dr. Charles E. Baker and Reverend John H. Killian with eulogy by Robert L. Hawkins, III—all either James' descendents or representatives of the Missouri Sons of Confederate Veterans—and proof copies of the published DNA test report and scholarly articles documenting the findings. Near the display of the scholarly papers (all under glass and, so, illegible—the existence of their argument, not its content, is the purpose of the display) is a copy of the April 5, 1882 *St. Joseph Daily Gazette* with 3 inch headlines declaring "Jesse, By Jehovah" as well as the 1995 copies of the same paper reporting the somewhat delayed but decidedly scientific verification of that claim. Finally, there are a series of typed pages hanging on the wall presenting a sworn affidavit by Dr. Jim Starrs, a professor of Law and Criminology, swearing that he, in no way, tainted the evidence of Jesse's body.[5] Clearly, the 99.9% certainty of the DNA testing did not quiet the skeptics.[6]

---

5. The DNA data was published in The American Bar Association Presidential Showcase Program, *The Trial of Jesse James—High Tech Meets the Wild West* (Chicago: ABA, 1996) and Anne C. Stone, James, E. Starrs and Mark Stoneking, "Mitochondrial DNA Analysis of the Presumptive Remains of Jesse James," *Journal of Forensic Science* 46, no. 1 (2001): 173–76. For an overview of the entire project, see Yeatman, *Frank and Jesse James*, 334–40.

6. For just two websites that dispute the veracity of the newspaper and eyewitness reports of Jesse's death, as well as the 1995 DNA analysis, see www.jessejamesintexas.com and www.theoutlaws.com.

Additionally, there has long been a dispute about whether or not Ford's bullet, which struck Jesse in the back of the head, had exited and struck the wall or had remained lodged in Jesse's skull. A rather gruesome debate, the question is not quite moot. On Jesse's death, a small hole was found in the wall, which many believed to be the bullet hole. Over time, relic-seeking tourists have carved splinters from the wall around the hole. It is now several inches in circumference and protected under glass. A plaster cast of Jesse's skull is on display in the house, along with clear-eyed declarations that the deadly bullet did not exit Jesse's head; there was no bullet hole in the wall.[7] Still, the house even now summons guests to "come see the bullet hole" in its advertisements, on its website and on signage facing the street. The wooden floors have also suffered from hungry relic hunters. Stains, declared to be drops of Jesse's blood, were found on the floorboards. Tourists immediately began chipping away splinters from the floor. The museum display still proclaims the gouges on the floor to be the areas formerly covered by the blood of the bandit, despite that documentation attests otherwise.[8] The Patee House in general, and the Jesse James Death House in particular, are, and likely always have been, much more depositories of lore and side-show exhibits, than they are "modern, historical" museums.

Clearly, the curators of the Death House have realized that the lure is the murder-room itself. That room is kept largely "as it was" on the day of Jesse's assassination, enabling one to stand where Ford stood (the floor is marked), face a chair "just like the one Jesse stood upon" and gaze at the "bullet hole" (which isn't, but which serves as a focal point for one's imagination) as if taking aim. Likely as hundreds of others before us had, we took turns staging a photo as Ford, our fingers luridly thrust out like a cocked gun. The purpose of the "murder-room" is to enter the site of history, but also to take a side, to take a role. The room is arranged so that the visitor plays the role of Ford, not James, since the chair and wall where Jesse stood is marked off by ropes barring access. One is being invited to imagine being a witness to history as a follower or a foe of the great man, perhaps to enter the role of the foil, but to imagine *being* the "great man" himself is too presumptuous.

Legends are difficult to kill and to bury, physically and metaphorically. In some ways, physical death actually leads to a more active life, since the legend is no longer bound by the body and the mundane laws of nature. At the time of his death, Jesse's body was identified, displayed,

---

7. Frank Triplett, *The Life, Times, and Treacherous Death of Jesse James* (repr. Samford, Conn.: Longmeadow, 1970), 293.
8. Yeatman, *Frank and Jesse James*, 276.

photographed and interred. None of this prevented that body from being seen hundreds of miles and decades removed from the assassination in St. Joseph.[9] As we will see in later chapters, even as Jesse's body "lay in state," banks were being robbed by bandits claiming his name. Rumors abounded that Jesse James had faked his own death, escaping to California or Mexico or Texas; for the next 50 years or so, figures would emerge claiming to be Jesse, or another wife, or an illegitimate child. There are even a few claims that Jesse reappeared supernaturally, as a ghostly visitor or in dreams. Even the physical Jesse has proven very difficult to keep buried. After a week of public display, his body was eventually buried. Jesse's wife and mother insisted on an open coffin to ensure that the body was buried intact.[10] Concern over relic hunters and tourists led to his disinterment and reburial. In the 1930s, he was quietly disinterred from the family plot (his head stone, however, was left behind), then reinterred in a local cemetery. Disinterred again in 1995 for DNA testing, Jesse was (finally?) laid back to rest alongside his wife, brother and mother in Kearny. Roughly every generation or so, Jesse has been dug up, poked, prodded, examined and reburied to address concerns that arise from the indomitable life of his legend and to assure everyone he is, in fact, still quite dead.

The first relic-hunting pilgrims, seeking to see for themselves just how dead Jesse might be, began arriving within days of his death. Later, James biographer Frank Triplett reports that the auction of Jesse's possessions began on the Monday afternoon following his death. "About ten dollars worth of rubbish brought near two hundred dollars. The chair...and duster...brought five dollars each," he reports.[11] Coincidently, a traveling Oscar Wilde was in the city in the days shortly following Jesse's murder, staying at the Patee Hotel. He wrote a series of letters about the excitement to his friends in New York and London, also including accounts of the relic-hunting throngs.[12] It took less than a week after James' assassination before newspapers, local and national, began to make comparisons between Bob Ford and Judas Iscariot. Jesse, though an outlaw, had become an icon of American myths of wildness, independence, masculinity and nationalistic fervor. Jesse's banditry was, to his own mind and those of many others, a form of active protest of

---

9. Yeatman (ibid., 272) tabulates multiple claims of Jesse involved in robberies for years after his death.
10. Triplett, *The Life*, 285.
11. Ibid., 311.
12. See Yeatman, *Frank and Jesse James*, 272. Oscar Wilde, according to his letters, was in St. Joseph on April 19.

Reconstruction-era politics. Jesse was hero to many for the very same reasons he was anathema to others. In the Bible-saturated American frontier, such ideas were bound to be cast in biblical language and imagery. In addition to playing a critical role in Jesse's own religious upbringing, the Bible was the basis for the common vocabulary of America in the 1880s; it was the central and formative text for discourse, perhaps the only book many (particularly on the Missouri frontier) would have ever read. Were this not enough, elements of Jesse's own narrative actually bear an uncanny resemblance to the Gospel accounts.

On the 14th or 15th of Nissan, sometime in the early 30s C.E., Roman soldiers nailed the body of Jesus of Nazareth to a cross on a hillside on the outskirts of Jerusalem. He had been betrayed by a member of his own gang. The form of death was one normally reserved for bandits and rebels against Roman rule; indeed, Jesus found himself, that day, flanked by two other bandits. According to biblical text, Jesus was mocked by Roman soldiers as "King of the Jews." His followers would pronounce him as the son of David, the rightful heir to the Jewish throne. It is hardly surprising his followers and his detractors made such connections. The idea of Jewish nationalism and independence had permeated the land since the days of the Maccabees. In memory (hewn in 1 Samuel, polished free of blemish by 1 Chronicles), David had been the paragon of both rebel and king. Beloved by God, David was, in many ways, God's own bandit. Fixed to the wood, Jesus was left to die, betrayed and abandoned by his own band beneath signage proclaiming him king and with the view of the "City of David" the last his eyes ever beheld.

Although less well known than other popular polarizing figures of his time (like John the Baptist), Jesus had a sufficiently powerful effect on the few who did know him to guarantee his legend. And as we have seen with Jesse James, both physically and metaphorically, legends are difficult to kill and to bury. The first written accounts of Jesus' career and ministry, the gospels, have been long known by scholars to be edited compendia of prior oral traditions about Jesus. Jesus' message existed in oral legend and folk tradition, circulating around the Levant, for decades before it began to be written down. The vigorous life of these traditions was fueled, in part, by the active life of Jesus' dead body. Crucifixion is propaganda. The State displays the dying rebel as a sign of its power. The dead bandit is left to rot, be eaten and scattered. His body, displayed in the throes of torture, is designed to vanish from public view after death. Yet not even one of the most brutal forms of execution ever devised prevented Jesus' body from being seen hundreds of miles and decades removed from its assassination site. Much like the later Jesse

James, the career of Jesus was, initially, largely oral. Again, like the later Jesse James, when elements of the career of Jesus began to be written down, they were composed in a context of exoticism, politics and dissent.

Jesse James and his partisans were familiar with and consequently invoked biblical traditions surrounding Jesus of Nazareth; similarly, Jesus and his followers were also familiar with and consequently invoked biblical traditions of a still earlier figure, David Bar-Jesse. Although comparisons between Jesse and Jesus remind us how Jesus' messianic claims were highly dissident in their time (messiahs are always/already rebels), one of the more obvious differences between Jesus and Jesse is that the latter was a killer and thief and the former is currently prayed to as the Incarnation of God. However, not only messianic progenitor and rebel, King David was very much a bandit, in the fullest sense of the word. Particularly during his early career prior to kingship, David roamed the wilderness, at odds with the law, living by his wits and violence. Indeed, in many ways, David is far more deadly than Jesse James ever was; though certainly calculating in violence and not above murder, there are no traditions stating that Jesse ever invaded and destroyed entire towns, killing everyone. David did. And David remained violent well after attaining the throne. Also, much like Jesse, later, popular memory of David worked to ground him in a nationalistic identity that downplayed the actual violence of his career. Many of David's pilgrim sites are also associated with Jesus. Few, if any, relics of his career remain, of course. Notably though, those that may—minor inscriptions which may or may not invoke David's name—are both venerated and vigorously debated.

Legends of David gave rise to legends of Jesus. Legends of Jesus give rise to legends of Jesse James. Legends of Jesse James re-cast the legends of David and Jesus alike. Jesse James, Jesus of Nazareth and King David intertwine in memory, image and legend. Each, a bandit to some, a redeemer to others, is memorialized in stories that escape text. We will examine the interconnections of our three messianic bandits as well as the methods of biography and folk literature (oral legends, images, songs and pop culture "iconography") that interpret their stories and animate popular imagination. We will also explore the methods and limits of history, particularly the "quests" for the "historical" figures of David, Jesus and Jesse James. Relics, pilgrimage, rumors of resurrection, invocation of biblical narrative: this nexus of religiously oriented practices, themes and texts, all surrounding the legend (even myth) of Jesses James, forms the subject of this work.

The Plan of This Work

In Chapter 1, "Bandits, Martyrs and Messiahs," we explore three crucial themes while also surveying relevant literature for our methodology. After a discussion of methodology, we explore to what extent Iron Age Judah, Roman Galilee, and Reconstruction-era Missouri invoke the context of colonial "territories" and areas of resistance. We then turn to the work of Eric Hobsbawm on social banditry. Bandits differ from rebels and thieves. They engage primarily in armed resistance to alterative forces, drawing both aid and encouragement from the surrounding, subaltern population using the rhetoric of alterity. Further, their acts of banditry are strategic resistance to authority. King David, Jesus of Nazareth and Jesses James, though facing initial attempts at official suppression, thrived in later memory and popular culture. Their memory and their work was perpetuated by the subaltern in folk stories, songs and legends. Popular construction of the stories surrounding each exhibit startling correlations and similar strategies. Each story is infused by popular culture and in turn constructs popular culture.

Chapter 2 addresses "David the Bandit." According to the books of Samuel, David lives the life of a bandit after he escapes from Saul, even gathering together a band of other disaffected men to raid unprotected towns along the border. Historically, the tenth century was an unstable time, with the waning of Egyptian domination and the waxing of the Philistine threat. Poised between these foreign powers, the people of Israel were attempting to forge new forms of political and social organization. Although overlooked in traditional readings, the outlaw period of David's career has been highlighted in a number of recent biographies. This chapter explores the bandit traditions in the context of the recent archeological reassessment of tenth-century Israel. Not only does the new archaeology shed light on the bandit traditions as they appear in the biblical text, but it also may explain why recent scholars have focused on David's more troubling traits, even labeling him "murderer," "traitor," "mercenary." As David's historicity is questioned, such characterizations serve to make him more "real." Finally, this chapter explores the ways in which David's legacy informs understandings of Jesus as Messiah "in the line of David."

Chapter 3, "Crossing Outlaws: The Legendary Lives of Jesse James and Jesus of Nazareth," explores the interconnections between Jesse and Jesus of Nazareth. Tracing the elements of the career of each, the chapter argues that, while narratives of Jesse clearly invoke Jesus as a romanticizing and legitimating motif, the comparison also exposes under-attended aspects of Jesus' ministry. Jesus is crucified by the Romans as a *leistein*, a bandit. In many ways, his ministry does, in fact, draw from elements of social banditry outlined by Hobsbawm. Recalling the "bandit"-laden context of Roman Galilee (as described by Horsley and others) and the context of other Jewish messianic figures, Jesus' ministry is far more ambiguous than gospel memory allows. The comparison reveals that the popular appeal of both Jesus and Jesse—past and present—arises in part from the role of each as a social bandit. It also suggests that dissidence and sedition are key aspects of both banditry and messiahship. Jesus was more bandit than we remember, and Jesse was more "messianic" than we often care to admit.

Chapter 4, "10 Cent Gospels," analyzes the overlap between constructions of the historical Jesus and the (pop) biography of Jesse James. The four most popular biographies of Jesse James present very different images of Jesse, all using the same "sources." The description becomes even more complicated by a survey of formal biography and popular memory and folk tale. The problems surrounding an accurate "biography" of Jesus of Nazareth are so pronounced they hardly need (re)articulation. David's memory, as well, has given biographers difficulties as they attempt to sort out sometimes conflicting (and often redacted) memories of David preserved in biblical text, alongside an absence of archaeological data. Once again, the popular, modern memory and images of Jesus and David complicate the process. This chapter explores the limits of biography for such figures and argues that many of these problems originate from the bandit context of the figures themselves. The process of making the "social bandit" or a "messiah" necessarily obscures the ability to glimpse the authentic figure in history.

The final chapter, "Bandits Beyond the Sunset," explores the "afterlives" of bandits in popular memory. We return as pilgrims to the key sites of Jesse's life and death to explore further the ways in which objects and places are transformed into relics and holy sites. Next, we read Ron Hansen's novel *The Assassination of Jesse James by the Coward Robert Ford* (1983).[13] Hansen's reconstruction of Jesse James is thoroughly informed by the lives of Jesus and David, biblical text and Christian story. Finally, we end with other literary afterlives of Jesse that are infused with similar sacred understandings.

---

13. Ron Hansen, *The Assassination of Jesse James by the Coward Robert Howard* (New York: Knopf, 1983; repr. New York: Norton, 1990; repr. New York: Harper Perennial, 1997; reissued 2007).

After viewing the museum and house, we took a late lunch of homemade sandwiches eaten in the car. Unable to resist the siren song of historical authenticity that rose to crescendo as we sat and looked down Lafayette, we could not help wandering over to see the "original" site of Jesse's rented home. We found little there, nothing at all related to Jesse James. The lot was empty of any structures, a grass and garbage covered knoll. It was difficult to be sure if we even had found the correct address. Atop the hill were only a few empty beer and whiskey bottles, a broken Judas Priest CD case and a dead garter snake. We talked, on the drive south to Jesse's family farm in Kearny, about how the Lafayette lot looked so generic, just another decayed lot in an old, run-down neighborhood of a highway town. Without the context of the "inauthentic" Patee Museum, the lot was meaningless. Yet the very desire to archive and preserve, to produce, uncritically disseminate and openly glorify oral and traditional history, which the Patee represents, has erased—in this case literally made barren—the site of history itself.

In many ways, this book is, ultimately, about that irony, that tension between the "authentic" events and the production and analysis of tradition, about the techniques and technologies of the production of popular historical memory. The "actual" past remains elusive, often precisely because of the process of historical preservation itself. We can't resist the impulse to "look behind" surviving stories, tourist-traps and partisan traditions to find the "real" past. Yet when we do, we find that much of it is irrecoverable; what we find is either meaningless, subsequent cultural flotsam or uncertain. It is tempting to argue that the layers of tradition and interpretation obscure history. We would argue, however, that these traditions and tales *are* history; they are what history consists of and what adds meaning to any surviving artifacts from the past or any present sense of self.

People live and die and in between they act, think, speak—both individually and in collective movements. But the interconnections between these events, the patterns of cause and effect and the meanings attached to those patterns are acts of interpretation that order afterwards. It is the *narrative* that emerges and survives, that moves through time and place, influencing other people who act and shape events; it is the *narrative* that becomes a force in and of history, it is the *narrative* that is history itself. We are not arguing that there are not real people and events behind the narrative—in most cases, there are. Nor are we suggesting that all historical investigation is equal, regardless of its presentation of these people and events. History can still be judged as accurate or adequate, challenged as erroneous or fraudulent, and opposing interpretations can still compete. But the narrative that exists in place of the people who have since died, the events that have since concluded, has an effect regardless of its accuracy. Sometimes the narrative is so powerful, the actual subject of the story is not only irrecoverable but also irrelevant. Archeological sites destroy as they uncover. In other words, ironically, in some cases the very quest for historical authenticity and evidence, which is prompted by engagement with historical narrative, actually erases by alteration the physical locus and artifact of history, even as the pursuit of authenticity is a requisite task for the construction of historical narrative. The finite flesh of David, Jesus and Jesse James has long since ceased to be; these men have lived and died. Yet, the stories of David, Jesus and Jesse James continue to be and it is these stories that reproduce, multiply and influence as they unfurl across time.

Chapter 1

BANDITS, MARTYRS AND MESSIAHS

What Has Kansas City to Do with Jerusalem?

This has been a difficult book to describe. We expected, and encountered, dubious looks from family. Little new in this. Despite their support and interest, a sense of bafflement regarding our work has always been present. The confusion expressed by colleagues in our own and other departments presented a different degree of concern. More than once we have encountered arched brows and the question "what can David, Jesus and Jesse James possibly have in common with one another?" Our answer has consistently been "Quite a bit, actually. You might be surprised." We then reviewed some of the parallels, many admittedly superficial, anticipating the eventual question "why do you think there are so many parallels, and are they important?" Our answer, for the most part, has been "we don't know. That's why we're working on this book."

In essence, the book that follows can be summarized as an exercise in comparative literature;[1] we pursue David, Jesus and Jesse with a posse of questions about why these similarities exist and if and how they matter. Our inquiry blends multiple strands of our training as biblical scholars. On one level, we use the standard, even conservative, elements of modern critical biblical interpretation: archaeology, form criticism, tradition criticism and reception history. We intend, however, to blend these traditional approaches with broader critical techniques of cultural studies and comparative literature, all within a framework heavily informed by poststructuralism.[2] We want to compare the careers—more accurately,

---

1. This project actually began as a comparative literature exercise. A very early draft of Chapter 3, the inspiration for this book, was first presented at the 2006 meeting of the American Comparative Literature Association in Princeton, New Jersey.

2. Both "poststructuralism" and "cultural studies" are terms widely varied in their meanings and use by biblical scholars. For our purposes, on poststructuralism and biblical studies, see The Bible and Culture Collective, *Postmodern Bible*

the traditional presentation of the careers—of King David, Jesus of Nazareth and Jesse James, with particular attention to the context, agenda and popular responses to each. At times, these parallels are the direct result of deliberate intertextuality; the followers of Jesus knew of the career of David, and grafted their stories of Jesus onto the roots of that tradition. Similarly, the contemporaries of Jesse James (and Jesse himself) were biblically literate. They drew from biblical text directly but also indirectly, from the types and archetypes present in Western culture and literature, patterns founded on biblical character and story. At times, the parallels among these figures are also very likely symptomatic of common problems and conditions of oral tradition and history; they also arise from some common elements in the general context of each figure. Comparison of the three traditions, then, reveals a standard, and very old, trope or motif in Western myth-making and traditional history which tends to arise given certain social and contextual cues and circumstances.

We are fundamentally engaged, here, in a work of comparative literature, resting our work on the fundamental assumption that these comparisons—despite substantial historical, linguistic and genre differences—are inherently provocative.[3] Along with producing a host of interesting potential "meanings," such comparisons across various communities, readers and texts can also potentially expose fundamental mechanisms

(New Haven: Yale University Press, 1995); Stephen D. Moore, *Poststructuralism and the New Testament: Derrida and Foucault at the Foot of the Cross* (Minneapolis: Fortress, 1994); A. K. M. Adam, *What Is Postmodern Biblical Criticism?* (Minneapolis: Fortress, 1995); Yvonne Sherwood and Kevin Hart, eds., *Derrida and Religion: Other Testaments* (New York: Routledge, 2005), Yvonne Sherwood, ed., *Derrida's Bible: (Reading a Page of Scripture with a Little Help from Derrida)* (New York: Palgrave Macmillan, 2004); and Jennifer L. Koosed, "Nine Reflections on the Book: Poststructuralism and the Hebrew Bible," *Religion Compass* 2 (2008): 499–512. Available online: http://religion-compass.com. On cultural studies and biblical criticism in general, see J. Cheryl Exum and Stephen D. Moore, eds., *Biblical Studies/Cultural Studies* (Sheffield: Sheffield Academic, 1998) and Philip Culbertson and Elaine M. Wainwright, eds., *The Bible in/and Popular Culture: A Creative Encounter* (Semeia Studies 65; Atlanta: Society of Biblical Literature, 2010). See below for further definition, discussion and bibliography of cultural studies.

3. For some recent work that foregrounds the role of the reader in the construction of intertextual connections between biblical text and other cultural products, see George Aichele and Richard Walsh, eds., *Screening the Scripture: Intertextual Connections Between Scripture and Film* (Harrisburg, Pa.: Trinity Press International, 2002), and Jennifer L. Koosed, *Gleaning Ruth: A Biblical Heroine and Her Afterlives* (Studies on Personalities of the Old Testament; Columbia: University of South Carolina Press, 2011).

for constructing meaning and sense. For example, we will argue that King David, Jesus of Nazareth and Jesse Woodson James are Hobsbawmian "social bandits," and it is from this bandit / dissident role that they both awakened fear from the standard authorities and popular support from the masses.

Yet a quick challenge to a comparison of Jesus to Jesse James—perhaps the main source of confusion regarding our project—lies in one central and obvious difference: the word "bandit." Jesse murdered and stole; Jesus did not. Most would assert, in fact, Jesus did precisely the opposite. While Jesse James was a popular figure who, as did Jesus, ignited public passions and imagination, he did not, as did Jesus, inspire religious devotion among his followers in any but a metaphoric sense. To put it bluntly, Jesus did not murder anyone, and no one ever prayed to Jesse James for forgiveness of sin. A secondary challenge arises from the comparison of David and Jesse James. David, some would assert, was a legitimate rebel leader who became king at his victory; he was not a "bandit" roving around with a small band committing larceny and wreaking havoc. Jesse was. Jesse died an outlaw; David died a king. Furthermore, concern over anachronistic reading and historical sense would suggest narratives about David and Jesus may inform narratives about Jesse, but not vice-versa.

There are reasons to believe that the Hebrew Bible's presentation of David has been glossed, his image photo-shopped to remove bandit blemishes. *Was* David a legitimate rebel triumphant, or was he a bandit who fought the law yet, somehow, also won? Jesus was tried and executed in the exact ways Romans dealt with roadside bandits and political rebels. Why? It is not sufficient to answer that the Romans mistakenly thought Jesus was a bandit. Why did they make *this particular* mistake (if, indeed, they did act in error)? Why *don't* more readers think of Jesus and his followers as dissident, rebellious, bandit movements? If Jesse James was not a religious figure, why does he still inspire many to engage in acts that, for every appearance, seem to be devotional? Why *don't* more Americans regard Jesse James in the same light as, say, the serial killer Ted Bundy or the terrorist Osama Bin Ladin? In other words, our comparison of both similarity and difference awakens many questions that cluster around the perennial dilemma of differentiating between "religious" and "secular" pop-devotion, sacred and tourist-pilgrimage. We assert that asking why *doesn't* anyone now pray to Jesse James is as legitimate as asking why people *do* pray to Jesus. Bringing Jesse James into the conversation helps highlight questions about how brutal and wild was a young David, about how close to violent revolt the early Jesus movement may have gotten, about how messiahs—divine or regal—are always-already civil dissidents and outlaws. Finally, such comparisons reveal similar structures of myth- and history-making along with the meaningfulness of certain types of texts.

Cultural Studies and Biblical Studies

Can the study of Jesse James tell us anything about the Bible? Is the study of Jesse James and his legends in any way related to biblical studies? What could we, as biblical scholars by both training and profession, find relevant to our work in a tour of western Missouri? Beyond discovering if or how legends of Jesse James use biblical texts or themes (and if or how they do so "correctly"), what interest could a biblicist have in the study of such a (comparatively) modern, pop-culture icon as Jesse James?

Methodologically, a central idea in the theory of modern cultural studies is the refusal to privilege any aspect of art or literature as "high culture" against "popular culture."[4] Such an equalizing of "high" and "low" culture is crucial for our study because interest in Jesse James lies principally in American popular culture around the reconstructed "Wild West." Such "low" culture is worthy of analysis because it reveals just as much about society as other more artistic cultural products, in many cases, more. For example, Jane Tompkins has argued very compellingly that interest in Western genre fiction and film is, de facto, American myth-making.[5] The stories, historical and fictional, of life in the West are constructing American notions of manhood, political sovereignty, destiny and fundamental ethical principles and both construct and reveal the mythic types and tropes for each that are present in our culture. These stories function as American political and social cosmogony and etiology.

---

4. For general introduction to the field of cultural studies, the following are seminal works: Simon During, ed., *The Cultural Studies Reader* (2d ed.; New York: Routledge, 1993); L. Grossberg, C. Nelson and P. Treichler, eds., *Cultural Studies* (New York: Routledge, 1992); T. W. Adorno, *The Culture Industry: Selected Essays on Mass Culture* (New York: Routledge, 1991); J. Baudrillard, *Le Système des objets* (Paris: Gallimard, 1968); P. Bourdieu, *The Field of Cultural Production: Essays on Art and Literature* (Cambridge: Polity, 1992); Richard Hoggart, *The Uses of Literacy* (San Francisco: Penguin, 1957); J. Fiske, *Understanding Popular Culture* (Boston: Unwin Hyman, 1989); J. Frow, *Cultural Studies and Cultural Value* (Oxford: Clarendon, 1995). The intellectual roots of cultural studies are in the soil of Hoggart's Birmingham Centre for Contemporary Cultural Studies. However, this rooting does not mean that current cultural studies critique can exclusively bear Marxist fruit(s).

5. Jane Tompkins, *West of Everything: The Inner Life of the Western* (Oxford: Oxford University Press, 1992).

Jesse appears in movie Westerns, "True West" documentaries, popular fiction and biography and tourist attractions of various levels of sophistication. Even during his lifetime, he was the central figure in a sub-genre of "dime novel" fiction. Instead of dismissing such cultural products as superficial and ephemeral, their analysis could reveal something deep and essential about American identity. Bible, of course, is within the genre of mythology, as well (traditional stories about the sacred). All three figures—David, Jesus and Jesse James—dwell in the realm of myth and archetype.

Cultural studies is currently enjoying a growing role in biblical criticism.[6] One critique among cultural studies approaches in English departments has been the explosion of dissertations on comic books, matched with the decline of dissertations on Shakespeare, leaving some critics to assert a major motivation behind cultural studies is the desire to work on something "new" in a field with a clear canon. The adoption of cultural studies methodologies within biblical studies (criticized by some for the same reasons) has followed a slightly different trajectory. More than a clear canon, biblical studies has a closed canon. For the most part, biblical scholars pursuing cultural studies have worked to locate and describe broader cultural appropriation (read: interpretation) of biblical language and literature.[7] Often, however, the overwhelming sense of any conversation between Bible and popular culture has been one-way, about how appropriation of the Bible reveals the intentions of the appropriator (disclosing the appropriator's interpretive moves), how Bible functions to construct cultural meaning, and how Bible, filtered through culture, has been received. We, instead, hope to also ask: How has the Bible played in the complex intersections of cultural and political hegemony

---

6. One of the earliest significant monograph-length examples (and still among the best) is Roland Boer, *Knockin' on Heaven's Door: The Bible and Popular Culture* (New York: Routledge, 1999). One of the most recent (and likely to be influential) is Culbertson and Wainwright, eds., *The Bible in/and Popular Culture*. For early bibliography, see Exum and Moore, eds., *Biblical Studies/Cultural Studies*.

7. Examples here could be Legion. We suggest: George Aichele, ed., *Culture, Entertainment and the Bible* (JSOTSup 309; Sheffield: Sheffield Academic, 2000); Timothy Beal and Tod Linafelt, eds., *Mel Gibson's Bible: Religion, Popular Culture, and "The Passion of the Christ"* (Chicago: University of Chicago Press, 2006); Michael J. Gilmour, *Gods and Guitars: Seeking the Sacred in Post-1960s Popular Music* (New York: Continuum, 2009); Adele Reinhartz, *Jesus of Hollywood* (New York: Oxford University Press, 2007); Erin Runions, *How Hysterical: Identification and Resistance in the Bible and Film* (New York: Palgrave, 2003). For excellent general survey, see John F. A. Sawyer, ed., *The Blackwell Companion to the Bible and Culture* (New York: Blackwell, 2006).

expressed in media and popular entertainment and discourse (ancient and modern). Exploring these three figures together exposes some of the working dynamics of canon and canonization.

Looking at the Bible's use in popular culture raises two questions. The first is how legends of Jesse James "cite" or mimic biblical legends of David and Jesus, both in elements of parallel structure and in patterns of formation, redaction and dissemination. How, in other words, does "low" or "secular" legend invoke or imitate "high" or "sacred" tradition? Yet the observation of parallels almost requires reflection on "accuracy" or appropriateness of parallel. We are tempted to ask if or how the parallel "gets it right," or if-or-how use of biblical images or processes are "accurate." This question exposes still another "high" and "low" bifurcation—between "correct" and "scholarly" readings of the Bible and biblical scholarship and "popular" or "naive" interpretation and use. Cultural studies is an overt challenge to these bifurcations, marking who is seeking control of whom, what concerns are ultimately at play, and reveling in the subsequent disruptions.

We, accordingly, are not primarily interested in whether a cultural product (in this case, Jesse's legend) gets the Bible "right" or "wrong." Instead, our approach will include comparisons that force reflection on whether borders and boundaries are, at best, porous—in particular, the borders between "high" and "low" art, literature and film, history and legend, religious and secular, even present and past. We are also interested in how these moments of intersection both form and reflect popular subjectivities. Comparison results in general insights about how forms of literature work, how form and meaning intersect; it also reveals both the limits and the potential of formal, critical biblical scholarship.

The reticence among biblical scholars to open up a two-way conversation between the Bible and other cultural products, textual and otherwise, is very much understandable. It arises, in part, from our training as biblical scholars; traditional approaches to our field have schooled us against eisegesis. Many biblical scholars long ago abandoned any ideas about the recoverability of authorial intention or any notion of clear demarcations between exegesis and eisegesis; many scholars who engage in cultural studies approaches to biblical text are exactly those scholars least likely to assume any priority to "authorial intention" for biblical meaning. Yet scholarship still often harbors misgivings about whether or not the analysis of contemporary popular culture can reveal any ideas of substance within biblical texts. When biblical scholars write about something or someone not in the Bible, it feels "wrong." It feels like something other than biblical scholarship.

Those of us who teach in the modern academy and in the contemporary synagogue or church have been exposed to hundreds of pre-critical readings of biblical texts. As professional biblicists, many of us have been wearied by reading and responding to countless undergraduate and earnest graduate papers outlining the biblical significance of any number of popular songs, films or cartoons. We have also been showered with random comments connecting the Bible and popular culture from students in lectures and discussion groups. Whereas students and congregants are often more informed about the most immediately current pop culture and can sometimes bring fresh insight to biblical stories, their interpretations also, unfortunately, reveal how unrestrained readings of biblical text have appropriated Bible themes, passages and mandates to undergird and disseminate a variety of prejudicial, racist, classist and homophobic arguments. We would like to see the contrast between the readings of the professional (biblical) critic and popular culture not as mutually exclusive alternatives but as a range of options which intersect and diverge. Popular culture is not completely a-critical; professional criticism is not isolated from popular reading(s).

Cultural studies has, in nearly every example, a moment of metacritical discourse built into it. Since its origins, the methodology asks serious questions not just about what appropriately falls within the literature, but about those schooled in defining what that canon might actually contain, even the very notion of "canon" itself.[8] To an extent, "Bible" is created by the very process of criticism. Further, this critical process, like the processes of the academic study of literature, art or aesthetics, tends to bifurcate "low" and "high" forms of criticism (as well as the things critiqued). The *sine qua non* of modern biblical studies is extensive study in ancient languages, culture and history. These tedious-yet-precious skills can offer substantial moments for insight, but they also construct notions of privilege for the status of the trained interpreter to establish borders to critical commentary and canon and irresistibly draw the eye of the biblical critic away from the present and toward the obscurity of the past. The popular challenge to the authority of the biblical scholar has been subdued in some corners by insistence upon a form of cultural studies/biblical studies where only a one-way discourse is allowed. The Bible may illumine popular culture; the critic may illumine the way popular culture is using biblical text. But the study of popular culture

---

8. A similar inquiry may be found in the work of George Aichele, particularly in *The Limits of Story* (SBLSS; Chico, Calif.: Scholars Press, 1985), and *The Control of Biblical Meaning: Canon as Semiotic Mechanism* (Harrisburg, Pa.: Trinity Press, 2001).

itself, as an end of its own, is bracketed off from the study of the Bible (in part by the very machinations of the biblical scholar's technical training, itself). The result is a bifurcation between "high" and "low" biblical scholarship. As poststructuralists, we can't help but scratch at the flair of an allergic response to these proposed (absolute) binaries. A serious commitment to poststructuralism and cultural studies must lead us to concede that biblical "meaning" can be constructed via means outside traditional, historically described methods of biblical criticism, that biblical criticism can be legitimately broadened to include the study and analysis of legends surrounding Jesse James.

We are fully aware that there are many other professionally trained biblical scholars who would find the study of Jesse James alongside David and Jesus to be interesting (perhaps), but not (most certainly) to be biblical scholarship. Further, we are aware that many would be concerned that cultural studies as we define it would mean biblical studies must include potentially any text or field, resulting in professional (and canonical) erasure by inclusion.

We would answer that resistance to a full-throated comparative literature or cultural studies approach to biblical criticism arises from that tenacious desire for controlled, methodological forms of reading; in other words, it comes from the desire to maintain "high" and "low" categories of interpretation. Many scholars still grant, implicitly and explicitly, privileged place to arguments about authorial intention in interpretive debates and concerns about a-critical or anachronistic readings which are often coded concerns and sublimated defenses of authorial (or institutional?) intention. Raising real questions about whether or not every modern attempt to interpret is always already anachronistic, we argue the slope toward total critical abandon is not, ultimately, so slippery. One can engage in cultural studies readings of the Bible where contemporary culture is used to interpret ancient text without total critical loss or defining biblical studies so broadly that everything, in essence, becomes biblical studies (though, in practical reality, perhaps biblical scholarship *could* address virtually anything in culture alongside its inquiry into biblical text). If nothing else, a biblical studies reading of Jesse James must invoke Bible or result in a deeper understanding of biblical characters, contexts, themes, structures, texts, reception, transmission, interpretation and influence. Our study of Jesse James explores all of these.

Perhaps the most substantial critique against our comparative reading is that it risks becoming mired in structuralism, particularly since we are comparing "texts" from such widely separate provenances. The accusation is not an idle one; the methodologies currently collected together as "cultural studies" have their origins, in part, in late twentieth-century neo-Marxism, a fairly structuralist ideology. Structuralism assumes that any commonalities between David, Jesus and Jesse (or, again to be most accurate, their legends) would arise from deep, endemic and intrinsic qualities present within myth, oral tradition and cultural/social needs.

In no sense do we argue that any aspect of language or literature or meaning manifestly exists universally. Nor would we necessarily assume any evolutionary structure to ideology. This does not preclude, however, an observation that some structures found in varied and disparate communities may, indeed, be similar, nor does it necessarily inhibit questions about whether correlations might have some sort of common causal context or relationship. Perhaps the most egregious element of structuralist thought lies in its confident assertions about "truth" and "reality." Indeed, the epistemology assumed by structuralism is exactly where it fails most. In a basic sense we will be avoiding this pitfall by avoiding any confident sense that our readings are "real." We fully acknowledge the transient, provisional and frankly rhetorical nature of our arguments. That is part of our point. When we assert that King David is a bandit like Jesse James, we openly admit the limited nature of our claim. We do not feel, however, that the comparisons we will make are, accordingly, "invalid." They provide both provocative and useful ways of understanding the activities of the figures we describe, despite the absent claim of absolute certainty and universality. Such are the mechanics of meaning and memory.

We have come to think of our method, in some ways, as a poststructuralist reinterpretation of traditional biblical source, form and redaction criticism, engaged in via contemporary cultural studies (and certain social-scientific analyses) and resting on New Historicist views of history and traditional biblical exegesis and hermeneutics.

Bandit-ridden Frontiers of Judea, the Galilee and Missouri: The Wild, Wild South, North and West

David, Jesus and Jesse thrived in "frontier" territories, under the influence of a political authority understood as "foreign," and in a context where that authority was alternatively absent and powerless then suddenly present and decisively violent. In the instability that resulted, figures such as David, Jesus and Jesse James were able to muster popular support and identification among the subaltern communities they lived within. Their popular support not only enabled their careers, but also shaped the forces that memorialized those careers. The political and social contexts of the Judean wilderness, Galilee and post-Bellum Missouri provided the fertile environments out of which these three bandit kings emerged.

As recorded in the books of Samuel, various tribes of Israel began to advocate for the unity of a state under the leadership of a king (1 Sam 8), likely sometime around the tenth century B.C.E. Saul, from the tribe of Benjamin, was anointed king by the popular priest and prophet Samuel because he was tall and handsome (1 Sam 9), because the people threw lots and the lot fell on him (1 Sam 10), and/or because of his military victories against the Ammonites (1 Sam 11). A shepherd's son named David entered Saul's court because Saul had headaches and David's musicianship soothed them (1 Sam 16:14–23) and/or David had a lauded victory over a Philistine warrior named Goliath (1 Sam 17). Eventually, David comes into conflict with Saul and escapes the court (1 Sam 19:12), thus initiating a cat-and-mouse game between the two men that continues until Saul is killed in battle against the Philistines (1 Sam 31) and David takes the throne, first in Judah (2 Sam 2:4) and finally over all of Israel (2 Sam 5:1–5).

Yet, as the cracks in the biblical narrative itself reveal, the course of establishing monarchy and dynasty did not always run smoothly, and the archeological record suggests even greater disunity among the peoples and regions of Israel than even the biblical stories allow. The period in question is one of great upheaval and transition, and the place in question is one of great austerity and isolation. As will be explored further in the next chapter, rather than becoming the brilliant capital of a flourishing kingdom, Jerusalem and its environs were wilderness territory. The area was wild, rough, barely inhabited because it was barely inhabitable. Geographically, its natural features isolate it from the rest of the Levant. Rocky hills run up its center like a spine. To the west, the hills drop off to more hospitable coastal plains, but these regions were inhabited by the Philistines. To the east, the hills drop off to the arid regions of the desert, and continue their downward plunge to the Dead Sea and the Jordan Valley, the lowest place on earth. Wide canyons and deep ravines, steep cliffs and jagged rocks define the landscape. Even in its most habitable areas, Judah's soil was poor, its land rocky and its rain unpredictable. The region had a sparse population (about five thousand), concentrated in a handful of small villages (no urban areas, not a single fortified town), living by subsistence agriculture with little manufacturing or trade.[9]

The northern region, on the other hand, had a gentler landscape and greater natural resources. The archaeological record reveals a bustling north with extensive agricultural development, including olive orchards

---

9. Israel Finkelstein and Neil Asher Silberman, *David and Solomon: In Search of the Bible's Sacred Kings and the Roots of the Western Tradition* (New York: Free Press, 2006), 33–37, 68.

and vineyards producing oil and wine for trade, and public works like storage facilities, all of which indicate a high degree of political administrative power and organization.[10] In the days of Saul, a picture emerges of a rich north attempting to exert control over a poor south, while the Judean people rally behind a local hero, more bandit than warrior, more rebel than king. Rather than an initial unity that disintegrates into two separate kingdoms in the ninth century—Israel in the north and Judah in the south—the two regions never were completely yoked under one rule. The strong, negative anti-Israel feelings of the south would persist for centuries as Judean prophets continued to decry the northern tribes as too cosmopolitan, too quick to foreign treaty, too wealthy and therefore neither uniquely and solely reliant upon their God. The entire Hebrew Bible is written from the perspective of the south.

As the story of the early career of David indicates, the Judean wilderness provided a fine location for David to hide from the armies of Saul. Such indicates something of the impassability of the terrain, the absence of cities, the difficulty of transportation of goods and materials. There is no doubt that the entire army of Saul could overwhelm David and his band of supporters through superior numbers, training, weaponry and organization. That they could not can only be explained by the inability of those troops to navigate successfully the mountains and to locate David and his entourage.

In many ways, the Galilee during the late Second Temple would seem radically different.[11] The geography and resources that made the north rich and powerful in the tenth century B.C.E. continued to obtain in the first century C.E. Rather than desert wilderness, the Galilee is famously the most lush region of Israel, well watered (comparatively), and thus able to support both agriculture and manufacturing. Further, it was located in the traditionally more urban northern regions of Israel and the region was bristling with major cities during the late Second Temple. The Roman-built Decapolis ("ten cities") planted a solid, cosmopolitan and urbane culture in the Galilee. The region served as a crossroads for northern, southern, and westward trade routes. From the reign of Herod, it also contained eastward sea ports on the Mediterranean. Consequently, the Galilee played a critical role in the control of the entire region.[12]

---

10. Ibid., 67–70.
11. On the history and culture of the Galilee, see Richard Horsley, *Galilee: History, Politics, People* (Valley Forge, Pa.: Trinity Press International, 1995).
12. See ibid., for extensive review of the history of the Galilee. We will treat this material in closer detail in subsequent chapters.

But the same resources that gave it independence in the tenth century, brought destruction and occupation from the eighth century through the Second Temple period. Galilee was long the locus for occupying troops and governments. Herod used it for his own capital, as did Philip. Trade routes were more important to control than southern wilderness, even if it surrounded Jerusalem. Indeed, foreign governments quickly learned that they governed Jerusalem best when they attempted to govern—or even dwell in—her the least. Richard Horsley's survey of Galilee reveals a largely agrarian economy, made up of small family units working as subsistence farmers.[13] These traditional farming communities were, however, under heavy pressures. Families were taxed at several levels—local magistrates, city taxes, taxes to the Roman emperor and taxes to Jerusalem to support the Temple.[14] Frequent uprisings and the threat of more resulted in sustained military occupation which consumed additional land and resources, creating even more pressures.[15]

Alongside these traditional agrarian communities were several cities, perhaps as many as 204.[16] These cities were essentially Greek in culture and occupied by Rome.[17] In the traditional agrarian communities, disputes were resolved by traditional, local governing bodies.[18] Cities, however, continued to assert their own legal and financial control. Horsley writes:

> As in most peasant societies, the living was barely subsistence for most. Households were economically marginal and susceptible to any disruption in the annual agricultural cycle... [S]everal sorts of disruptions... could have a major effect on the economic and social viability of peasant families, from suddenly disruptive military expeditions through their territory to the steady escalation of economic pressure in the form of new demands from additional layers of rulers. Interestingly enough, it is precisely in times of such disruptions, for which we have evidence in Josephus, that overt social conflict erupted in Galilee, whether escalating banditry, peasant strikes, or widespread peasant revolt.[19]

Horsley devotes substantial space to discussions of these uprisings and revolts.[20] Galilee was culturally and militarily occupied. This culture was consistently seen as foreign, imposed and at odds with Jewish identity. Under the Romans, with the rise of the urbanization of Galilee, we find

13. Ibid., 189, 202–14.
14. Ibid., 220–21.
15. Ibid., 192, 196–97.
16. Ibid., 191, 215–16.
17. Ibid., 192, 240.
18. Ibid., 232–34.
19. Ibid., 201.
20. Ibid., 256–75.

a series of revolts and messianic movements. In addition, the Galilee seems to be a fertile location for religious extremism. Galilee, though in many ways different from the Judean wilderness, shared a common quality—each was a territory under foreign control. In each case, signs of "foreigners" were ubiquitous. Yet, in each case, the military forces of the foreign government were not able to completely police the populous, and regional, local disputes were resolved by local, indigenous people. Galilee was a frontier, the border lands between various, clashing ways of life, notions of government and expectations of order. It was both accessible and inaccessible to martial control. It was a breeding ground for banditry.

Jesse James' Missouri was also a land on the margins of government and civilization. Missouri has a complicated history of occupation despite never being "occupied" in any formal sense—claimed as territory by the French despite its native inhabitants, bought by Thomas Jefferson for the United States as part of the Louisiana Purchase, quickly settled by Europeans with the aid of enslaved Africans. As it was the gateway to the Louisiana Purchase, after the explorers Lewis and Clark, it became the first leg of a major roadway to the West for subsequent travelers and settlers.[21] Missouri was admitted entrance into the Union in 1821.

Slavery was legal in Missouri, and remained so as part of the Missouri Compromise (1820). This compromise, put forward as an attempt to forestall dissolution of the United States, fixed slavery to states / territories below the Mason-Dixon line (36 degrees, 30 minutes) and mandated that, for each free state admitted to the Union, a southern slave state must also be admitted. Clearly, given that the Western territories were all decidedly anti-slavery, this compromise would have resulted in the eventual decline of slavery in the United States. With the repeal of the Compromise in 1823, tensions between the settlers of the state of Missouri and its western neighbor, the territory of Kansas, heightened. Under the Randolph Act of 1823, each new territory admitted to the Union as a state would decide for itself if slave ownership would be legal. Individuals living in New England who opposed the spread of slavery organized colonization companies, sending abolitionists to stake a claim and reside in Kansas and, when the time came, vote opposing the legalization of slave ownership.[22] Missouri residents sympathetic to slavery (if not slave owners, themselves—actual practice in Missouri

---

21. In many ways, Missouri still performs this role. St. Louis boasts its Arch, the "Gateway to the West."

22. Thomas Goodrich, *War to the Knife: Bleeding Kansas, 1854–1861* (Mechanicsburg, Pa.: Stackpole, 1998), 9–10, 20–25.

varied) and highly antithetical to "back easterners" (who were seen as too "civilized" for rugged life on the frontier and, therefore, weaker in character) began to cross the border and interfere with elections. Without any sense of irony, they crossed into Kansas to commit election fraud and intimidate anti-slavery settlers, who were legal Kansas residents, in order to resist what they saw as the "foreign intrusion" of these settlers into Kansas politics.[23]

Tensions escalated. Conflict between Missouri and Kansas resulted in border wars marked by various massacres, coercive use of rape and arson, murder and other atrocities.[24] Though initially instigated by Missourians, the violence quickly became mutual. The conflict would play a critical role in escalating national tensions leading up to the cession of the Confederate States and the onset of the American Civil War. Missouri, however, although a slave state, would not become a part of the Confederacy, as it had long since been heavily occupied by United States federal troops sent in to quell the escalating Kansas–Missouri border war.

The topography of Missouri played an essential role in shaping the federal response to its political crises. Missouri, as noted before, played a key role as the first stage of the road westward. The Mississippi River, the great watercourse linking North to South and dividing the United States into eastern and western regions, established Missouri's eastern border. Into the Mississippi ran the Missouri River, the main artery crossing west across the northern third of the state. The settlements of St. Louis and Kansas City early emerged and grew—St. Louis where the Missouri leaves the Mississippi, and Kansas City near the confluence of several other rivers both north and west and where the Missouri turns north to establish the state's northwestern boundary. Early railways and roads roughly followed the course of the Missouri River across Missouri and Kansas, and river and rail transit offered settlers, manufacturers, farmers, traders and federal troops a means for rapid deployment westward. In short, Missouri played too important a role in American expansionist plans to be left lawless. As a result, Missouri found itself occupied by federal troops, considered by the local residents as agents of

---

23. Ibid., 32, 34–36.
24. See, in general, Wiley Britton, *The Civil War on the Border* (New York: Putnam's, 1899) for the classic "of the moment" account, along with Goodrich. Both are sources of primary and anecdotal history. For critical reflection, see Patrick Brophy, ed., *Bushwackers of the Border: The Civil War Period in Western Missouri* (Nevada, Mo.: Vernon County Historical Society, 1980); and Jay Monaghan, *The Civil War on the Western Border* (Boston: Little & Brown, 1958).

a "foreign" and "hostile" government, before, during and after the Civil War. These troops were particularly concerned about controlling the regions of St. Louis and Kansas City and the intervening shipping and rail routes. The relatively crude state of infrastructure and hostile citizenry meant that these same troops had a much more difficult time controlling the population living "in country," away from major cities or the major rivers. East to West, travel was rapid. North to South, it was not.

Jesse and Frank James began their careers as guerrilla soldiers during the Missouri–Kansas border wars. They had grown up "in country," familiar with the major urban centers (particularly Kansas City) but not immediately under their influence. They continued to ride as guerrillas during the Civil War under the leadership of William C. Quantrill.[25] Many Missourians saw these guerrilla armies—literally bandits and terrorist groups—as Missouri's only form of "regular army." Occupied by federal troops from before the war's beginning, Missouri never had the option of secession. The "black flag" troops were seen as Missouri's own unofficial militia, defending the home rights of Missouri citizens. At the war's end, since those who rode with Quantrill and other guerrilla generals were not "regular army," they did not qualify for Lincoln's amnesty program. Some were captured and prosecuted. Most left Missouri or changed their identity. A few others, like the James brothers, continued their life as marauders, this time as bandits, during the era of Reconstruction.[26]

25. Don R. Bowen, "Guerrilla War in Western Missouri, 1862–65," *Comparative Studies in History and Society* 19 (1977): 30–51. On guerrilla warfare in Civil War-era Missouri, see also Richard S. Brownlee, *Grey Ghosts of the Confederacy Guerilla Warfare in the West, 1861–1963* (Baton Rouge: Louisiana State University Press, 1958); Albert E. Castel, *William Clarke Quantrill: His Life and Times* (New York: Fell, 1962); William Elsey Connelley, *Quantrill and the Border Wars* (repr. New York: Pageant, 1956); Michel Fellman, *Inside War: The Guerrilla Conflict in Missouri During the Civil War* (New York: Oxford University Press, 1989); Edward E. Leslie, *The Devil Knows How to Ride: The True Story of William Clarke Quantrill and His Confederate Raiders* (New York: Random House, 1996). The two most famous militia/guerrilla "generals" were Bill Anderson and William Quantrill. They seem to have attempted to outdo one another in savagery.

26. On the pressures of Reconstruction Era Missouri, particularly vis-à-vis the restrictions faced by former Confederates or Confederate sympathizers, see Edward L. Ayers, *The Promise of the New South: Life After Reconstruction* (New York: Oxford University Press, 1992); William E. Parrish, *Missouri Under Radical Rule, 1865–1870* (Columbia: University of Missouri Press, 1965). Yeatman, *Frank and Jesse James*, 88, 89 discusses the Drake Construction of Missouri, post-1865 which required loyalty oaths for ex-troops and "all clergy, educators, corporate officers and lawyers."

All three figures, David, Jesus and Jesse James, lived and worked within areas that were under control of governments deemed foreign. These foreign governments ruled by superimposition of ideology and practice, and this superimposition was maintained by martial force. The exchange, then, was not mutual but one of external, hegemonic domination. Each local government was also largely involved in commercial and economic activities that supported the foreign government. There was a sharp cultural difference among the local and foreign communities, where the former was considered less civilized and refined by the latter. In other words, structurally and functionally, all three figures inhabit a colonial space.

Though only the Galilee is actually described as a "colony" occupied by an "empire," the functional characteristics of colonial control are more critical than the presence or absence of the words "colony" and "empire" officially employed. All three regions are, in effect, "occupied" by foreign rulers, hegemonic over a local (largely agrarian and peasant) population, seeking to extract natural resources and carry on an economic program to the benefit of the occupying power. Further, in all three cases, there is clear imposition (often violent) of "foreign" cultural and political values and practice. Yet there are also problems with calling these three regions "colonial." As, perhaps, Missouri best illustrates, hegemony, extra-regional economic and martial control, and definite bifurcation into altern and subaltern classes can most certainly occur in contexts where both local "colonized" and "colonizer" share a common language, ethnicity and "race" and, indeed, even a common governance and constitution.

By establishing Iron Age Judah, Roman Galilee, and Reconstruction-era Missouri as colonial spaces, it may seem that we are going to employ postcolonial interpretation, arguably a critical sub-genre of cultural studies.[27] Though we will occasionally engage postcolonial literature (particularly mining it for useful equivalent structures, methods and terms), we will not, however, be engaging in a postcolonial reading of any of our texts. The complexities of the Missouri context and the notion

---

27. The location of postcolonialism as a genre of cultural studies critique is, we acknowledge, debated. Postcolonial critique is within the line of discussion begun by Hoggart and others at Birmingham. However, the work of scholars such as Homi Bhabha and Gayatra Spivak—in their concepts of Hybridity, Mimicry and Mockery—are grounded in poststructuralism. Ultimately, while we do recognize that much cultural studies critique has been rooted in Marxism (and, therefore, structuralism) we understand cultural studies critiques such as the location of "culture," *auteur* notions about the composition of "popular," the analysis of "high" verses "popular" art and literature, are questions that also may be addressed via poststructuralism.

of "race," in particular, makes us reticent about the application of post-colonialism to biblical criticism in our study. "Race," as understood by postcolonial critics such as Edward Said, Gayatri Spivak, Homi Bhabha and, within biblical criticism, R.S. Sugirtharajah, is a nineteenth century construct, mostly rooted in emerging "scientific" notions of genotype-phenotype control, eugenics, and rudimentary linkage between anthropology and genetics. In two of our contexts, "race" was more about ethnicity—language, god, perhaps dress and cultural values. It was a product of locale and heritage, not genetics; its markers were cultural, not physiognomic. Modern notions of race, particularly of racial identity as an automatic and necessary manifestation of birth, are critical to the tensions described by, for example, Bhabhan hybridity or Spivak's views of subalterity and such notions of race simply do not exist in Israel either in the Iron Age or in the Roman Era. In the Missouri context, race is a significant factor although the "colonial subjects" that are the focus of our study are of the same race as the "colonial powers." In Missouri, those who perceive themselves as oppressed by the federal government were equal party to the racist ideologies and systems of that government. A simple postcolonial critique will not work in our analysis. Being cautious in our use of postcolonial concepts does not mean, however, that we will be disregarding the complex inter-relationships between altern and subaltern communities in a political context fraught with both unequal power and cultural conflict. To the contrary, they are central to our argument. We largely assume a Gramskian model of cultural hegemony, and it is this social, cultural and political tyranny that is ultimately opposed by the social bandit.

Social Banditry, Martyrs, Messiahs and the History of Memory

Eric Hobsbawm's *Bandits* was first published in 1969.[28] Hobsbawm was certainly harbinger (if not originator) of a great deal on interest in bandit and insurgent movements by late twentieth-century historians and social scientists.[29] For Hobsbawm:

---

28. Eric Hobsbawm, *Bandits* (rev. ed.; New York: New Press, 2000).
29. Rather than detail the numerous works on banditry and social banditry, we instead note a few works particular to biblical studies and Jesse James: Horsley, *Galilee*, 256–75; Eric Thurman, "Looking for a Few Good Men: Mark and Masculinity," in *New Testament Masculinities* (ed. Stephen D. Moore and Janice Capel Anderson; Semeia 45; Atlanta: Society of Biblical Literature, 2004), 137–61; Brent Shaw, "Bandits in the Roman Empire," *Past and Present* 105 (1984): 3–52; Pat O'Malley, "The Suppression of Banditry: Train Robbers in the US Border States

> [S]ocial bandits...are peasant outlaws whom the lord and state regard as criminals but who remain within peasant society, and are considered by their people as heroes, as champions, avengers, fighters for justice, perhaps even leaders of liberation, and in any case as men to be admired, helped and supported. In cases where a traditional society resists the encroachments and historical advance of central governments and states, native or foreign, they may be helped and supported even by the local lords. This relation between the ordinary peasant and the rebel, outlaw, and robber is what makes social banditry interesting and significant. It also distinguishes it from two other kinds of rural crime... Underworld robbers and raiders regard the peasants as their prey... It would be unthinkable for a social bandit to snatch the peasants'...harvest in his own territory.[30]

Foreign governments claim, and exert, some local control; yet they cannot completely suppress all resistance:

> Before the nineteenth century no state with a territory larger than could be walked across in a day or two, possessed sufficient knowledge, regularly updated, of who lived in its territory, was born and died there... No state, before the railways, and the telegraphs, ancestors of the modern communications revolution, could know what happened in its remoter corners or move its agents rapidly to take action... The weakness of power contained the potential for banditry.[31]

Bandits and banditry arise when the imposed state power challenges some aspect of local culture, making it illegal or economically impossible. The state power, however, lacks sufficient martial control of the given region to completely enforce its will. "Banditry simultaneously challenges the economic, social and political order by challenging those who hold or lay claim to power, law and control of resources... They

---

and Bushrangers in Australia," *Crime & Social Justice* 16 (1981): 32–39; Kent L. Steckmesser, "Robin Hood and the American Outlaw," *Journal of American Folklore* 79 (1966): 348–55; Richard White, "Outlaw Gangs of the Middle American Border: American Social Bandits," *Western Historical Quarterly* 12 (1981): 387–408. Some key critique comes especially from Alan Blok, "The Peasant and the Brigand: Social Banditry Reconsidered," *Comparative Studies in Society and History* 14 (1972): 495–504; *The Mafia of a Sicilian Village: A Study of Violent Peasant Entrepreneurs 1860–1960* (Oxford: Blackwell, 1974), 97–102. T. J. Stiles, *Jesse James: Last Rebel of the Civil War* (New York: Knopf, 2002), 382–89, 391–92 is particularly critical of applying the notion of "social bandit" to Jesse James. Hobsbawm answers Blok and several of his other critics in the recent edition of *Bandits* (pp. 168–85).

30. Hobsbawm, *Bandits*, 20.
31. Ibid., 15, 16.

only become outlaws, and punishable as such, when they are judged by a criterion of public law and order which is not theirs."[32]

The bandit, tied to the community by strong family and ethnic bonds (here, the bandit's origins among agrarian kinship communities becomes critical) is finally compelled to take to the wilds and resist, often attracting a band of followers.[33] This group of outlaws lives by violence and theft. They direct the bulk of their hostility against forces representing the encroaching power of the foreign state, often seen as "taking from the rich" to support the interests of the poor (Robin Hood is, indeed, a prototype).

These bandits become "social bandits" (and not mere brigands or thieves) because they claim or are understood to represent local protest, local power. They are in the wild *because of* the impression of inappropriate control by the state. In the wilderness, they fight for the local peasantry, at times vicariously enacting the resistance that others desire but are too timid to engage,[34] and at times directly enforcing local justice, resolving local disputes and protecting the oppressed. In return, the local community shelters the bandits, offering them protection, food, news and concealment. Hobsbawm notes that the "social bandit" has difficulty existing in contexts where modern communications facilitate deployment of state troops who can move more rapidly than local rumor. Social bandits are often christened folk heroes within their own lifetimes or within the first generation of their contemporaries, and are popular figures in oral legend and folklore. Further, they blend various strands of folklore and folk tradition into their own narrative.[35]

The bandits meet their end only rarely by victory (driving out the invader); their public career is normally two to three years long.[36] More often, they melt back into the community once the most immediate and egregious imposition of foreign power is neutralized. Another common fate is betrayal to state authorities, usually by a community outsider who

32. Ibid., 7–8.
33. Bandits are also normally, though not exclusively, male. On female bandits, see ibid., 146–49. Women are most notably the bandits' paramours or "doubles," not necessarily sexual partners, but parallel figures to the (often lead) male bandit.
34. Hobsbawm identifies one type of bandit as the "Avenger." These hyper-violent figures offer catharsis as much as justice. Ibid., 71–73.
35. Ibid., 157, 160. Though, note, p. 154: "[T]he more remote the public was—in time or space—from a celebrated brigand, the easier it was to concentrate on his positive aspects, the easier to overlook the negative. Nevertheless the process of selective idealization can be traced back to the first generation."
36. Ibid., 59.

for a variety of reasons has managed to become ensconced within the bandit group. Social bandits are geographically contained, as well. If they attempt to move beyond their immediate sphere of support, they are regarded as simply dangerous dissidents and not noble resistors and they do not enjoy local support or aid; consequently, they are unable to be successful in their banditry. These social bandits are long remembered by their communities, celebrated in song, folklore and oral tradition. In subsequent memory, their unique talents (intellectual and martial), endurance, vigor and even charm are lauded.

Hobsbawm is correct and astute to observe that local banditry is often a response to foreign power, entered into by individuals (not exclusively, but predominantly, men) who, at some level, see themselves and are seen by others as the local voice of protest to the foreign rule.[37] At minimum, the violence, mayhem and disorder brought about by banditry is seen as more tolerable to locals than is the idea of handing over a few more "good, hometown boys" to representatives of foreign law. Bandits need support. They need places to store and exchange stolen goods. They need weapons. They need transportation. They need shelter and seasonal clothing. They need food. They need to know where state troops are searching or stationed. They need to know if state troops are approaching. They can accomplish none of this without local support and help. Doubtless, by their willingness to engage in violence and their local knowledge, they can intimidate some into providing what they need (or, at minimum, not hindering the bandits in acquiring it for themselves). But, even more clearly, the bandit must have at least some if not most of the community offering support out of a sense of loyalty.

Local, popular support for the social bandit arises, in part, because the bandits perform services for the community such as avenging wrongs and providing a check to state power. They also, however, provide a vicarious release for an oppressed peasantry, and that boldness awakens genuine admiration. Bandits may do wrong, but at least they are doing *something*. "Banditry itself is therefore not a programme for peasant society but a form of self-help to escape it in particular circumstances... Banditry is freedom."[38]

---

37. Though, note: "[B]anditry as a mass phenomenon can appear not only when non-class societies resist the rise or imposition of class societies, but when traditional rural class societies resist the advance of other rural...or urban or foreign class societies, states or regimes... All resist the encroaching power of outside authority and capital" (ibid., 9)

38. Ibid., 29, 30.

Returning to our triptych of figures—David, Jesus and Jesse James—we find that a general outline of the career of each reveals similarity to Hobsbawm's Social Bandit model. The geo-social and political context of each figure conforms to the conditions described by Hobsbawm. All three operate largely in rural areas on the fringes of urbanized communities that are largely governed by "alien" authorities. All three have agrarian roots and community ties. Each attract followers even as (perhaps "largely because") conflicts arise with the state. Each is seen as a leader of an alternate state/kingdom that challenges the legitimacy of the dominant government and voices questions about that government's ability to rule ethically. Each is engaged, knowingly and defiantly, in illegal activity (as defined by the state). David eventually takes the role of legitimate king (that is, if the biblical record is trustworthy at all in its narrative), but Jesus and Jesse James are betrayed by their own followers while they are relatively young men at the apex of their fame and popular appeal.

One central problem in Hobsbawm is his lack of clarity regarding where and how he sees the idea of "social banditry" forming. It is not clear whether Hobsbawm sees the social bandit as an actual figure reoccurring in various diverse locations in history, or whether the social bandit is an *ex post facto* rhetorical construction, a folk type or motif. For example, Hobsbawm begins his book by noting the surprisingly high number of bandit figures who share a relatively standard bandit *cursus* (dis)*honorum*. They begin among a disempowered agrarian peasantry living in a peripheral region of a dominant state power. Hobsbawm notes that social bandits occur in a huge array of communities, varied by time and geography. At times, he seems to suggest that social banditry is a socio-historical phenomenon. Social banditry seems the almost inevitable outcome of several economic, geographic and socio-political ingredients.

> Social banditry...is one of the most universal social phenomena known to history, and one of the most amazingly uniform. Practically all cases belong to two or three clearly related types, and the variations within these are relatively superficial. What is more, this uniformity is not the consequence of cultural diffusion, but the reflection of similar situations within peasant societies whether in China, Peru, Sicily, the Ukraine or Indonesia.[39]

---

39. Ibid., 21.

Yet, Hobsbawm also acknowledges the role of legend in the construction of the bandit stories. Hobsbawm identifies his three sub-genres of social bandit as the Noble Robber, the Avenger, and the *Haiduks* (a Turkish term for, essentially, peasant *ronin*). In his description of each (particularly the first two), he is quick to note that, while the bandits all fall into a remarkably consistent career path, their exploits are overwhelmed by legend. Hobsbawm, for example, openly admits Robin Hood (his paradigm for the Noble Robber) cannot be historically recovered and is "pure myth."[40] He considers stories that Jesse James, like Robin Hood, stole from the rich to give to the local poor to be pure folklore, noting that an identical story is told about another bandit.[41] He is also dubious that Jesse James was hesitant to kill anyone, contrary to local rhetoric that asserted the James brothers only resorted to mortal violence when absolutely required.[42]

It would seem clear that the actual career (not to mention the motivation) of the social bandit is shrouded by legend, lore, ballad, and local (political) sensibility. This local story-telling is subject to the normal "rules" of folk culture and oral literature. Bandits and other parties are often aware of their respective roles in the script.[43] Not surprisingly, these stories will manifest motifs and types. Hobsbawm never seems resolved on the question of whether or not the "social bandit" is a type, constructed and maintained by communities (perhaps even, at times, also believed in by the bandit himself), or if the social bandit simply "is." Hobsbawm can write that "very little about the historical reality of social banditry, let alone the career of any actual bandit, can be inferred from the context of the myths told about them or the songs sung about them."[44] But he also writes that "the set of beliefs about social banditry is simply too strong and uniform to be reduced to an innovation…or even as a product of literary construction."[45] It would seem, at first reading, that Hobsbawm is confusing social and historical reality with analysis of folklore and oral tradition. Hobsbawm, however, does seem aware of the issue, noting that "for the bandit myth, the reality of their existence may be secondary."[46]

---

40. Ibid., 46.
41. Ibid., 48–49.
42. Ibid., 52.
43. Ibid., 151.
44. Ibid., 182.
45. Ibid., 158.
46. Ibid., 10.

His point is subtle. Can the history of a bandit, particularly a popular one, ever be separated from the legend? In a sense, there is a substantial argument to be made that it is exactly the sort of popular reception and regard that makes a social bandit a *social* bandit (and not merely a serial killing, hyper-violent, thieving thug). Popular reception, is, of course, mediated by folk and oral tradition. The "myth," then, *is* the history and the mechanism of social construction. The point of accounts of social banditry is not so much reporting of what actually happened as it is an offer of a heuristic for a peasant community to articulate something about itself in relation to a foreign power, particularly when that peasant community is almost certainly going to "lose" the conflict.[47] The only reason stories of social bandits exist is because a larger (subaltern) community constructed stories about them, and, once these stories have been constructed, the actuality of the social bandit is over-written. The "actual" of history—locations, activities, names, dates, witness narratives, artifacts, etc.—becomes intertwined with the narrative of legend and lore. Lore, which makes the "historical" worth reporting, obscures the actual even as it depends upon it. History erases as it writes.

In many ways the character of the social bandit resembles the character of the martyr. Martyrologies have stock narrative patterns, tropes and motifs, as well. Much like social bandits, martyrs are seen as the local defiance of the subaltern against an encroaching foreign power. Like social bandits, the stories of martyrs are steeped in violence. Much like social bandits, martyrs depend upon a broader community for "success." Martyrs, by definition, cannot write their own histories and require the community to preserve their memories and interpret the meaning of their actions.

One may, of course, ask whether or not social bandits themselves understood their actions in terms of socio-political protest. The same may be asked of martyrs. Certainly some individuals in history have died at the hands of the state, believing they were persecuted solely for their ideology and social protests, yet they failed to leave a community following who venerated them—or perhaps even identified them—as martyrs. Others may well have been killed by the state for a variety of reasons, none of which were related to suppression of a political or religious idea or protest. Yet the communities these individuals left behind told the stories of these deaths in ways that constructed a martyr. The same must be true of social banditry. Some outlaws intended, via violence, to effect some larger idea of "rightness" but failed, in the end,

---

47. Our point is that, at one level, all history is etiological myth.

to convince anyone that they were anything other than common brigands and thugs. Others, intent on a career of violence to achieve power or to become wealthy, were identified as local heroes. In the case of both the martyr and the social bandit, it is the community memory, then, that creates the larger ideologically driven dynamic that both bestows and actually creates the identity of the martyr and the bandit. In both cases, opinions will vary. To the state, the social bandit or martyr (or messiah, for that matter) are all outlaws and threats. Yet, to their communities they are regarded as heroes precisely because of this dissent and the courage it represents.

In the case of both the martyr and the social bandit, it is this later, communally constructed and bestowed identity that becomes the historical "fact" of the event for their communities, even as the state struggles to preserve its own narrative. One cannot pry beneath the veneer of the martyrology to see the "real" martyr; only scant, skeletal data, all already interpreted by conflicting interests, remain. In a similar case, one cannot fully unveil the "historical" social bandit; too many anecdotes, folk traditions, state issued descriptions, anti-state rhetoric and general cultural tropes and forms from oral narrative overlay his career. In the case of both martyrs and bandits, the social memory, the folk tradition, the oral tale, the ballad, the cultural and historical "memory" *are* the history and they intertwine with the "official" narrative.

Elizabeth Castelli has explored this aspect of martyrology as "memory."[48] She writes "the notion of collective memory allows one to move past often unresolvable questions of 'what really happened' to questions of how particular ways of constructing the past enable later communities to constitute and sustain themselves."[49] Castelli, relying on the work of Maurice Halbwach,[50] sees "memory" as a social construction "the product of the individual's interaction with his or her group... [I]ndividuals remember things only in relation to the memories of

---

48. Elizabeth A. Castelli, *Martyrdom and Memory: Early Christian Culture Making* (Gender, Theory and Religion; New York: Columbia University Press, 2004). "My thesis is that memory work done by early Christians on the historical experience of persecution and martyrdom was a form of culture making whereby Christian identity was indelibly marked by the collective memory of the religious suffering of others... Martyrdom has to do, foundationally, with competing ideas about the character and legitimacy of different systems of power" (p. 4).

49. Ibid., 5.

50. In particular, *Les cadres sociaux de la mémoire* (Paris: Alcan, 1925); *La mémoire collective* (2d ed.; Paris: Presses Universitaires de France, 1968); *La topographie légendaire des évangiles en terne sainte: Étude de mémoire collective* (Paris: Presses Universitaires de France, 1941).

others."[51] Memory is narrative and story-telling. It is mutually, communally constructed reality. Moving beyond analysis of subjectivity resulting from philosophies of cognition,[52] Halbwach argued that the gospels, particularly in their role as redacted transcriptions of oral tradition, were central examples of "social memory" and demonstrated the difficulties in separating "memory" from "history." Castelli, critiquing Halbwach, applies his central arguments about the gospels to early Christian martyrology.[53] She observes "the task of early Christian historians was the production of Christian collective memory, a memory characterized by striking degrees of continuity... One might even go so far as to argue that they did not simply *preserve* the story of persecution and martyrdom, but, in fact, *created* it."[54] She notes that martyrdom is a method of protest of power, particularly power that is foreign and imposed.[55] But martyrdom is also a performance.[56] Castelli notes:

> Martyrdom is not simply an action. Martyrdom requires audience (whether real or fictive), retelling, interpretation, and world- and meaning-making activity. Suffering and violence in and of itself is not enough. In order for martyrdom to emerge, both the violence and its suffering must be infused with particular meanings. Indeed, martyrdom can be understood as one form of refusing the *meaninglessness* of death itself, of insisting that suffering and death do not signify emptiness and nothingness.[57]

To demonstrate her point, Castelli concludes her volume with the story of Cassie Bernal.[58] Bernal was a student at Columbine High School, Littleton, Colorado. On April 20, 1999, two disturbed young men, Dylan

---

51. Castelli, *Martyrdom and Memory*, 11. On memory, history and myth as categories with overlap and distinction, see pp. 28–32. Note, also, p. 26: "...critical engagement implies acceptance of particular contemporary historiographical standards, such as the supremacy of the rules of evidence and the importance of veiling or minimizing perspective. It is helpful to remember, however, that these standards are conventional and themselves hardly specific. This is not to diminish their value for the professional work of historians, but it does suggest that it is unhistorical to hold ancient sources to these standards... One does not need to venture far into the ancient historiographical project to recognize different governing values at work." We would move this even more broadly into the realm of popular history and literature.
52. As per Locke, for example.
53. Castelli, *Martyrdom and Memory*, 13, 19–26.
54. Ibid., 25.
55. Ibid., 39–52.
56. Ibid., 52–55.
57. Ibid., 34.
58. Ibid., 172–96.

Klebold and Eric Harris, arrived at their school with several weapons. They began a killing spree which ended with their own suicide. Bernal was one of the slain. According to early reports, Bernal was asked by Klebold if she believed in God. When she said yes, she was shot in the face.

Bernal and her family were devout evangelical Christians. They quickly began to celebrate, in the midst of the unthinkable tragedy that pervaded Littleton, the courage of Bernal in her testimony. Literally facing death, she would not betray her faith. Her parents would eventually publish Bernal's biography—with a particular focus on her faith and her final moments of courage—in a bestselling work titled *She Said Yes*.[59] Bernal's family and thousands of other evangelical Christians regard Bernal as a modern-day martyr.

As time has continued, reports have revealed that Klebold and Harris asked several students questions about their belief in God, heaven and hell and shot their victims without regard to the answer. Those who said yes were shot, as were those who said no. The assassins also asked an assortment of irrelevant questions. Clearly, they were not targeting people of faith. At present, it is not entirely clear, despite early reports, if Bernal had even been among those actually asked questions about her faith, and none of the other students who were questioned are regarded as "martyrs." Klebold and Harris were not engaged in a rampage against people of faith, and the earliest memory of the community of survivors was not that this was a moment of martyrdom. Yet, none of these facts seem to matter. For countless evangelicals, Bernal is a martyr. What "really happened" or why it happened is not relevant; what the community remembers and how the community interprets or understands that memory is what matters.

The same conditions that surround martyrs seem to be true of both bandits and messiahs, particularly those who also delve into the folk patterns of the martyr and the bandit. Self-appointed messiahs, simply put, are not successful if they do not manage to convince others of their messianic status. They certainly do not persist in communal memory beyond their own deaths without achieving a community of followers who preserve, disseminate and most likely construct the messianic identity. Those later identified as messiah figures, though certainly aware of a high influence on others, may never have made such claims of their own. Historical Jesus research has revealed how difficult it can be, for

---

59. Misty Bernall, *She Said Yes: The Unlikely Martyrdom of Cassie Bernall* (New York: Pocket, 2000).

example, to recover, via conventional tools of historical inquiry, any precision and certainty regarding the actual self-understanding and claims of Jesus of Nazareth. Even further, should we decide simply to grant the claims of the gospels that Jesus presented himself as messiah, the gospels alone offer exceptionally little specific information to enable any reconstruction of the full, systematic doctrine of what he, and others, might have meant by "messiah."

Hobsbawm addresses in several locations aspects of social banditry that appear to overlap with religious devotion. He notes several twentieth-century bandit movements that are openly linked with messianic expectations.[60] For example, *Rampok* bands of Indonesia and the 1945 Javanese movement were openly religious. Hobsbawm notes multiple moments of "religious cults around the graves of some dead brigands in Argentina."[61] The borders between bandits, messiahs and martyrs becomes thin. All three seem to be forged by similar pressures. All three are honed by public memories.

Bandits, Messiahs and Martyrs

We are comparing the public memories of David, Jesus and Jesse James because the borders between the careers of bandit, messiah and martyr are as unpoliced and wild as the home of their lead characters. Monarchs, martyrs, messiahs and social bandits are made by public memories. They are made by the way they are inscribed, written, in-and-by popular culture. These constructions are similar because they are forged in similar cultural and political foundries.

As the remainder of this book unfolds we will explore further how each figure—David, Jesus and Jesse James—are social bandits. All three are engaged in activities deemed illegal by the state as a form of protesting the state's authority. All three become figures of later communal narrative. David is ideological forefather of both Jesus and American mythology captured in "Wild West" film, art, literature and popular narrative. We argue that there are also critical overlaps in the career-arc of Jesus and Jesse James and the narratives of these two figures, narratives crafted from the amalgamation of oral legend perpetuated in the context of political resistance, and we reveal the problems of discovering the "real" Jesse James and Jesus of Nazareth, problems arising from the intersection of inter-text, communal memory structures and similar

---

60. Hobsbawm, *Bandits*, 110–11.
61. Ibid., 160.

"afterlives." Drawing from cultural studies, we will argue that many of the distinctions imposed on these figures are artificial, imposed by arbitrary binaries of "high" and "low" culture, "scholarly" and "popular" interpretation, and "religious" and "secular" phenomenon.

We are comparing these figures because the comparison illuminates how wild the borders are around each category and how the memories of such robust-seeming men are, in reality, delicate and fragile. We are comparing these figures because the comparison reveals that their characterizations and constructions, crafted by public memory, arise as much, if not more, from the needs and contexts of their memorializers than from their actual careers. We are comparing these figures because the comparison reveals how much history relies on, is made up of, memory. We are comparing these figures because, in the comparison we realize how, seen in the right light, it can be very difficult to tell if we are looking at David in the Judean Wilderness, Jesus entering Jerusalem, or Jesse James approaching Kansas City.

> *He pressed his right hand against his closed eyes and rubbed. They were red and tired. For the briefest moment his shoulders drooped. He exhaled and seemed to repossess himself. He rolled his hand around to first rub, then scratch his chin as he opened his eyes to regard the city lying below him.*
>
> *He turned his head toward a hand that touched against his arm, one of his men handing him water. Without making eye contact, he took it and drank, tasting the steel cold water and limey road dust that coated all of his clothing, his face, everything. He kept his eyes on the town below. It bustled with activity as its citizens went about their ordinary day. By instinct, he counted the number of soldiers he saw, noting how thinly spread they seemed for the size of such a place. He drank again, then passed the water back.*
>
> *He could work here. People would help; his reputation had traveled further and faster than he did. Many who wouldn't help would be too frightened to interfere. True, this wasn't quite the same as the work on the wilderness, but that was the point. New opportunities. A victory here would solidify his control of the region. His work on the margins was going well, but it wasn't long-term. He was as far as he would be able to go, and he had spent years now biting road dust and homeless. If he ever wanted this to change, he needed to go forward, toward town, toward the conflict that was absolutely certain, a conflict he was wagering he would win in the end.*
>
> *He looked casually over his shoulders, noting through his peripheral vision that his band was with him, watching him, ready to move when he did. Their views were split about the wisdom of what he was doing, but they would come with him anyway. The opposition, to be sure, was also*

1. *Bandits, Martyrs and Messiahs*

ready. The soldiers would certainly act to do their jobs. The only uncertainty, and the critical uncertainty, was how the crowds would react. He sniffed and spurred his mount forward, deciding that the only way to know was to find out. One by one, his band followed him forward, down to the town below and the last confrontation. He almost turned to look behind him, sensing that one of them tarried more, seemed an odd mixture of resolution and hesitation. The city glittered below, with its hope of dinner and a bed; he dropped his eyes back down and put the matter from his mind and rode toward the crowds now forming below, awaiting him, singing already about his life.

Chapter 2

DAVID, THE BANDIT

King of the Wild Frontier

The narratives took shape thousands of years ago—an underdog triumphs, a hunted man finds refuge in the wilderness, an unexpected savior appears upon the horizon, a promise of a once and future king—the strands tangle together and then come unbound, forming and reforming in different configurations, knotting around one figure and then another. David did not begin the story, since his tale drew on ancient Near Eastern stories already in circulation, but his particular narrative becomes the foundation for the story in Western culture. So integral is the biblical story of David to our religion, our politics and our arts that recent investigations that call the historicity of his story into question have caused uproar in the academy, in synagogues and churches and even in the secular streets.

Textual excavation of David has intensified at the same time and at the same pace as archaeological investigation, fueled in part by the argument between the so-called minimalists and the maximalists. Minimalists and maximalists position themselves at opposite ends of the historiographic pole. Minimalists rely primarily on archaeological and extra-biblical inscriptions to reconstruct the history of Israel. If a biblical event or character cannot be substantiated with non-biblical evidence then the event did not happen and the character did not exist. Maximalists believe in the basic historical reliability of the biblical text. Extra-biblical evidence trumps the biblical account only if it directly and explicitly contradicts it; in cases of extreme maximalists, not even then. In terms of the United Monarchy of Saul, David and Solomon, minimalists argue that it is entirely legendary and that David is no more real than King Arthur.[1]

---

1. For three prominent minimalist studies, see Philip R. Davies, *In Search of "Ancient Israel"* (Sheffield: Sheffield Academic, 1992), and Thomas Thompson,

Whereas maximalists do not regard the Bible as accurate on every point (few, for example, think that David's kingdom stretched as far as the Euphrates River, as it does according to 2 Sam 8:3), they do hold that the United Monarchy did indeed exist and that David was Israel's most glorious king. In search of Saul, David and Solomon, shovels and picks have dug down to the tenth century B.C.E. all over the land of Israel.

David dominates the controversy because David dominates the Hebrew Bible—more biblical text is devoted to him than any other figure. In fact, some scholars theorize that the first written stories in the Bible were the stories of David. The rest of the biblical text, then, serves as a foreword and an afterword to his stunning career.[2] Long after Israel loses political independence and the Davidic line disappears from history, the shepherd turned king continues to haunt. Various messianic ideas develop in early Judaism based upon the divine promise that David's house will be eternal (2 Sam 7:11–16). Isaiah, for example, writes:

> A shoot shall come out from the stump of Jesse, and a branch shall grow out of his roots. The spirit of the Lord shall rest on him, the spirit of wisdom and understanding, the spirit of counsel and might, the spirit of knowledge and the fear of the Lord. His delight shall be in the fear of the Lord. He shall not judge by what his eyes see, or decide by what his ears hear; but with righteousness he shall judge the poor, and decide with equity for the meek of the earth; he shall strike the earth with the rod of his mouth, and with the breath of his lips he shall kill the wicked. Righteousness shall be the belt around his waist, and faithfulness the belt around his loins. (Isa 11:1–5)

According to the genealogies in the gospels of Matthew and Luke (Matt 1:6; Luke 3:31), Jesus is this shoot. Part of his messianic credentials is his physical descent from David, and thus the Israelite king is integrated

---

The Bible in History: How Writers Create a Past (London: Cape, 1999), and *The Mythic Past: Biblical Archaeology and the Myth of Israel* (New York: Basic, 2000).

2. David's name appears over one thousand times. His story is told in 1 and 2 Samuel and 1 Chronicles. He is referenced repeatedly in 1 and 2 Kings and 2 Chronicles; many of the Psalms are attributed to him; his name and reign are integral to the work of the prophets; and several New Testament writers understand Jesus as a descendent of David. The theory that the Bible began as stories about David suggests that these stories were written by a court historian, who also wrote the parts of the Torah attributed to the J-source. For a discussion of this theory see Jonathan Kirsch, *King David: The Real Life of the Man Who Ruled Israel* (New York: Ballantine, 2000), 9–11. Kirsch provides a popular distillation of recent scholarship. See also Richard Elliot Friedman, *The Hidden Book in the Bible* (San Francisco: HarperSanFrancisco, 1998), and Harold Bloom and David Rosenberg, *The Book of J* (New York: Grove Weidenfeld, 1990).

into Christian theology.[3] Although messianic expectation is a focus of only a small segment of the Jewish populace, the idea that a son of David will return still weaves its way in and out of many prayers and songs. And regardless of religious conviction, the United Kingdom in general and David's reign in particular figures into the politics of Zionism and the State of Israel. Part of Israel's definition of and claim to the land rests in its understanding of David. Consequently, much is at stake in the textual and archeological investigation of this famed king.

The acclamation of David in religious and political contexts alike is not the result of a perfect character. David's flaws have always been evident, especially that nasty episode with Bathsheba and Uriah (2 Sam 11). Yet, from the biblical text itself to modern "biographies," David's bards have attempted to obscure, explain and apologize for his bad behavior. Although whitewashing is particularly evident in devotional literature, it has also been a feature of more secular and academic studies. Recently, however, studies that explore the more sinister side of the king have proliferated.[4] He has been called traitor, mercenary, terrorist, pirate, murderer, extortionist… The model of the bandit has also influenced the reconsideration of David's portrait; he has lately been called a "bandit-chief"[5] and a "brigand king."[6]

As his crimes accumulate, the debate over whether or not he even existed grows more acute. The recent reassessment of his character takes place against the backdrop of the minimalist–maximalist debate. The biblical story paints a picture of the incredible wealth and power of David and his son Solomon. Ruling over substantial territories, known internationally, engaged in spectacular building projects, the record of

---

3. Note, however, that Matthew and Luke relate Jesus to David in different ways—Matthew through the royal line and Luke through sons of David who never sat on the throne. In addition, despite the idea of the virgin birth, both Matthew and Luke connect Jesus to David through Joseph and not Mary, thus further complicating an already contrived connection.

4. David has had decriers before the recent turn in scholarship. Beginning in the seventeenth century, critique of biblical morality focused on the crimes of David. According to Yvonne Sherwood and Stephen D. Moore, the genesis of modern biblical scholarship can be found in Enlightenment critiques of David's character by writers such as Pierre Bayle (1647–1706) whose work portrays David "as a Nero-like monster of depravity" (*The Invention of the Biblical Scholar: A Critical Manifesto* [Minneapolis: Fortress, 2011], 52). Major shifts in biblical scholarship are intertwined with reassessments of David's character.

5. Finkelstein and Silberman, *David and Solomon*, 31.

6. Baruch Halpern, *David's Secret Demons: Messiah, Murderer, Traitor, King* (Grand Rapids: Eerdmans, 2001), 479.

their reign should be obvious in any archaeological investigation. Yet, neither king nor country is mentioned in the political records of any other tenth-century state, and the evidence in Israel for a great and wealthy kingdom is ambiguous at best. Jerusalem, the capital of the great United Kingdom, appears to be no more than a small village without imperial building and without luxury goods in the tenth century. Some claim to have found Solomon's gates in cities such as Megiddo, Gezer and Hazor; others disagree and date those gates to later periods in Israel's history.[7] Certainly, by the ninth century, a dynasty ruled in Jerusalem that called itself the "House of David," if the inscription found at Tel Dan is a reliable indication of political reality.[8] But a ruling family that claims the name of David over a century after he is alleged to have lived is hardly definitive proof that he did, indeed, live. Like Jesse James and Jesus, biography and story intertwine; unlike Jesse James and Jesus, the knots of legend may unravel leaving nothing but frayed rope behind.

With David, all we have is words: stories in scriptures, letters carved in stone. "The accounts of David's activities and experiences belong to the realm of literature rather than to historical documentation, and the David depicted in them must be seen as a literary figure rather than a historical one. The real David has generated a literary one. He may have transmitted some characteristics to his heir, but we do not know which," writes Shimon Bar-Efrat.[9] And according to the earliest words about

---

7. For a discussion between two perspectives on the tenth century, see Israel Finkelstein and Amihai Mazar, *The Quest for the Historical Israel: Debating Archaeology and the History of Early Israel* (Atlanta: Society of Biblical Literature, 2007). Finkelstein dates the gates and the monumental buildings at Gezer, Megiddo and Hazor to Omri's reign in the ninth century, whereas Mazar defends the traditional chronology which ascribes these building projects to Solomon in the tenth century. See also the appendices of Finkelstein and Silberman, *David and Solomon*, 267–88 for a more detailed analysis of the tenth-century archaeological data; compare to Halpern's appendices (*David's Secret Demons*, 427–78). Halpern also defends a more traditional chronology.

8. The initial reports on the Tel Dan inscription were published by Avraham Biran and Joseph Naveh, "An Aramaic Stele Fragment from Tel Dan," *Israel Exploration Journal* 43, no. 2–3 (1993): 81–98; and "The Tel Dan Inscription: A New Fragment," *Israel Exploration Journal* 45, no. 1 (1995): 1–18. For a taste of the subsequent (vitriolic) debate see Philip R. Davies, "'House of David' Built on Sand: The Sins of the Biblical Maximizers," *BAR* 20 (July/August 1994): 54–55; David Noel Freedman and Jeffrey C. Geoghegan, "'House of David' Is There!," *BAR* 21 (March/April 1995): 78–79.

9. Shimon Bar-Efrat, "From History to Story: The Development of the Figure of David in Biblical and Post-Biblical Literature," in *For and Against David: Story and History in the Books of Samuel* (ed. A. Graeme Auld and Erik Eynikel; Leuven:

David (the books of Samuel), his life of crime began well before he was crowned king. The biblical tales are up-front albeit brief about this time in David's life. Wanted dead by Saul (1 Sam 19:1, 11), David escapes the court with the help of Saul's children, Jonathan (David's best friend) and Michal (David's wife). Like any fugitive, David uses deception to get the supplies he needs before he heads to his hideout in the hills. He convinces the priest Ahimelech of Nob that he is really on a secret mission for Saul (1 Sam 21:3). Or was Ahimelech more intimidated than conned as Jonathan Kirsch and Robert Alter suggest?[10] The priest hands over both bread (the consecrated bread from the alter, no less) and weapons (appropriately, Goliath's sword) to the outlaw (1 Sam 21:7, 10). Next, David comes into the realm of the Philistine King Achish of Gath where he feigns madness by drooling in order to avert capture and certain death (1 Sam 21:14). Succeeding in the ruse, "David left there [Gath] and escaped to the cave of Adullam; when his brothers and all his father's house heard of it, they went down there to him. Everyone who was in distress, and everyone who was in debt, and everyone who was discontented gathered to him; and he became captain over them. Those who were with him numbered about four hundred" (1 Sam 22:1–2). Well-armed, well-fed and free of the Philistines, David wipes off his chin and becomes a bandit-chief.

In many ways, the stories of David in the books of Samuel conform to the model explicated in Eric Hobsbawm's seminal work on banditry. David is a "peasant [in this case shepherd] outlaw whom the…state regard[s] as a criminal…"[11] He emerges in a time of great change and social unrest, accompanied by "economic crisis."[12] Regardless of the exact configuration of the emerging Israelite monarchy, the transition from loose confederacy of tribes to nation state disrupts traditional social, economic and political structures. The men who gather around David are disaffected by the transitioning social, political and economic

---

Peeters, 2010), 49. This collection of essays explores many of the literary ambiguities of the portrait of David as well as the complexities of attaching the literary character to a historical person.

10. "Was David now reduced to begging a country priest for a handout? Or was he extorting provisions for himself—and perhaps a few cohorts who were traveling with him—with an oblique threat of violence?" Kirsch, *King David*, 79. Robert Alter, *The David Story: A Translation with Commentary of 1 and 2 Samuel* (New York: Norton, 1999) suggests that Ahimelech may suspect that David is a fugitive (p. 131). Jesus references this story to justify his own redefinition of Sabbath law (Mark 2:23–28).

11. Hobsbawm, *Bandits*, 20.

12. Ibid., 26.

order. They are alienated from their communities and hide out in the "mountain and pastoral regions...the classical zones for such outlawry."[13]

Frontier spaces are the borderlands between states and civilizations, where the forces of law and order grow weak as the terrain grows rough. David was born in such country, for Bethlehem is in the Judean hills. After he fled Saul's execution order, he again made such frontier spaces his home. As the biblical text records, "David remained in the strongholds in the wilderness, in the hill country of the Wilderness of Ziph" (23:14a); "David and his men were in the wilderness of Maon, in the Arabah to the south of Jeshimon" (23:24b); "When Saul returned from following the Philistines, he was told, 'David is in the wildernesses of En-gedi'" (24:1). David and his bandit band run free at the fringes of Saul's kingdom.

Ziph, Arabah, En-gedi...most contemporary readers have little more than a passing familiarity with such place names and may even be completely ignorant of the routes and landscapes they describe. But such attention to detail is more than just the work of an ancient writer with a fancy for cartography and geography. Finkelstein and Silberman note "The sheer weight of geographical information and long lists of place-names interwoven in [the Hebrew Bible's] stories testify to a familiarity with the ancient landscape of Judah and Israel."[14] The writers as well as the early readers knew these areas and the place names had a character just as evocative as, say, the Mississippi River or the Rockies do for American readers today. The place names and locations functioned as a sort of short-hand: "Thus the frequent appearance of place-names and geographical terms in David's tale in the first book of Samuel...speak in a coded language of familiarity with contemporary landscapes of power..."[15] Like the "arid and rugged" desert terrain with its "[t]wisting ravines" and "rough, deep canyons pocked with caves,"[16] David himself was free, rugged and untamed.

After escaping to Israel's desert wilderness and gathering a band of other disaffected and disenfranchised men around him, David begins his bandit career. He remains a fugitive, eluding and evading Saul again and

---

13. Ibid., 36.
14. Finkelstein and Silberman, *David and Solomon*, 33.
15. Ibid. Finkelstein and Silberman also use the geographic information to help date the text. The "wild south" that is essential as the setting for these stories was not so wild by the late eighth century when Finkelstein and Silberman argue the stories were written down. Therefore, they conclude, the bandit tales date back before the end of the ninth century (pp. 38–39) and circulated as oral traditions.
16. Ibid., 36.

again. Saul's inability to capture him demonstrates that the state is "remote, ineffective, and weak."[17] In between episodes of escape from Saul, David and his men conduct raids on border towns. One of the first targeted towns illustrates the ambiguity in the biblical text concerning David's actions. In ch. 23 David and his men "deliver" the town of Keilah from the Philistines. On the surface, it looks like David is acting the hero, protecting the small town from the ravages of their enemies. But a few notes in the text betray that this simple picture is more complex. After David's desperados "liberate" Keilah from the Philistines, they also "liberate" some of the people's possessions: they drive off the cattle of the Philistines and end up with the ephod of the Lord (1 Sam 23:5–6).[18] In addition, rather than welcoming David as a hero, David worries that the people of Keilah will hand him over to Saul. When he inquires of God, his worries are validated (1 Sam 23:12). The liberators are not welcomed with open arms; they are treated as criminal invaders. Hence, David and his men take their spoils and again head to the hills.[19]

Other incidents are portrayed with less ambiguity. In a discussion of the relationship between bandits and their communities, Hobsbawm notes that "not only must local men of wealth or authority come to terms with bandits, but in many rural societies they also have a distinct interest in doing so."[20] David and his men approach Nabel and try to convince him of this fact (1 Sam 25). They boast to him of their "good" deeds—they did not harm his shepherds and they did not steal his flocks; therefore, he owes them provision (25:7–8). "The request really amounted to extortion—'protection money' paid to a mafioso."[21] Nabal (whose name means "fool") dismisses David but his wife Abigail is a wiser reader of the situation. She pays proper tribute to David (25:23–31), her husband somehow drops dead (25:23–24) and Abigail runs off with the outlaw (25:40–42). Once David and his men cross the border to escape further the long arm of the law, their actions become not only treasonous and mercenary, but even brutal and murderous.

By this time, David has six hundred men under his leadership (27:2), and he seeks the protection of Achish, the Philistine king of Gath (and the same man in front of whom he feigned madness just a few chapters

---

17. Hobsbawm, *Bandits*, 59.
18. The exact possessors of these items and how they come into the hands of David and his men is ambiguous.
19. Kirsch, *King David*, 88–89; Steven L. McKenzie, *King David: A Biography* (New York: Oxford University Press, 2000), 93.
20. Hobsbawm, *Bandits*, 99.
21. McKenzie, *King David*, 97.

earlier). As Hobsbawm discusses, such a relationship can accrue benefit to a regional ruler: "a local reservoir of uncommitted armed men who, if they can be induced to accept the patronage of some gentleman or magnate, will greatly add to his prestige and may well on a suitable occasion add to his fighting or vote-getting force."[22] Unlike Nabel, the king of Gath recognizes Hobsbawm's wisdom and David and his men come under his protection. They enter into his service and conduct a series of raids along the border. According to the text, David tells Achish that he is raiding the towns of Israelites and their allies when he is really raiding the settlements of the Geshurites, the Girzites and the Amalekites.

> David struck the land, leaving neither man nor woman alive, but took away the sheep, the oxen, the donkeys, the camels, and the clothing, and came back to Achish. When Achish asked "Against whom have you made a raid today?" David would say, "Against the Negeb of the Jerahmeelites," or "Against the Negeb of the Kenites." David left neither man nor woman alive to be brought back to Gath, thinking, "They might tell about us, and say, 'David has done so and so.'" Such was his practice all the time he lived in the country of the Philistines. (1 Sam 27:9–11)

The political game may be to deceive the king of Gath, but David's machinations leave behind a bloodbath of the innocent.

In addition to these bandit raids, David barely avoids going to war explicitly and officially against Saul and the Israelites. He voluntarily joins the king of Gath (28:1–2) as he prepares for war against Saul and the people of Israel. However, the other Philistine lords refuse to march against Israel with a gang of "Hebrews," so David and his men are sent home (1 Sam 29).[23] The use of the word "Hebrew" in v. 3 to describe David and his cohorts by the Philistine lords is an unusual designation in the Samuel material and may be an additional indication of their bandit status. The word "Hebrew" may be related to the word *hapiru* as found in other ancient Near Eastern texts like the Armana letters. Whereas scholars first thought that the word named an ethnic group, further study suggests that the word is a sociological designation. The *hapiru* were bands of people disaffected politically and/or economically from the

---

22. Hobsbawm, *Bandits*, 100.

23. Some scholars argue that David did indeed participate in the war and thus was involved in the death of Saul and Jonathan. The biblical writer constructs this story in order to exculpate David from the crimes of regicide and usurpation. See Halpern, who calls the story of the Philistines' rejection of David's help "a dissertation of denial!" (*David's Secret Demons*, 78).

colonial powers that controlled the ancient Near East. They were implicated in raids, thefts, murders and general lawlessness. In other words, they appear to be bandits.[24]

Most scholars position themselves somewhere in between the two radical poles of maximalist and minimalist. Yet scholars who stake out very different positions in the maximalist–minimalist debate surrounding David converge in their attention on David's frontier adventures after his daring escape from Saul. Positioning themselves as a "middle way" through the minimalist–maximalist controversies, Israel Finkelstein and Neil Asher Silberman actually begin their study with the assertion, "the true, historic David, as far as archaeology and historical sources can reveal, gained his greatest fame as something of a bandit chief."[25] They continue:

> As a guerilla force, David's men are quick and mobile. They come to the rescue of beleaguered villagers, humiliate an arrogant local strongman, outsmart the ruler of a powerful neighboring Philistine city, and evade the relentless pursuit of King Saul again and again. Extortion, seduction, deception, and righteous violence are David's methods. His story is filled with larger-than-life ironies, comic episodes, and entertaining events. It is a classical bandit tale of a type known all over the world, then and now, in which popular rebels—like Robin Hood, Jesse James, and Pancho Villa—use bravado and cunning to challenge the corrupt, brutal powers that be. The exploits of some bandits have been gradually forgotten, but the tales of others have grown steadily more vivid over time. Modest events are transformed into astonishing achievements; unique personal trails are exaggerated to a mythic scale. In the case of the biblical narrative, the tales of David's early bandit days merge into the national history of Israel. When King Saul dies on the battlefield, David is proclaimed king of Judah and proceeds to conquer Jerusalem and establish it as his seat of power. His destiny is to become king of all Israel, yet his days of banditry remain an essential part of the legend of the man.[26]

Positing that David and Saul may have had overlapping rather than consecutive reigns—Saul holding the northern areas and David the south—a picture emerges in Finkelstein and Silberman's historical reconstruction of a southern state resisting northern colonial aggression, led by an outlaw who has a less than perfect moral character—considered a hero by some and a murderous traitor by others.

---

24. Finkelstein and Silberman, *David and Solomon*, 40–50. See also Niels Peter Lemche, "Habiru, Hapiru," *ABD* 3:6–10.
25. Finkelstein and Silberman, *David and Solomon*, 31.
26. Ibid., 32.

2. David, the Bandit

Finkelstein and Silberman argue that David did indeed exist, but the United Kingdom did not; the stories of the glorious United Kingdom took shape over the course of several centuries (ninth through seventh) in part to buttress the national reforms and revivals of Hezekiah and Josiah.[27] But even scholars who argue for the historicity of the United Kingdom have come to regard David as a bit of a bandit. After all, it is difficult to see any other way to read this period in David's life. What else does one call the leader of a posse of disaffected men living in caves at the fringes of society, raiding outlying villages, plundering their properties and murdering their inhabitants?

For example, Baruch Halpern has been quite critical of the minimalist perspective.[28] In his 2001 study *David's Secret Demons*, he certainly argues that there was a United Kingdom, that David did rule over it and that 1 and 2 Samuel were written during Solomon's reign (at the latest) to clear David's name and garner support for his dynasty. Good, solid maximalist presuppositions. Yet, Halpern goes well beyond the traditional suspicions that some of the details in 1 and 2 Samuel—like David's kingdom stretching to the Euphrates—are hyperbole and propaganda.

Halpern subtitles his book *Messiah, Murderer, Traitor, King*, and his portrait of David emphasizes the "murderer." In this provocatively titled study, he seeks to understand how David's enemies perceived him.[29] He argues that 1 and 2 Samuel are an apology and that the various murders that happen around David were actually committed by David. Nabel did not just drop dead—he was murdered by David or by Abigail for David;[30] Joab did not murder Abner to settle a personal vendetta—he murdered the advisor of David's rival on David's order;[31] God and the Gibeonites did not demand the death of Saul's remaining descendents to expiate a crime committed by Saul—they were executed by David to eliminate all rival claims to the throne.[32] The bodies amass in Halpern's portrait of "King David, Serial Killer."[33]

In conclusion, Halpern writes:

---

27. Ibid., 91–177.
28. Halpern has earned his maximalist credentials with such articles as "Erasing History: The Minimalist Assault on Ancient Israel," *BR* (1995): 26–47, which was part of the Tel Dan brawl.
29. Halpern, *David's Secret Demons*, xv.
30. Ibid., 77.
31. Ibid., 82–84.
32. Ibid., 84–87.
33. The title of Halpern's chapter on these cases.

David's enemies regarded him as a non-Israelite. Specifically, they thought of him as the Gibeonite agent of Philistine masters. They accused him of importing a foreign icon, the ark, as his state symbol. He consistently allied with foreign powers to suppress the Israelites whom he dominated. He spent most of his career as a brigand-king, and, where he ruled, he did so by employing murder and mayhem as tools of statecraft. In fact, the only murder in the books of Samuel of which he was probably innocent is the one murder of which he stands accused in the apology [the murder of Uriah]. His enemies considered him a mass murderer.[34]

David did usurp the throne from Saul, and he was involved in Saul's death. Halpern's suspicions run so deep that he doubts the paternity of Solomon. The episode with Bathsheba was constructed by the apologist to prove that Solomon really was David's and not Uriah's son. With maximalists like these, who needs minimalists?

The scholars who have downplayed David's more sinister side have been controlled by the dominant ideology of the material in Samuel–Kings and Chronicles—David is God's own beloved. He is handsome, charismatic, irresistibly charming. God is on his side and the readers should be too. The scholars who have recently reassessed David are free of the control of the text's dominant ideology but they are operating under agendas of their own. By focusing attention on the negative aspects of his character, such portraits make David more human, more real. If David were only a literary figure (so the argument goes), he would be more idealized, the text would not be trying to cover anything up, and he would truly be "a man after God's own heart." Halpern's portrait may be a character assassination but it is a character assassination that saves David's historicity, lending it even more credibility.

However, the bandit traditions do not necessarily prove historicity. Once the bandit pattern is established, story-tellers can either plug an already established figure into the pattern, shaping his biography according to the bandit plot, or they can easily construct a fictional character. Looking again at Finkelstein and Silberman's work, they compare David to "Robin Hood, Jesse James, and Pancho Villa." Jesse James and Pancho Villa were certainly real, historical men (although their stories are also thick with legend). Robin Hood, on the other hand, was not. Even though Hobsbawm discusses Robin Hood, even categorizing a

---

34. Halpern, *David's Secret Demons*, 479. See also McKenzie for the argument that David was responsible for the deaths of his various political enemies and opponents. The first scholar to argue that the biblical story was largely an apology was P. Kyle McCarter, "The Apology of David," *JBL* 99 (1980): 489–504.

whole group of bandits as "Noble Robbers" or "Robin Hood types," he also notes that "Robin Hood is pure myth."[35] The pattern of David's career was already part of the fabric of ancient Near Eastern royal ideology. In his study of messiah myths, Thomas Thompson chronicles the precursors to David's story. In particular, Thompson notes, "The pattern of Idrimi's story [a Syrian ruler] has long been seen as a forerunner of the story of David's rise to the throne."[36] The Syrian Idrimi prefigures the Israelite David: he is the youngest among his brothers; when Idrimi's life is in danger, he flees to the desert and lives among the *hapiru* for seven years; yet he returns from the wilderness to take the throne, build a palace and restore the cult of his ancestors. The ambiguities that emerge in Hobsbawm's work about whether or not the "social bandit" is a historical or a literary figure is even more acute when trying to access David's biography, since the only extant David is in words. History and mythology are inextricably intertwined in all of these tales—from Idrimi to David, from Jesus to Jesse and back to David again.

David Goes West

The stories of the American West—both textual and cinematic—are deeply shaped by America's biblical inheritance. From the opening lines of Genesis through the horrors of Revelation, the Bible has left an indelible stamp on the ways we think, write and picture our western frontiers. Although not as obvious a presence as other biblical characters and motifs, David has also left his mark on western stories and images. In particular, the bandit traditions of Israel's greatest king have shaped the messianic mythologies of the American West.

Owen Wister's *The Virginian* (1902) is widely considered the first Western novel, but it was the work of Zane Grey, especially his *Riders of the Purple Sage* (1912), that really established the Western as a genre. On the surface, the novel sets Christianity (in particular, Mormonism) in opposition to the gunman's ethic. The opening scene is iconic. The protagonist Jane Withersteen is besieged by the Mormon elders who want her large and prosperous ranch. Her best hired hand Bern Venters, who is not a Mormon, is about to be whipped. Jane helplessly stands by:

---

35. Hobsbawm, *Bandits*, 46 n.
36. Thomas Thompson, *The Messiah Myth: The Near Eastern Roots of Jesus and David* (New York: Basic, 2005), 154; see also Halpern, *David's Secret Demons*, 20.

> Once more her strained gaze sought the sage-slopes. Jane Withersteen loved that wild and purple wilderness. In times of sorrow it had been her strength, in happiness its beauty was her continued delight. In her extremity she found herself murmuring, "Whence cometh my help!" It was a prayer, as if forth from those lonely purple reaches and walls of red and clefts of blue might ride a fearless man, neither creed-bound nor creed-mad, who would hold up a restraining hand in the faces of her ruthless people.
>
> The restless movements of Tull's men suddenly quieted down. Then followed a low whisper, a rustle, a sharp exclamation.
>
> "Look!" said one pointing to the west.
>
> "A rider!"[37]

A stranger—clad in black leather, carrying two black-handled guns, riding a fine sorrel horse—rides into the conflict. He is the notorious gunman Lassiter.

In Jane Tompkins' work of Western criticism, she argues that the Western arose in protest to a Christianity exemplified by the wildly popular novel *In His Steps* by Charles M. Sheldon (1896). In this novel, a minister's sermon writing is interrupted one morning by a knock on his door. When he opens it, he sees a young homeless man looking for work. The minister turns him away and then returns to his sermon writing. That next Sunday in church, the disheveled man returns to tell his story and ask the congregation to live up to its own ideals and act according to the teachings of Christ. After his challenge, he collapses from hunger and dies a few days later. This encounter transforms the minister who subsequently embarks upon a life of service. The Western, according to Tompkins, needs to be understood as a response to Sheldon's novel and others of its kind. In short, the Western is "a rejection of Christianity."[38] She continues, "What the Western shows us, among other things, is that Christianity had to be forcibly ejected. When the genre first appears on the scene, therefore, it defines itself in part by struggling to get rid of Christianity's enormous cultural weight."[39] Tompkins then uses the opening scene of *Riders of the Purple Sage* to illustrate her point:

> In her hour of need, the heroine, a Christian woman who dresses in white, loves children, and preaches against violence, turns her eyes to the hills. Grey deliberately invokes the biblical reference, and just as deliberately rejects it. Instead of help coming from the Lord who made heaven and earth, as in the psalm, it arrives in the form of "a horseman, silhouetted

---

37. Zane Grey, *Riders of the Purple Sage* (San Francisco: HarperCollins, 1992; first published by Harper & Brothers, 1912), 17–18.
38. Tompkins, *West of Everything*, 31.
39. Ibid., 32.

against the western sky, come riding out of the sage" (8). An emanation of the desert, this redeemer is not from heaven but from earth, connected to the natural world by his horse and to the world of men by his black dress and black-butted guns. He is Lassiter, a famous gunman whom everyone fears, the savior as Antichrist.[40]

Tompkins makes a strong argument that Lassiter is a kind of "Antichrist," that he replaces God as the savior of both Jane and Venters, that Ben Venters "represents the men of the nineteenth century who have been enfeebled by the doctrines of a feminized Christianity,"[41] and that risking death through gunfight is what confers masculinity not forgiveness and turning the other cheek. Tompkins misses, however, other aspects of both the Western and Christianity. In the Western, there is still an affirmation of core Christian values; in Christianity, violence is at the heart of the biblical story.

By evoking Ps 121 which opens "I lift up my eyes to the hills—from where will my help come?" and answering the prayer not with God but with the feared outlaw, Grey is certainly displacing a certain type of religiosity and replacing it with the hard and violent realism of life on the frontier. However, he is not disputing the core values of Judaism or Christianity. As the scene continues to unfold, Grey lays the foundations for the characterizations of both Jane and Lassiter in their first exchange. Before Lassiter notices the prisoner, he politely asks Jane for water for his horse. When she responds in the affirmative, he hesitates. Maybe if she knew who he was, she would not give his horse water. Jane counters that it does not matter who he is, and extends her hospitality to the man himself, inviting him into her house for food and drink.[42] Jane does precisely what the minister of *In His Steps* failed to do, the act held up by the novel as the *sine qua non* of Christian morality—offer hospitality to a stranger in need. In this scene there are also overtones of John 4, where Jesus approaches an unknown woman at a well and asks for water. The woman demurs because she is a Samaritan and he is a Jew, two peoples who are hostile to one another. Jesus responds to her surprise by stating that if she knew who he was, she would have asked him for living water (John 4:10). In both scenes, hospitality is requested by an unknown traveler and hesitancy is expressed based upon the identity of the traveler

---

40. Ibid.
41. Ibid., 33.
42. Grey, *Riders of the Purple Sage*, 9–10. She repeats the offer after the Mormon elders have left and Ben Venters has been freed. The biblical connection is even more explicit as she urges Lassiter to "break bread" with her (pp. 15–16).

("if you knew who I really was..."). In one case, revelation of true identity may result in a refusal of hospitality; in the other case, revelation of true identity may result in a reversal of hospitality. In both cases, the core value of hospitality (even excessive hospitality) to strangers is affirmed.

Lassiter is called "stranger" seven times in the couple of pages it takes between his appearance and the revelation of his identity. In Lev 19:34, the Israelite is enjoined to love the stranger, and in Lev 19:18 to love the neighbor. Jesus highlights this later law as one of the Greatest Commandments (Mark 12:31; Luke 10:27; Matt 19:19; 22:39). Much of the Israelite ethic addresses the treatment of the stranger, which forms the foundation of both Jewish and Christian morality. The opening scene of *Riders of the Purple Sage* contains a deep irony—one that would not work if it were just disavowing Christianity. The men who have been endowed with ecclesial title and power are about to whip (probably to death) an innocent man because of a potent combination of jealousy, greed and prejudice whereas the woman and the gunman manifest Christian love, outside of institutions, dogmas and expectations. The citation of a *psalm*, the biblical genre traditionally ascribed to David, could not be more apt. David, not Jesus, is the figure that resonates with the character Lassiter—a complex man who has a good heart but is not shy to violence, a man who leaves home and family to become an outlaw riding at the fringes of society, a man who will ultimately ride in to save the day. Lassiter is not just an outlaw; he is a messianic bandit.

Jane Withersteen and Lassiter engage in a struggle throughout the narrative over her protection of the Mormon Elders who are persecuting her. She begs Lassiter to spare their lives and Lassiter continually accuses her of being blind to the realities of the situation. Tompkins is correct that "In place of the gospel of forgiveness, Lassiter installs the reign of an eye for an eye,"[43] but "an eye for an eye" is not a biblical precept advocating violence (which is what Tompkins means) but one enjoining justice. Jane Withersteen has to free herself not from Christianity but from the thrall of her Mormon religion and the power of the ecclesial hierarchies. Lassiter does reject mercy, but he does so in the name of justice. These men have amassed multiple crimes: murder, the kidnapping of Lassiter's sister and her child, cattle rustling and other thefts, extortion. They have also blinded Lassiter's horse with hot irons. In the end, they kidnap Jane's adopted daughter, Fay, in an attempt to force Jane into marriage with Elder Tull and Jane is ready to submit in order to

---

43. Tompkins, *West of Everything*, 33.

be reunited with her little girl.[44] Jane's mercy is misplaced because it allows crime after crime to accumulate in her community. The shoot that springs from the stump of Jesse in the oracles of Isaiah not only lauds the righteous and the meek; Jesse's descendent also "kill[s] the wicked" (Isa 11:4). In *Riders of the Purple Sage*, it is only when Jane finally frees herself from the institutions of Christianity that she becomes truly Christian in ethic and action; it is only when Lassiter takes up his guns, that justice prevails.

There is one other reference to the psalms in *Riders of the Purple Sage*. Jane Withersteen is the embodiment of "goodness and mercy,"[45] an allusion to Ps 23, one of the most famous prayers attributed to David. Psalm 23 proclaims that "goodness and mercy shall follow me all the days of my life" because the speaker trusts in the Lord (v. 6). Throughout the novel, Jane helps people in need, particularly the poor and outcast; she is kind to children; she restrains both Venters and Lassiter from violence (at least for a time). Lassiter may be the messianic bandit, but Jane is the Christ figure. At the end of the novel, Jane has abandoned her ranch and she is fleeing with Lassiter from the Mormon elders. While on the run, they encounter Ben Venters and a strange young woman (who ends up being Lassiter's missing niece), who are also fleeing the Mormon authorities. When it is revealed that Venters is engaged to the young woman, Jane unleashes her fury at being deceived. As the conversation between the four continues, Jane overthrows the hate that had temporarily risen up in her soul.[46] She asks forgiveness. At the end of the encounter, she gives the only two possessions she has remaining to the young lovers—her beloved horses. This act of munificence and material sacrifice is also potentially an act which will sacrifice her and Lassiter's lives. Venters and his fiancée are sure to escape on the fast horses; Lassiter and Jane are sure to be caught without them. Venters protests her generosity but she insists. "Then in the white, rapt face, in the unfathomable eyes, Venters saw Jane Withersteen in a supreme moment. This moment was one wherein she reached up to the height for which her noble soul had ever yearned… Jane Withesteen was the incarnation of selflessness. He experienced wonder and terror, exquisite pain and rapture."[47] As she transforms into the incarnation of selflessness, she becomes the Incarnation, and Venters responds with veneration.

---

44. Grey, *Riders of the Purple Sage*, 313–14.
45. Ibid., 361.
46. Ibid., 336.
47. Ibid., 345–46.

Tompkins is correct that a certain type of Christianity popular in the nineteenth century is rejected by the Western genre, but the biblical tradition is affirmed in more than just hospitality, love and self-sacrifice. The violence of the Western is not anathema to biblical religion; it is integral to it. Jesse's lineage includes David's bandit ways and Jesus' violent death, a death which, according to Christian theology, was ordained by a God who requires blood. The New Testament then ends with God's beaten son, resurrected and ready for revenge, unleashing murder and mayhem throughout the world in the book of Revelation. Westerns do reject a "feminized Christianity," as well as the institutions of religion associated with both Europe and the East. But in highlighting sacrifices that save and justice achieved through violence, Westerns are reliant on the deep structures of the messianic ideal and the theology of Christianity.

Examples of the centrality of Christianity abound in Westerns. The themes sounded in Zane Grey's first novel are expressed through to his last. In *The Vanishing American*, Grey eviscerates Christian missionaries and writes a powerful exposé of their corrupt and criminal conduct on Indian reservations.[48] At the same time, however, the protagonists—a Native American named Nophaie and a young white woman named Marian who becomes his wife—embody the core biblical ethics, and Nophaie even converts to Christianity at the end of the novel. Another Western that frames its story through the use of a Psalm of David is the Clint Eastwood movie *Pale Rider* (itself a remake of the movie and novel *Shane*; *Pale Rider* is a reference to the fourth Horseman of the Apocalypse in Rev 6:8). As Lassiter appears just as Jane is finishing praying Ps 121, Eastwood's character rides in while a girl whose family is in distress is reading and commenting on Ps 23. When Eastwood accepts the hospitality of the family and comes inside to wash, the viewer sees the wounds on his back and side. The messianic careers of both David and Jesus converge in Eastwood's character—he is savior and avenger. The branch that grows from Jesse's tree wears "righteousness" and "faithfulness" on a belt around the waist and loins (Isa 11:5) like two guns in a holster. David and Jesus ride in and out of Westerns more often than one would expect. Contra Tompkins, the Western is not a rejection of Christianity; rather, the Western highlights the violence inherent in Christianity and it performs the undercurrent of criminality in the messianic traditions and legends.

---

48. Zane Grey, *The Vanishing American* (rev. ed.; New York: Pocket, 1982; first published by Harper & Row, 1925).

Land and Character

The intertextual threads that connect bandits and messiahs, biblical story and Western genre, also wind around the landscapes where outlaws run wild. As discussed in the previous chapter, certain geographies contribute to the creation of social bandits and their bands. At the narrative level, the ways in which the land is described is also entwined with the ways in which these men are characterized. Finkelstein and Silberman assert that the landscapes of David's outlaw days would have been deeply evocative to ninth-century readers,[49] but since they only have the text to read and not ninth-century readers to ask, their interpretation depends on unverifiable data. Instead of the minds of the original audience of Samuel, Finkelstein and Silberman's characterization of David reflects the ways in which landscape establishes character in the stories of the American West. Their interpretation demonstrates the intertextual tangle of narratives, moving back and forth across time and through genres both scholarly and literary, "a vast stereophony"[50] of rugged and untamed men and terrain. Lassiter's face, for example, has "all the characteristics of the range rider's—the leanness, the red burn of the sun, and the set changelessness that came from years of silence and solitude."[51] He is marked by sun and silence, like the great desert wilderness itself. He is deeply and irrevocably a rider of the purple sage, just as David is a man forged by his own desert wildness.

There is a particular affinity with the way the wilderness functions in the biblical stories and the way the wilderness functions in the stories of the Western. The connection is not coincidence. Western writers use biblical allusion in their creation of the Western mythology. Specifically, Tompkins argues, "Western landscape reflects the Old Testament sense of the world at creation… God creates the heaven and the earth and then the light, the constituent elements of the Western landscape. In the Western as in Genesis, the physical world comes first."[52]

Even a cursory survey of Western movies demonstrates the primacy of the land—generally, the opening shot of the movie is an empty landscape. This landscape is a desert and it evokes a variety of meanings,

---

49. Finkelstein and Silberman, *David and Solomon*, 36.
50. The phrase comes from Roland Barthes' description of intertextuality in *Image–Music–Text* (trans. Stephen Heath; New York: Hill & Wang, 1977), 160. See Sherwood and Moore for a discussion of Barthes, intertextuality, and biblical studies.
51. Grey, *Riders of the Purple Sage*, 9.
52. Tompkins, *West of Everything*, 70.

all with biblical resonances. The land is pristine and pure, evocative of Eden. Owen Wister writes in *The Virginian*, "A world of crystal light, a land without evil, a space across which Noah and Adam might come straight from Genesis."[53] There is also a sense in the Bible and the Western alike that primordial chaos lays just below the surface of the natural order. Adam is expelled from the garden when creation itself betrays him in the form of a snake, and Noah's world is destroyed when God unleashes the watery chaos of flood. Even more profoundly, the earth creates the man and the man returns to the earth. Adam is created out of earth and when he dies he will return to dust. In the Western, the rough landscape "creates" the man as he strives to imitate "the qualities that nature implicitly possesses—power, endurance, rugged majesty..."[54] Despite the Western hero's brief mastery of his surroundings, it is the land that ultimately succeeds—the desert that forges the man will triumph over him through death and decomposition. Westerns are littered with the bodies of the dead; tombstones and dry bones are as integral to the landscape as cacti and mesas.

Land produces legend; biography transforms into mythology; legend and mythology produce history, in layer upon layer of meaning-making. The "fiction" cannot be separated from the "fact" in the stories of our bandits for such distinctions dissolve in the making of meaning. The biblical stories have wrought the mythology of the American West which in turn has shaped our understanding of biblical narrative and character. Finkelstein and Silberman are not the only two writers on David to name him an outlaw, root his characterization in the description of the land and compare him to Jesse James. They do, however, go further than most in their description of the political context. Judah is a southern state with its own fragmented political identity, resisting northern colonial aggression, led by an outlaw who is considered a hero by some and a murderous traitor by others—it is difficult not to hear echoes of the life of Jesse James and his bifurcated American context. Jesse and David blend all that is brutal and romantic, criminal and heroic about the identity of the rebel. In this sense, then, David the bandit is not just son of Jesse of Bethlehem, but son of Jesse of Missouri, son of Jesse James.

---

53. As cited in ibid.
54. Ibid., 72.

Chapter 3

CROSSING OUTLAWS:
THE LIFE AND TIMES OF JESSE JAMES AND JESUS OF NAZARETH[*]

The Betrayal of a Bandit

Jesse Woodson James was shot in the back of the head with a .45 Colt Navy revolver by Robert Newton Ford on April 3, 1882. Wanted posters dotted the territory promising $5000 for Jesse's seizure or murder with an additional $5000 upon his arraignment. Bob Ford and his brother Charlie had recently joined James' gang of bandits and were staying with Jesse in his home. Despite the fact that Jesse was worth more alive than dead, the risks of capturing and transporting the nation's most famous bandit, as opposed to simply killing him unawares, must have entered the Ford brother's calculations. There are indications, as well, that the Ford brothers had been commissioned by Missouri authorities to kill, not capture, James.

Describing the scene from the public testimony of Bob and Charlie Ford, the biographer Frank Triplett writes:

> On the morning of April 3rd, 1882, Jesse James stood in a chair, brushing some pictures with a feather duster. His coat was off, as the weather was warm; the door was open to admit the breeze, and he feared that suspicion might be attracted if he continued to wear his belt containing one pistol… Laying his belt aside, as he had often done before…he got upon a chair to use a feather duster, and here he committed the fatal mistake of turning his back to the Fords.[1]

Bob Ford fired the fatal shot. Charlie, according to later testimony, drew but did not fire; neither brother spoke a word of warning or arrest. Jesse

---

[*] An early version of this chapter appeared as "Crossing Outlaws: The Lives and Legends of Jesus of Nazareth and Jesse James," in *Sacred Tropes: Tanach, New Testament and Qur'an as Literary Works* (ed. Roberta Sterman Sabbath; New York: Brill, 2009), 361–71.

[1]. Triplett, *The Life, Times and Treacherous Death of Jesse James*, 224.

heard them as they drew and cocked their revolvers but offered only a slight turn of his head; he made no attempt to defend himself, flee or shout a warning to his wife in the next room. He simply stood and waited.

Capturing the public outrage against the deed, Triplett condemns the assassination by decrying it as

> ...the most diabolical plan ever conceived and adopted to rid the State of an outlaw since the world began. Even had Jesse James been guilty of all with which he was charged, and his dearest friends do not claim that he was innocent of all the crime laid to his door, yet would it have been better for him to have still run and rioted on his career, rather than that the fair name of the State should have been stained by so foul a deed, originated, sanctioned and perfected by her chief magistrate and his accomplices... That an outlaw shall pillage is to be expected; that in his wild and crime-stained career even red-handed murder and cruel assassination may stalk companion-like beside him would cause surprise to no one; but that the Governor of the State, the conservator of the liberties of her people, and the preserver and executor of her laws, should league with harlots, thieves and murderers to procure assassination, is astounding almost beyond belief.[2]

The crimes of Jesse could not compare to the black sin of betrayal, perpetrated by his own friends in league with an illegitimate state.

Jesse James

That Jesse died as a victim of violent betrayal is no surprise. The career of Jesse James and his outlaw companions certainly bore every potential for tragic end; in many ways, it is more surprising Jesse James lived as long as he did. Missouri, then and now, was a state caught between southern, western and midwestern identities. As we saw in Chapter 1, during the Civil War, the white populace was divided in its sympathies for the North and the South. The state was prohibited from forming militias for either side, and the federal troop presence increased. Missouri's statehood and identity were integrally tied to national identity and civil union. According to all records, the core of the James–Younger band—Jesse and Frank James, Bob, Cole, and Thomas Younger—began their careers as outlaws while in their early teens, riding along with any of a number of loosely organized "black flag" units of Confederate sympathizers. Jesse and Frank rode with the ruthless Arch Clemmens

---

2. Ibid., 219.

and William Clarke Quantrill, seeking revenge for atrocities, some real, some imagined, committed by Union loyalists. According to their later reports, Cole and Bob Younger enlisted in one such unit in response to a midnight raid against their family farm. In later years, both men would reflect on the pivotal impact of a single night raid where they, as teenage boys, were forced to witness the burning of the family barn, the destruction of family stores and livestock and the serial rapes of their mother and sisters. Driven to revenge these and similar other atrocities, many of the Missouri outlaws enlisted in these renegade bands and exacted a vengeance every bit as savage as the motivating offence and frighteningly vigilante.[3]

After the war's end, the offer of general amnesty which was extended to formal combatants affiliated with the confederacy, of course, did not extend to these guerrilla bands. Furthermore, the severity and savagery of their assaults—assaults, it must be remembered, against citizens still living in the region who were ideologically allied with post-war government and judicial bodies—elicited severe legal penalty. Unable to hope for any official clemency, most members of these guerrilla bands who managed to escape capture and hanging were forced to melt into the general population or, if they had been particularly notorious as resisters, to relocate to neighboring states of Arkansas, Illinois, Ohio and Kentucky. Motivated as many were by intense loyalties to their home state of Missouri, some would prefer a life on the legal margins and the risks of eventual capture and capital punishment to abandonment of home. Throughout their career as outlaws and bandits, the James–Younger gang would continually insist that their life of crime was foisted upon them by forces beyond their control and was perpetuated by their certainty that they would never face a fair judicial review. Unable to return to civil or domestic life, they were forced to banditry to survive. Whether or not their previous war careers really prohibited their peace time resettlement (most "black flag" soldiers did not take up outlawry), it did train them in precision, planning, timing, tactics and it most certainly established bonds of inter-gang trust and communication. It also made them exceptionally violent and ruthless when need arose. The James–Younger gang was effective in outlawry because they were, in effect, special forces gone rogue.

---

3. The accounts on both sides invite suspicion because of their clear tendentiousness. The conflict was likely mutual, though it does seem that the most vicious acts were, at least initially, perpetuated by Missouri. It would seem reasonable, however, to think of the conflict both more and less atrocious than the literature recalls.

Jesse's and Frank's career as bandits was famous for its excessive violence and boldness, celebrated in paeans to Missouri manliness by the newspaperman John Newman Edwards in the *St. Louis Dispatch*. In addition to years of editorials, in 1877 Edwards published *Noted Guerrillas, or the Warfare of the Border*.[4] Edwards singles out Frank and Jesse James for particular praise, even though the latter rode as a guerrilla only for a very brief period while he was a young teen, and thus could not have made much difference to Quantrill's platoon. Edwards' account of Jesse's post-war career, particularly his apology for Jesse's criminality—that the brothers, as successful guerrillas and not "regular army" Confederates, would have never been allowed to reintegrate into civil society—has become the standard explanation of the James brothers' career. Edwards' *Noted Guerrillas* in many ways defined the James–Younger band, and Jesse in particular, as corollaries to the Kansas border violence. Implicitly, Edwards argued Jesse was an outlaw because of Federal law itself.

According to Edwards and to newspaper letters and editorials claiming James' signature, Jesse James and his cohorts saw themselves not just as brigands, but as bandits still engaged in guerrilla resistance to a foreign army. While incarcerated in the Minnesota State Prison, an elderly Cole Younger composed "The real facts about the Northfield, Minnesota 'Bank Robbery'" (the last and one of the most dramatic robberies attempted by the James–Younger brothers in 1901). Even at this late date, more than 20 years after his last attempted robbery and almost 40 years after the end of the Civil War, Cole continues to identify himself and his compatriots as guerrillas, driven to the margins of civil society and into brigandage by forces beyond their control. Cole writes:

> I have only to say that there is no heroism in outlawry, and that the man who sows is sure to reap. After Lee surrendered I tried my best to live at peace with the world and earn a livelihood. I'd been made a guerrilla by a provocation that few men could have resisted. My father had been cruelly murdered, my mother had been hounded to death, my entire family had been tormented and all my relatives plundered and imprisoned... [The guerrilla warrior] was made what he was by such outrages as Osceola, Palmyra and by a hundred raids less famous but not less infamous, that were made by Kansas into Missouri during the war... As for myself and

---

4. John Newman Edwards, *Noted Guerrillas, or the Warfare of the Border* (St. Louis: Brand & Co., 1877). He had also written two earlier works: *Shelby and His Men* (Cincinnati: Miami Printing & Publishing Co., 1867); and *Shelby's Expedition to Mexico* (Kansas City: Kansas City Times, 1872), celebrating Confederate causes and leadership.

brothers I wish to emphasize that we made an honest attempt to return to normal life at the close of the war, and had we been permitted to do so the name of Younger would never have been connected with the crimes that were committed in the period immediately following the war... That my life was good or clean I do not assert. But such as it was, it was forced upon me by conditions over which I had no control.[5]

Jesse also had a story used to justify his continuing criminal actions. On or around May 15, 1865, as the Civil War was slouching to its close, Jesse James, a guerrilla militant riding under the command of Arch Clement, was shot by Union soldiers outside of Lexington, Kentucky. Jesse would report that the soldiers, drunk, had attacked him and a very small band of other riders without provocation as they were riding to negotiate terms of surrender.[6] Jesse was shot with a .50 caliber musket ball through the chest and his horse was killed. The thumb-sized bullet remained in his lung, a permanent wound leaching lead into his body with every heartbeat and breath. The story would later be cited as justification for Jesse's refusal to surrender; he insisted, citing May of 1865 as his evidence, that he would not be given fair hearing and that he may even be murdered.

Somehow he managed to escape the immediate battleground and find local farmers who aided his escape to the care of kinfolk. Jesse was sent back first to Kansas to convalesce. Worried he would die outside Missouri (not an idle concern given the gravity of his injury), Jesse was secreted back to the St. Joseph area to die.[7] He was in the general vicinity still healing (and very much in hiding), when the Bank at Liberty, Missouri was robbed on February 13, 1866.[8] Jesse's grave wound would be cited as his proof of his own innocence. Yet, even as James' body lay near death, Jesse's legend was born.

The criminal exploits of the James–Younger gang reflect some of the bandit-guerrilla quality to their missions and self-understanding. Jesse James was most noted for his bold, daylight robberies of railroad trains, stage coaches and banks. Each of these, while ready suppositories of cash, jewelry and other valuables, were also associated in popular sentiment with federal, particularly "Eastern," industries and interests. The banking and transportation industries were seen as tools for moving in

---

5. Thomas ColemanYounger, "Real Facts About the Northfield, Minnesota, Bank Robbery," in *Convict Life at the Minnesota State Prison, Stillwater, Minnesota* (ed. William Caspar Heilbron; 2d ed.; St. Paul, Minn.: Heilbron, 1909), 125–26.
6. Yeatman, *Frank and Jesse James*, 76.
7. Ibid., 83.
8. Ibid., 85–88.

federal supporters, troops and resources and for shipping out local wealth, property and produce. The banking industry, in particular, was considered synonymous with the federal government. Bank and train robbery began during the Civil War as Confederate attacks against pro-Union and federal organizations. The first ever day-light bank robbery was undertaken by a group of Confederate "special forces" troops.

Even after the Civil War, the federal government continued to "intrude" in ways resented by white rural Missouri. In the decades between the end of the Civil War and the beginning of the twentieth century, the rate of change in Missouri was break-neck. The incursion of the railroad was crucial to this change. From 1851 to the end of the Civil War, there were only 925 miles of track laid in Missouri, and all but one of the railroad companies had gone bankrupt. In 1870, there were 2000 miles of track, by 1880 there were 4000, by 1890, 6000 and by 1909, there were 8000 miles of railroad tracks.[9] The railroads changed everything by making it cheaper and easier to ship goods, thereby expanding markets. Consequently, the population of Missouri exploded as new people moved in to take advantage of the changing economic climate; forests were cleared, coal mines expanded, and a lot of money was made. These changing economic structures (industrialization and market capitalism) were resisted in a variety of ways by the people of Missouri. In his book *Paths of Resistance: Tradition and Dignity in Industrializing Missouri*, David Thelen argues:

> The central mechanism for popular resistance, however, was less a law of development than a pattern of folk memories that Missourians drew upon to keep alive values and traditions that the new order threatened... It did not matter that the "traditional" family or religion or craft that Missourians sought to preserve included some components rooted in the reality of the recent past, other components whose existence was so old that no one could date them, and still others that may never have existed. What gave force to the tradition was not the reality on which it had been based in the past—how a thing was made, how particular people related to each other, when the reality had existed—but the ability of people to use that memory or tradition to project resistance in the present. By providing the means to evaluate loss, folk memories energized struggles to regain control over the processes of change.[10]

The use of Missouri folk memories was dynamic; they created a new reality rather than re-creating a fixed past.

---

9. David Thelen, *Paths of Resistance: Tradition and Dignity in Industrializing Missouri* (New York: Oxford University Press, 1986), 29, 31.

10. Ibid., 5.

There was a general crisis of law and authority in Missouri after the Civil War. The fight over railroad bonds illustrates the deep divisions between the people and the government, Missourians and those perceived as outsiders. The public did not want to pay more in taxes to finance the railroad, but in community after community, such taxes were imposed upon them. Even, sometimes, after such bonds were voted down in an election, judges and/or politicians would overturn the results of the election and issue the bonds anyway. To fight back, communities sometimes stole the tax records and burned them. There were even a few cases where angry mobs rioted and the violent clashes resulted in several deaths. The tax burden of the railroad was exceedingly high. In some counties, a single railroad subscription cost more than all other taxes combined over the course of a decade.[11] As the new railroad promoters clashed with the citizens of Missouri,

> each side believed the other to be "robbers" and "traitors." The collision of values was too fundamental to be resolved by political institutions, whose legitimacy in any case had collapsed during the Civil War. In the end the central issue was whether the railroads had enough military, economic, and political power to secure their property from taxpayers, workers, and bandits who had concluded, with the public's agreement, that collective, direct, illegal action was the only alternative to submission to the railroads' world.[12]

Jesse James and the rest of the James–Younger gang, notorious in folk tradition as both bank and train robbers, attacked precisely these instruments of economic change and exploitation. Even their daylight robbery of the Kansas City Fair was symbolic of Jesse's assault on industrialization and the new market capitalism, since the fair had been staged to promote economic development. At the same time, the James–Younger gang tapped into the Missourian traditions surrounding love and protection of family. Jesse was reported to have been a loving and devoted son, father and husband and to have carried a Bible around with him all of the time.[13] As Hobsbawm notes, "The James brothers...specialized in banks and railroads...there was probably no redneck in the South-west and few prairie farmers anywhere in times of depression who would not have regarded this as natural and just."[14] The James–Younger gang perfected a form of brigandage that was rooted in secessionist guerrilla strategies

11. Ibid., 63.
12. Ibid., 59.
13. Ibid., 74.
14. Hobsbawm, *Bandits*, 186. Thelen (*Paths of Resistance*, 70) also calls Jesse James "America's Classic Social Bandit."

and directed against industries affiliated with federal control. From this vantage, Missouri of the nineteenth century can be read as a colonial context, and there is some credence to the James–Younger claims of banditry/ brigandage as their modes of resistance to a foreign, usurping colonial power.

By the late summer of 1876, the James–Younger gang was at its apex. Despite being the most wanted men in America, the gang continued to ride and rob across Missouri, Arkansas, Kentucky and Tennessee with relative impunity. For unknown reasons, the gang decided to branch out beyond their secure regions and methods and engage in a robbery in Northfield, Minnesota under the advice and guidance of Bill Stiles, a far less experienced bandit. Stiles brought along two other men to supplement the ranks of the James–Youngers. The raid, conducted on September 7, went terribly awry. According to later reports of survivors, the extra men, grown nervous, had become drunk waiting for the robbery to begin. The bank staff was not cooperative; the main safe was closed. The frustrated robbers began to grow more dangerous. Meanwhile, the robbers on lookout outside the bank were noted by suspicious townspeople. Once it became apparent that the bank was being robbed, locals, using sniper positions enjoying the protection of cover, began firing upon the outlaws exposed in the street. Those still inside the bank were pinned down; the robbers outside in the street were cut down. By the end of the confrontation, three men—Bill Chadwell, Charlie Pitts and Clell Miller—were dead; nearly all the others were wounded, several gravely.

As they fled, the Youngers and Jameses split up, a tactic they had often used to elude posses in the past. The surviving Youngers—Cole and Bob—would be captured rather quickly. The Jameses, with Jesse severely wounded, only one horse between them, no supplies and no guide for the territories, managed to make the 500 mile journey back to the safe regions of Missouri, despite what became the largest manhunt in United States history to that date. The return journey of Frank and Jesse James—with no food, essentially weaponless, no friends, no supplies, one horse and severe gunshot wounds—is one of the most incredible (and yet documented) feats of James' career.

Apparently, the devastating defeat at Northfield took some of Frank James' desire for banditry. He seems to have wanted nothing more than to retire, marry and settle in Nashville (a frequent hiding place for both brothers). By 1880, Jesse persuaded him to return for a final "tour of the battlefield" culminating in a very ineffective train robbery in Danville, Missouri. Jesse and Frank had cobbled together a small band consisting of some distant (and very young) cousins mixed with local ruffians, including the Fords. Their intelligence regarding the train was flawed. The brakeman and baggage-man were resistant; the gang missed several thousand dollars hidden in the mail car and were reduced to trolling the passengers for cash and jewelry (even here, by all reports, they missed several hundred dollars). After this rather bland robbery, more notable for its echoes of former glory than for any real achievement, Frank made good on his intentions to retire leaving a listless Jesse, aging, troubled by old wounds and hiding in a tiny house in St. Joseph under the alias "Thomas Howard," to revel in his past triumphs with his new band of sycophants.

Jesse's attempts to live as anything but a bandit had often been marked by tension. According to anecdote, very likely modified by memory, Jesse's time as "Mr. Howard" in Nashville and Missouri had been marked by flashes of his barely contained bandit temperament.

> On a few occasions Jesse was reported to have displayed his marksmanship with a revolver. Once during a barbecue at the Humphreys County fairground, a dog managed to filch some meat. Someone said the dog should be killed, and Jesse instantly obliged... Another time a contest was held at the county fair in which a candle was placed on an upturned barrel, and the locals tried to shoot it out. Jesse was apparently rather exasperated with the display and is said to have snuffed the candle with one shot, again to the amazement of onlookers. "Light it again," he said, and shifted the gun to his left hand and repeated the feat.
>
> There were other episodes, as well. One day while racing horses at the Link place an argument over a bet developed between Jesse and another racer, Jim Ward. Ward began to curse "Mr. Howard," using language that was anything but sacred, and it appeared he wanted to fight. Jesse got his saddlebags, tossed them over his left shoulder, and slipped his hand under the flap of one of them. He walked up to Ward and said: "Jim, when I came up here I had my mind made up to kill you, but I've changed my notion. You can call me anything you want, but if you hit me I'm going to shoot you. Now what are you going to do?"
>
> Ward resumed telling Howard off, but he never struck Jesse.
>
> The outlaw listened with a grin on his face and then mounted his horse and rode away laughing... Jesse had a similar run in with D. B. Thomas... Thomas had hired one of Jesse's black field hands out from under him. When Jesse told Thomas he wanted his man back, Thomas lost his temper. Jesse reached for his gun then stopped, suddenly turning his horse, and again rode off laughing.[15]

Jesse's temper was mercurial in the best of times; he could flare up in deadly rage, then just as suddenly collapse in laughter. The preservation

---

15. As reported in Yeatman, *Frank and Jesse James*, 199 (without sources).

of these (oral) anecdotes about Jesse also reveals the tensions felt by those who lived near him, permanently on edge with fears of Jesse's dangerous presence yet still tellingly in respectful awe of him. Toward the end of his life, in St. Joseph, Jesse's moodiness and paranoia seem to have again taken over. There are hints Jesse was also slowly going mad. He was ill. He had been diagnosed with malaria in March of 1879.[16] In the months before his death, Jesse grew suspicious of, then killed, a gang member named Frank Miller. He began to grow suspicious of another, Dick Liddil.[17] According to Bob Ford's later testimony, "Jesse...had outlived his greatness as a bandit, though not as an individual robber... As a leader he was dead. There were few who would place themselves in his clutches... It was his tyranny among his fellows that wrecked his empire."[18] Jesse had died before the body of James stopped breathing. He was unable to illicit respect and intense loyalty among his followers. Ominously, it was exactly at this time when Jesse's potential capture was at its most profitable, that Jesse began to alienate and frighten his followers, shaking their loyalty. Ironically, his paranoia was justified, yet he was suspicious of exactly the wrong people at exactly the wrong time.

Bob and Charlie Ford had been in and out of close association with James' gang of bandits. Although both brothers were staying with Jesse and his family in St. Joseph, Jesse trusted Charlie, but was ambivalent about Bob. There is ample reason to suspect that both Ford brothers were in league with then Missouri governor Thomas Crittenden, the sheriff of Clay County, Missouri and the marshal of St. Joseph, to capture or assassinate Jesse James. Certainly Frank Triplett and the earliest biographers of Jesse James were assured that Crittenden had worked along with Craig and Timberlake to execute James.[19] Liddil was also likely involved. Though these historians are highly tendentious, there is ample reason to believe them here and most modern James biographers do. Triplett reports secret meetings between the conspirators in the St. James Hotel in Kansas City.[20] He suggests that the Fords entered Jesse's gang as "undercover" informants for Crittenden; the Governor, Triplett declares,

16. Ibid., 207.
17. Ibid., 265.
18. As quoted in ibid., 265.
19. Triplett's biography of James, published by the end of the year James died (1882), and largely suspected to have been co-written by Jesse's mother and wife, was the first "official" biography of James. Triplett was highly sympathetic of James and highly critical of Crittenden. There are reasonable suggestions that Crittenden worked to suppress the publication and distribution of the volume.
20. Triplett, *The Life, Times and Treacherous Death of Jesse James*, 225. He fails, however, to note the irony.

knew of Jesse's whereabouts and activities for more than a week before James was finally shot; officials, if they truly sought James' arrest, could have taken him at any time.[21] For his part, Triplett describes Jesse as haunted by dreams and premonitions for the weeks between having met the Fords and his own death.[22] For Triplett, the action of Bob Ford reflects "the old, old tale of the serpent taken in and warmed, only to turn and strike its benefactor."[23]

After his assassination, Jesse "lay in state" for nearly a week and (for the period) an astonishing number of photographs exist of his body. Local, state and even national newspapers followed the story and the subsequent trial of the Fords with close attention. Crowds of the curious assembled for days. Local conversation and newspaper editorials argued about the governor's role in the execution, but public opinion was firmly set against the Fords, branding them not only traitors who violated every element of hospitality by sharing Jesse's table even as they plotted his execution, but also as cowards who attacked an unarmed and outnumbered man from behind with his wife and small children in the very next room.

Bob Ford, in particular, was not celebrated as the bringer of law and as the ender of a terrible crime spree; he was excoriated in popular opinion and routinely compared with notable traitors of history, particularly Judas Iscariot. Edwards, then writing as editor for the *St. Louis Dispatch*, wrote, "such a cry of horror and indignation…is…thundering over the land that if a single of the miserable assassins had either manhood, conscience or courage, he would go, as another Judas, and hang himself."[24] Hanging was not an idle possibility. Both Bob and Charlie were tried for the murder of James, found guilty, and sentenced to hang; only a pardon by Governor Crittenden kept them from the gallows.

The Fords never collected the full amount of Jesse's bounty and they were so hounded by popular hatred that they had to leave the entire region. They developed a stage show called *How I Shot Jesse James* that re-enacted the murder with Charlie playing Jesse and Bob playing himself. They toured the eastern United States for over a year. The play did not rehabilitate their image. Returning to Missouri in 1884, Charlie Ford, suffering from tuberculosis and addicted to morphine, shot himself in the chest. Newspapers and popular presses describe Bob Ford as

21. Ibid., 214.
22. Ibid., 225.
23. Ibid.
24. William A. Settle, Jr., *Jesse James Was His Name* (Lincoln: University of Nebraska Press, 1966), 120.

serpent-like, a fiend and an enemy of heaven. Literally "demonized" by popular opinion, Ford eventually settled in Crede, Colorado where he opened a saloon. He, in turn, was shot to death by Edward O'Kelley.[25]

For his part, Governor Crittenden went on record early declaring his full support of the Fords' actions and even suggesting that much had been pre-arranged. In an interview for the *Kansas City Times*, April 5, 1882, Crittenden responded to his accusers by asserting "when your house is burning, you stand not upon the method of extinction."[26] Crittenden took credit for having set in motion events that, in his opinion, corrected a serious problem for the state of Missouri.

> After I became Governor I determined to overthrow this bold night rider and his gang, by any and all means known to human ingenuity; and within eight months from the time I inaugurated my policy, I am glad to say, despite much opposition which should not have existed, the lawless leader and his gang have been driven to death, to the prison and to submission to the law and its officers.[27]

Hardly intimidated by immediate public reprisals, Crittenden declared to the *St. Louis Republican*:

> I have no excuse to make, no apologies to render to any living man for the part I have played in this bloody drama, nor has [St. Joseph Marshal] Craig, nor has [Clay County Sheriff] Timberlake. I am not regretful of his death, and have no censure for the boys who removed him. They deserve credit, it is my candid, solemn opinion.[28]

Crittenden wrote on behalf of the Fords to the railroad companies and others who had promised monies to support Jesse's bounty. In time, Crittenden would deny any support of the actual murder (as opposed, presumably, to the capture) of James. However, he immediately pardoned both Bob and Charlie of any criminal charges, an act that many suggested seemed premeditated, as if scripted in advance of the Fords' trial.[29]

As to the Youngers, Bob died in September of 1889 of tuberculosis, still a prisoner in Minnesota. Jim and Cole were released in 1901. Jim, still physically suffering from his poorly healed wounds and unable to

---

25. Edward O'Kelly (or Kelly) was sentenced to life for the murder, but was released in 1902. In 1904, he himself was shot by a police officer. See Yeatman, *Frank and Jesse James*, 292.
26. Triplett, *The Life, Times and Treacherous Death of Jesse James*, 258.
27. Ibid.
28. Ibid., 259.
29. Ibid., 259–61.

marry because of his status as parolee, drank excessively and committed suicide by gunshot to the head in 1902. Cole returned to Missouri. The Youngers were not prominent in Edwards' history of the period, *Notable Guerillas*. Cole still enjoyed some modest fame, however. Frank James and Cole reunited in 1903 for a Wild West show, but their tour fizzled to an end after only a few months. Frank died at the family farm in 1915. Cole's pardon restricted his ability to profit from stories of his crimes. He occasionally lectured on the vacuity of a life of crime until his own, rather quiet death in 1916.

Most James biographers and historians accept the Edwards apology for James. Even those who do not concede that Jesse was compelled to become a bandit still seem to accept that Jesse—from the beginning of his career of outlawry—understood himself to be a guerrilla. It seems evident, however, that this particular bandit-apology was first crafted (retrospectively) by Edwards and was rooted from the very beginning in political identity. We would point out that we have no idea what the "historical Jesse" thought about anything. Editorials written in his name need not be taken at face value. In addition, every argument/apology for Jesse's banditry is offered retrospectively. There was no programmatic document issued at the outset. Certainly, something about Jesse's career inspired local support and some admiration. Yet we have no idea what Jesse thought of himself at any given moment in his infamous career; we certainly have no reliable evidence at all as to what prompted it.

Even so, there are reasons to suspect that popular opinion among the citizens of Missouri agreed in many ways with the James–Younger outlook on resistance. Jesse James, in particular, lived as an outlaw for more than 20 years, uncaptured, unarrested and with largely uninhibited travel. His family owned property and continued their agrarian work largely unmolested. Some records suggest that both Frank and Jesse returned to help with domestic chores and harvests. When finally arrested, despite stunning circumstantial and material evidence and a withering number of separate accounts of armed robbery and theft, Frank James was acquitted of all charges. After his death, Jesse James was almost immediately "canonized" as a local hero while Bob Ford was vilified mercilessly as Judas. Memory of such popular support remains today among citizens of Missouri border counties; the number of restaurants, hotels, and parks which are affiliated with James' exploits remains high and are well attended.[30]

---

30. Review, for example, the tableau of locations identified on the James–Younger Historical Society web page.

Support for and pivotal debate over the James–Younger gang was not limited to popular or grass roots conversation or concerns. The gubernatorial election of 1876 brought the exploits of the James gang into the center of national attention. Republican political rhetoric centered on the general lawlessness of the state of Missouri and noted that the James gang, in particular, was wildly brutal and produced a climate that held external investment in and settlement of Missouri to the most minimal levels. Democrats countered that, while the James gang were outlaws, they at least represented a Missouri courage and popular character that was worthy of both admiration and emulation. Seizing on a noted reticence among Missouri democrats to eschew James and his actions, Republicans hammered home their claims of lawlessness and the debate was picked up by Eastern and urban newspapers in both Chicago and Washington D.C. where it provided evidence to those readerships of the violence inherent in the border states and the imperative need for Eastern and Northern control and supervision. James came to represent, internally, a symbol of Missouri freedom, independence and courage. Externally, he was a foil for arguments for further supervision of Missouri governance by outside forces and of the righteous superiority of Republican policies and agencies. These tensions were represented, even within the state of Missouri, by a divided representation of James and his exploits in the leading St. Louis newspapers. Those with Democrat affinities continued to argue for James' innocence and character; those that were Republican insisted that James and his company graphically illustrated the need for firm legal control and for aggressive re-establishment of law and order. Were this not complex enough, James also captured urban and eastern romantic fascination with the "Western outlaw" and soon became a regular trope and leading figure in dime novels of the American West.

Death did not resolve these conflicts and tensions; in many ways, death exacerbated them. Those who had opposed Jesse James (either for his lawless campaigns or for personal reasons) circulated stories about his involvement in numerous crimes and murders, some of which occurred on the same day in places more than one hundred miles apart; his supporters and friends denied these and other charges, the most extreme nearly suggesting that James had never been involved in any criminal activity at all or in any violence since his days in the confederacy. After his death, stories circulated that the man shot for Jesse James was an imposter or that James had faked his death in order to finally avoid the authorities and leave his life of banditry. Sightings continued for decades. As the final chapter will explore further, James began to resurrect in legend and popular culture almost from the moment of his execution. In life and death, James became a cipher in public rhetoric—either a noble, populist brigand resistor of "foreign" rule and economics or a savage robber, thug and serial killer who represented everything wrong with secessionist ideology and allegiance.

Jesus of Nazareth

The basic elements of Jesus' life as recounted in the gospels are perhaps more widely known to the audience of our book than the biography of Jesse James. As described in the first chapter, Jesus' career began in Galilee, a region fraught with tensions between Roman rule and indigenous Jewish culture, a tension aggravated by memories of the successful Maccabean revolt less than two centuries prior. At the beginning of the first century, Galilee was in the midst of rapid development and faced high rates of taxation. Jesus' early years were spent in the company of John the Baptist, a popular apocalyptic preacher who had his own troubles with the law; Jesus' subsequent ministry was equally apocalyptic in tone and equally troublesome from the perspective of the government. John the Baptist's execution at the hands of Herod Antipas exemplifies the reality of movements that advocated apocalypticism and/or messianism (whatever that term might have meant in context); they were deemed illegal by the state but both John and Jesus engaged in them anyway. Jesus became famous among a largely peasant group of followers for both extraordinary powers and a message of defiance of the state authority. Whatever his exact meaning, both John and Jesus' advocacy of the Kingdom of God certainly challenged the legitimacy of the Kingdom of Rome, and Jesus' movement alienated the Roman rulers and the Temple authorities alike. Local leaders who were installed by and sympathetic to foreign rule plotted with the Roman governor Pilate to remove Jesus.

Just like Jesse's story, there are many points in Jesus' story that are contested and debated among historians. Even if the plot as summarized above is historically unreliable, the Jesus movement doubtless put pressures on local Rome-affiliated governors to demonstrate their ability to control the populace (read: perpetuate an environment favorable to Roman economic, military and political interests). Otherwise, Jesus would not have been executed by Rome, one of the few biographical details agreed upon by all New Testament scholars and historians. Also like Jesse, the actual life of Jesus matters less than the stories told about him after his death. Regardless of how he regarded himself, he was surrounded by legend, much of which celebrated his resistance to the state. Whether or not he preached an apocalyptic Kingdom of God, his followers proclaimed an apocalyptic message immediately following his death. Jesus was supported by locals because by doing so they expressed their own opposition to the state. Oral legends of Jesus venerated him after his death in ways that continued to articulate opposition to Rome.

Jesus' basic career arc is similar to Jesse James' own narrative. In part, this may be because Jesus' career has become a cultural type. Yet, as we realize that claims to messianism are always-already illegal, we may ask if the parallel arc exists because Jesus is, in some ways, a social bandit like Jesse James. It is worthwhile, then, to examine some of the elements of Jesus' career in closer detail, beginning at his own betrayal.

On the 14th or 15th of Nissan, after dinner, Judas Iscariot led a group of armed men to where an unarmed Jesus and his band were encamped. Signaling to the authorities which man was Jesus by embracing him, Judas' action became the paradigm of treacherous betrayal (Mark 14:41–46). The gospel writers who follow and use Mark's account struggle with Judas' motivation. Dissatisfied with the paucity of the story, Matthew adds details that have come to define the story of Judas' betrayal. For Matthew, Judas does it for the money (Matt 26:14–16). Matthew also expands Judas' story with by adding his remorse, return of the money and suicide by hanging. Perhaps in answer to the obvious questions Matthew's account raises—how could Jesus choose a man of such low character to be one of his disciples—Luke's and John's accounts introduce Satan. The devil made Judas do it in Luke in conjunction with the reward money (Luke 22:3–6), and in John in lieu of the reward money (John 13:2). The writer of the Gospel of Luke concludes the Judas episode at the beginning of Acts—Judas buys a field, somehow falls down, and bursts apart (Acts 1:16–19). There is a developing oral tradition where Judas' death gets increasingly more gruesome.[31]

The comparisons between Jesus of Nazareth and Jesse James, the men and their movements, neither begin nor end with their treacherous deaths. The career of Jesus of Nazareth, according to the gospels, was bracketed by attempts on his life and brushes with the government. According to Matthew, his infancy precipitated a state-sponsored massacre of children under the age of two (Matt 2:16–18). The Gospel of John narrates Jesus'

---

31. There is one account of Judas' fate outside of the New Testament. The second-century bishop Papias of Hieropolis writes that Judas' body bloated grotesquely, his excrement was full of pus and worms, and he "died after many tortures and punishments, in a secluded spot which has remained deserted and uninhabited up to our time" due to the malodor that still clung to the area where Judas expired.

"cleansing" (better: "assault") of the Temple at the beginning of his ministry (John 2:13–16), an event located in the last week of Jesus' life by the other three gospels (Mark 11:15–17; Matt 21:12–13; Luke 7:16). Even though no other gospel but Matthew records Herod's gruesome order, there is no evidence for Herod's slaughter of the innocents, and it is dubious that Jesus twice became violent in the Temple, these legends are still historically telling. Violence and hostility to state authority completely surrounded the career of the Prince of Peace.

This is more than a storyteller's sense of irony. Widely accepted as a historical datum, all four gospels note that Jesus began his career among the followers of apocalyptic and active John the Baptist, a spiritual Quantrill-like raider. Such an association would no doubt have been dangerous in Roman controlled Galilee. Jesus then engages in a career of "teaching and ministry" (the content of that teaching, notably, was outspoken opposition to the local spiritual and political authorities) which consists largely of wonder-working and exorcism, both of which attract crowds. To these crowds, Jesus preached a message that defies the "kingdom of Rome" (*baseleia tou Romanou*) by espousing the "kingdom of God" (*baseliea tou theou*). The exorcisms in particular are politically provocative. There was a long-standing tradition equating Roman colonial rule with Satanic rule.[32] In the Gospel tradition, especially in Mark, Jesus' exorcisms are coded as an assault against Rome (the most obvious example being the exorcism of the Gadarene/Geressene demoniac in Mark 5:1–20; note that the name of the demon is "Legion," a direct reference to Roman military occupation). To collaborate with the ruling powers, therefore, was seen as tantamount to collaboration with Satan. According to the gospels, Jesus' message contained outbursts of fiery indictment. He took for himself (or was given by his followers) the titles "savior," and "bringer of peace," favorite monikers of the emperor Augustus who had established the "Pax Romana."[33] He demanded a loyalty and allegiance greater than the one given to Rome.

It is not surprising that the Gospels report that Jesus' followers, at times, became confused, expecting an armed insurrection against Rome. In the gospels, Jesus is depicted as attracting radicals and rebels to his

---

32. Thurman, "Looking for a Few Good Men," 147.

33. On imperial titles and veneration of the Roman emperor in the first century C.E., see S. R. F. Price, *Rituals and Power: The Roman Imperial Cult in Asia Minor* (Cambridge: Cambridge University Press, 1987), and Steven Frieson, *Twice Neokoros: Ephesos, Asia and the Cult of the Flavian Imperial Family* (Religions in the Greco-Roman World 116; Leiden: Brill, 1993).

inner circle of followers (Luke 6:15; though Horsley, as discussed below, is surely right in his suspicion that the zealot party did not exist until mid-century). Peter carries a sword (Matt 26:51; Mark 14:47; Luke 22:50; John 18:10). James and John call for the destruction of cities (Luke 9:54). They were so fiery that, according to Mark 13:3, they were nicknamed "sons of thunder," fitting bandit titles, indeed. According to the Gospel of John, the peasants (twice) attempt to start an armed rebellion with Jesus as the head (John 6:15). In the context of Roman rule, messianic claims were, strictly speaking, illegal; the resultant unrest and unapproved public assembly were also explicitly against the law.

In the last week of Jesus' life, he arrived in Jerusalem during Passover. The holiday, celebrating Jewish independence, drew tens of thousands of pilgrims to the city. Tense already over holiday preparations and city over-crowding, pilgrims were also surrounded by politically volatile rhetoric. They chanted hymns to independence and God's deliverance as they fought through the crowds and climbed the steps of the Temple to worship within the very shadow of occupying Roman garrisons and troops. Tensions were high and both popular rhetoric and public liturgy were exasperating them. Violent conflict between Jewish worshipers and Roman guards was inevitable.

Ominously, it was in this context that Jesus began to alienate and frustrate his followers. In this climate, Jesus assaults the Temple courts chasing out money lenders. He repeatedly and publicly voiced invective against the cities rulers and elites (Mark 11:27–32; Luke 20, 22; Matt 21). The gospels all reveal signs of dissent between Jesus and his followers. They seem confused about his mission and unsure of his plans (see Mark 4:14, 41; 6:6, 51–52; 8:17–21, 27–32; 9:17–29, 32–34; 10:24, 37–45, for examples). In time, they will abandon him when the final conflict begins. The crucifixion of Jesus could hardly be a surprise to the ancient readers of the gospels.

A convention of scholarship in "New Testament Backgrounds" has been to identify the polarized society of early first-century C.E. Palestine and to stress the importance of "parties" within Judaism (a term supplied by the historian Flavius Josephus). These "parties"—the Sadducees, Pharisees, Zealots and Essenes—were all organized ways for Jews to deal with the various pressures of being part of Roman society. Judaism of the late Second Temple has long been regarded by gospel scholars as concerned with separation and ritual purity. The tensions arising from the collision of liturgical separation and Roman cultural and political hegemony prompted some Palestinian Jews to accommodate and compromise their religious views (the Sadducees and Temple authorities) which in turn prompted some to withdraw to the desert turning to ascetic separatism (the Essenes), some to rural household-based expressions of hyper-piety and separation (the Pharisees) and a few to threaten hostile revolt (the Zealots).

Horsley has argued compellingly that it is fallacious to see the Zealots and their subgroup the Sicarii as a constant community in the first half of the first century C.E.[34] Much as scholarship has revealed that there was no uniform expectation of "Messiah," there is little to suggest a uniform and organized protest to Rome prior to the '60s. Certainly, there is ample evidence that many Jews opposed the occupation by Rome, and Roman intrusion may have brought cultural and economic pressures that, according to some, made conventional Jewish religious observances more difficult. Yet there is no real evidence for the sustained existence of a party of organized insurgents who practiced public assassination as a means of instigating war with Rome, and it is difficult to imagine Roman patience with such a clearly defined and identifiable group extending for decades. Further, there are political and ideological reasons modern scholars might want to posit such a community. Such a hypothetical community has been posited, in many ways, to stress the peaceful nature of Jesus' career. Jesus' peaceful "spiritual rebellion" offers a contrast to the imagined consistent calls for violence from the Zealots, even as the Zealots provide the rationale for an argued Roman hypersensitivity to rebellion which would result in confusion over Jesus and state over-reaction. Instead of a sustained (though oddly ineffective for decades) campaign to provoke Roman invasion by one (and only one) "party" within Judaism, Horsley and others observe that the actual history of Palestine under Roman occupation was one of serial uprisings. Palestine was volatile. In many ways, so was Jesus.

The Jesus movement, since Reimarus, has long been regarded by scholarship as having aspects of political protest and political dissent. Modern reconstructions of the historical Jesus foreground this aspect of his work. Beginning with Reimarus, moving through Wrede and Schweitzer, and ending in contemporary historical reconstructions of Jesus such as E. P. Sanders or John Dominic Crossan, the "Temple event" of Jesus' career is widely seen as the act that precipitates Jesus' arrest and defines Jesus' antipathy to the state and the state-sympathetic Temple. According to these readings, Jesus' "cleansing of the Temple," attested in all four gospels (Mark 11:15–19; Matt 21:12–16; Luke 19:45–58; and John 2:13–16), was actually an act of insurrection

---

34. Horsley, *Galilee*, 258–59.

and unrest.[35] Indeed, this political protest seems to be one of the few common elements in hypothesized reconstructions, and many scholars suggest that this event, more than any other, precipitates Jesus' arrest by the Romans.

The suggestion that Jesus was acting like a bandit is certainly not new—Pilate himself leveled it during Jesus' own lifetime. The charge upon which Jesus is arrested and under which he is killed is, essentially, insurrection. The charge of pretention to being "king of the Jews" pervades the trail scene in all four gospels, another rare moment (like the assault on the Temple) of an event that transcends both Synoptic and Johannine traditions (Mark 15:2, 9, 12, 18, 26; Matt 27:11; 29, 37; Luke 23:3, 37–38; John 19:3, 19–21). In the Synoptic tradition, Jesus remarks that, because he is taken in the middle of the night by armed men, he is being treated as a *leisten* (Mark 14:48; Matt 26:55, Luke 22:52). The Greek *leisten* has the dual meaning of "robber, highwayman, bandit" or "revolutionary, insurrectionist, guerilla." Bauer's *Greek–English Lexicon* cannot, in fact, choose between the meanings in the translation of the gospel verses noted above.[36] These two meanings slide into each other throughout the first-century literature on the phenomenon (Josephus, for example), yet the two meanings are radically divergent today. Although "bandit" may still carry some political overtones in contemporary English, a "robber" is simply a criminal, one who steals from others with no socially or politically redeeming message to the act. Note how the connotations shift in English when *leisten* is translated as "insurrectionist" in Mark's verse: "Then Jesus spoke: 'Do you take me for an insurrectionist, that you have come out with swords and cudgels to arrest me?'" (Mark 14:48). In addition, Jesus was crucified—a form of punishment reserved for revolutionaries/bandits—in between two revolutionaries/bandits. Jesus was treated as an outlaw.[37] And, frankly, to the Romans, he was.

---

35. An argument central in Albert Schweitzer, *The Quest for the Historical Jesus* (New York: Macmillan, 1973) and E. P. Sanders, *The Historical Figure of Jesus* (London: Allen Lane/Penguin, 1993); *Jesus and Judaism* (Philadelphia: Fortress, 1985); and Bart D. Ehrman, *Jesus: Apocalyptic Prophet of a New Millennium* (New York: Oxford University Press, 1999); Richard A. Horsley, *Jesus in Context: Power, People and Performance* (Minneapolis: Fortress, 2008); John Dominic Crossan, *Jesus: A Revolutionary Biography* (San Francisco: Harper Collins, 1989).

36. BAGD, 594.

37. Martin Hengel, *Crucifixion* (Grand Rapids: Eerdmans, 1977), is still the seminal, grisly, work on this subject.

First-century Palestine was a state living under Roman occupation and a variety of movements and strategies emerged to resist the colonizers. The Galilee in particular was a rebellious region. It had a long tradition of resisting the control imposed by any centralized government whether that political influence came from Jerusalem or a foreign empire. Throughout the history of the region, Galilee was on the margins of the states and empires that rose to power around it. The Galilee was a frontier state and the Galileans "had a keen sense of independence, periodically resisting or outright revolting against" any outside control.[38]

Bandit bands form in areas where there is little centralized political control; where the local social, political, and economic systems have been disrupted often by the attempts of outsiders to establish control; and where the subsequent violence that accompanies such outsider incursions has displaced segments of the populace. This describes the conditions under which the Galileans lived, particularly during the reign of Herod the Great and on into the first century, up to and including the First Jewish Revolt against Rome. During this period especially, there was a confluence between robbery and revolution. A bandit was not just someone who robbed and sometimes murdered travelers. Rather, such acts were also considered crimes against the state. They disrupted the Roman peace, targeted the wealthy and powerful, and sometimes raided such state-controlled institutions as grain repositories (as, for example, John of Gischala against whom Rome sent troops). Drawing on Eric Hobsbawm's social scientific studies of the general phenomenon of banditry, Horsley calls the marauding activity of these Galileans "social banditry" thus underscoring its political valence.[39] In fact, social banditry is a "prepolitical form of social protest against particular local conditions and injustices."[40] This does not mean, however, that every gang was a revolutionary band. For the most part, banditry does not escalate into rebellion because it lacks a unified inspired and inspiring vision of social change. In other words, bandits tend simply to react against and disrupt the status quo, rarely striving towards or enacting an alternative social system.

There are, of course, exceptions to this general rule of banditry, and several of these exceptions can be located in first-century Palestine. Along with the Galilee's strong independent streak, there was a long-standing Israelite tradition of charismatic kingship. Unlike its sister state

---

38. Horsley, *Galilee*, 276.
39. Ibid., 257.
40. Ibid., 258.

of Judah, Israel never established a ruling dynasty. Kings were charismatic leaders who rose up from among the general populace and were maneuvered into power usually through armed insurrection. Ironically, this describes David's own career. Even though the biblical writers condemn the northern kingdom of Israel for not having a Davidic monarch on the throne, their pattern of choosing a leader more closely matches David's own rise than does the subsequent history of Judah's kings. Josephus chronicles at least three politicized bandit gangs emerging in the Galilee in the first century, gangs in which, perhaps harkening back to the Israelite tradition of charismatic monarchy, their leaders were proclaimed "king": Judas son of Hezekiah (the brigand chief of the last generation), Simon and Athronges.[41] These three movements are in addition to the one surrounding John of Gischala—who, while never proclaimed "king," fomented a general peasant rebellion against Rome and the leaders of Jerusalem—and Judas the Galilean who was involved with the protests against the census in 6 C.E.[42] During the First and Second Jewish Revolts there were also figures around whom messianic fervor swirled: Simon bar Giora and Simeon bar Kokhba, respectively. Conditions were such in the Galilee that any "stabilized and legitimate definition of 'law and order'" was lacking.[43] Consequently, "who viewed whom as 'outlaw'" constituted "a fluid relationship among the people, tradition, and rivals for power in Jerusalem."[44] The Galilee can certainly be regarded as the "Robber State" of the Roman colonies. It was the wild, wild North.

Where does the Jesus movement fit, then, in the social banditry of first-century Galilee? Judas son of Hezekiah's revolt took place immediately after the death of Herod the Great; the other named messianic pretenders followed with increasing fervor throughout the '40s, '50s, and '60s until a full-scale rebellion broke out in '66. Sandwiched in between these two notable times of unrest some have argued that Jesus' own time period was quiet and peaceful. However, it seems unlikely that a single generation of tranquility would emerge untouched by the documented unrest of the generations that immediately precede and follow it. There may have not been a figure that achieved the notoriety of Judas son of Hezekiah during Jesus' lifetime (apart, that is, from both John and Jesus—both of whom, we argue, are bandit-like insurrectionists),

---

41. Ibid., 269.
42. Horsley argues that Judas son of Hezekiah and Judas the Galilean are two different people.
43. Horsley, *Galilee*, 262.
44. Ibid., 263.

3. *Crossing Outlaws* 83

but the stories of his brigandry and the effects of his insurrection had to have circulated in the environs of the Galilee. Jesus was a social bandit. Certainly, his followers did and do not regard his activity as merely criminal but this is one of the most fundamental characteristics of a social bandit (and, indeed, what sets them apart from general brigands).

Jesus most certainly was regarded as a bandit by the governing authorities and his movement shares many of the key elements of Judas' revolution. Jesus was the leader of a roving band of Galilean rural poor; he is proclaimed king over and against the rule of both Rome and Jerusalem; his followers attempt armed insurrection at least once (if John's account in 6:14–15 has any historical underpinnings); and he is taken and executed like any other first-century outlaw. In frontier regions during times of war, one man's bandit is another man's revolutionary; one man's revolutionary is another man's prophet.

The gospel writers all in their own way associate Jesus with banditry. They do not describe Jesus as robbing, pillaging and murdering his way across the frontier. As Eric Thurman (influenced by Ched Meyers) argues, Mark in particular associates Jesus with banditry. For example, when Jesus is first questioned about his ability to exorcise demons, he is characterized as an "'outlaw' of sorts, breaking and entering into 'the strong man's house,' tying him up, plundering property, and so bringing Satan's dominion to an end (Mark 3:22–27…)."[45] Jesus the outlaw then, literally, rides into Jerusalem as messiah, and raids the Temple, hence "culminat[ing] his banditlike activity."[46] Jesus' actions in the Temple pivot on the symbolism of the bandit/revolutionary. He accuses it of being a house of insurrectionists (*leistein*), contrasting his own type of banditry (symbolic and against Satan) with the banditry of revolution (violent and against the Roman Empire). The pardon of Barabbas, a violent insurrectionist, whose name literally means "Son of the Father," just prior to—indeed as a substitute for—Jesus' crucifixion makes the same contrast.

Jesus' actions at the Temple bring him to the attention of the governing authorities. He is taken by armed men in the middle of the night, and crucified amidst other outlaws. "Like a bandit or an insurrectionist, Jesus

---

45. Thurman, "Looking for a Few Good Men," 147.
46. Ibid., 148. He also cites George Aichele, *Jesus Framed* (Biblical Limits; New York: Routledge, 1996), 183–84; Richard A. Horsley, *Hearing the Whole Story: The Politics of Plot in Mark's Gospel* (Louisville: Westminster John Knox, 2001), 148; Ched Myers, *Binding the Strong Man: A Political Reading of Mark's Story of Jesus* (Maryknoll, N.Y.: Orbis Books, 1997).

resists Satan's colonial control on behalf of an alternative imperial male power."[47] At the very least, the Gospels are highly invested in the question of Jesus' banditry, asserting that he was not, at least, a typical bandit, even though, perhaps in a "spiritual sense," he was.

Crossing Outlaws

Within days of the assassination of Jesse James, Bob Ford was compared to Judas Iscariot. Like the gospel writers themselves engage in speculation about Judas' motivation, the question of exactly why Bob Ford betrayed Jesse James is also open. "Was it the prospect of the reward that had motivated Bob Ford to kill Jesse James? Probably."[48] And yet, there is no firm historical data about how much the reward money was, where it came from, how or to whom it was distributed. He was certainly in communication if not conspiracy with the governing officials, and he came close to ending his life hanged like the Matthean Judas. Although Jesse's betrayer neither hangs himself nor bursts apart in a field, Bob Ford does meet his demise in an "appropriate" manner. As recorded in one of the earliest ballads written about the incident, "And then one day, the papers say,/ Bob Ford got his rewarding:/ A cowboy drunk his heart did plunk./ As you do you'll get according."[49]

Much like the parallels between the legends of Bob Ford and Judas, there are significant overlaps between the career arcs of Jesse the Bandit and Jesus the Messiah. Further, in their ends, Jesse was shot from behind, unarmed, without protest and partly unrobed, as he stood cruciform against the wall. Jesse, like Jesus, is taken unarmed, after a meal, and betrayed/denied by two of his followers. The two were about the same age and died around the same date on the Jewish calendar (April 3, 1882 was 14th of Nissan 5642). Both were hounded by a "foreign" governor struggling to bring order to a region of political unrest. Both figures divided the opinions of the populace, a populace burdened by taxation and deeply concerned about the decline of their traditional way of life and values due to outside domination, during their careers and after their deaths. Both opposed the oppressive rule of a "foreign" government. Both attacked manifestations of that foreign rule (via exorcism in one case and train and bank robbery in the other). Jesse's life was largely preserved in short, pithy stories about his exploits, many of which reflect political/regional tensions of the day; many other stories preserve

---

47. Thurman, "Looking for a Few Good Men," 147.
48. Settle, *Jesse James Was His Name*, 119.
49. Ibid., 174.

short, often humorous sayings. The study of the formation of the gospels reveals how stories of Jesus first circulated as "pronouncement stories," "miracle tales," parables and narratives of conflict. The oral skeleton of the preserved biographies of both figures is often obvious. In the gospels, the trial and execution of Jesus reveal complex ways in which Jesus was viewed by his contemporaries, both those who supported his mission and those who regarded him as a threat to civil and religious order. The death of Jesse James, and particularly the press accounts that followed it and the editorials of Jesse's life that perhaps inspired it, likewise reveal the tensions of identity and description that surrounded the bandit figure. The social conditions of Reconstruction-era Missouri and Roman-occupied Galilee have key similarities. The careers of Jesse James and Jesus of Nazareth met similar responses from the state. Indeed, in many ways, from the perspective of the state, Messiahs are bandits by another name. Jesus and Jesse James have similar career arcs because both are social bandits.

Of course, Jesus' fans assert(ed) his unique status and hold him up as a moral exemplar. Jesse's fans too assert(ed) his unique status and defend his moral character. Despite the absence of corroborating evidence, Jesse James was quickly labeled a Robin Hood, and legends began to circulate about how he stole from the rich and gave to the poor.[50] Early biographers, such as Triplett and Edwards, work very hard to argue that Jesse James was morally innocent (at least, circumstantially compelled) and showed a marked preference for non-violence. The fact that the James–Younger band lived and moved throughout the region in relative security was in part due to Jesse's reputation of championing the rural poor of frontier Missouri. Jesus was proclaimed "messiah" and "king" in imitation of earlier Galilean insurrectionists and bandit movements. His protection and popularity while in Galilee attest to the broad appeal of his message among the rural poor; the Gospels concur that, even in Galilee, Jesus was most likely surrounded by the marginal, the poor, and the powerless. When coming south to the more central territory under the sway of Jerusalem, Jesus is on a sure course for arrest and execution.

"Assassination at the hand of a traitor did much to raise him to heroic standing."[51] Young, cut down at the height of their careers, both betrayed by a close follower, enmeshed in the political and social unrest of their day, legends quickly accrued around Jesus and Jesse. In fact, the public

---

50. See ibid., 171–72, for example.
51. Ibid., 123.

reaction to Jesse's death was quicker and more widespread than that of Jesus—though we might attribute this fact to the technological advancement of the newspaper. As we outlined earlier in the Introduction, within a week of the death of Jesse James, his home in St. Joseph was opened to the curious public and his fence and stables were taken apart, splinter by splinter, by relic seekers.[52] Fearing that the relic hunters would not be content with pieces of wood, Jesse's mother had his grave dug on her farm where his body remained until 1902.[53] When Jesse's body was finally moved to a public cemetery, the obelisk that marked his grave was set upon by relic seekers and they chipped it away until the stone completely disappeared. Even today, a casting of Jesse's bullet-shattered skull sits on display in the front room of his former home, now turned museum.

Rumors circulated that Jesse's death had been a hoax, a way of circumventing the law so that he could retire in peace and obscurity. There were many who refused to believe that he was really dead, that he could really be taken by an inferior like Bob Ford. Within a year of his death, a local farmer reported that Jesse had appeared in Clay County.[54] Throughout the years, Jesse appeared all over the country, and numerous people came forward claiming to be Jesse James himself. But perhaps fueling the legend of Jesse James more than his personal afterlife appearances was his resurrection in American folk ballads, dime novels and finally the silver screen. The Gospel's accounts of post-crucifixion appearances by Jesus could scarcely be more difficult to harmonize; from the open/empty tomb to the ascension, they are among the most contradictory portions of the entire narrative.

Both Jesus' and Jesse's bi-polar status in popular imagination while living thwart attempts to discover their "real," historical identity. As betrayed bandits, such identification becomes even more nebulous through their treacherous deaths. "Resurrected" in public memory, they continue to elude capture by historians. The exact specifics of a "historical" Jesse are as difficult to describe as the qualities of any potential "historical" Jesus; this specificity is frustrated most acutely by the remarkably conflicted communities who told stories of their passing and by the glorification of oral traditions. Jesse and Jesus exist, now, in stories. Privy through story to the intimate workings of their mission, even modern hearers of their stories become attuned to their resistance and determined not to be identified with their final betrayers; no one

52. Ibid., 127.
53. Ibid., 166.
54. Ibid., 169.

wants to become a Bob Ford or a Judas. Sensing the resistance inherent in both Jesus and Jesse, later communities of story-tellers begin to interpret their resistance in ways that awaken freedom, hope, inversion of oppressive power structures and trickster-like evasion.

Both Jesus and Jesse James are social bandits. Jesus' activity was illegal in its context, as was Jesse's. Of course, Jesus' followers would argue that he was following a higher morality than that of the state. So did Jesse's. Indeed, this is practically the sine qua non of the social bandit—that the bandit's community sees the bandit's actions as either morally legal or at least as an illegal route to the manifestation of a higher good. In "crossing" these two double-crossed outlaws, we see how similar social dynamics were in play in their resistances and in the oral stories which preserved their memory. Further, we see how the moment of treacherous death—betrayal to a literal cross or to a corrupt and harsh legal system—functions to perpetuate the mystique of their appeal. Jesse James and Jesus of Nazareth have become figures larger than history and integral to the identities of entire historical epochs; the romance of their resistance, and the potential freedom from "order" and constraint that it inspires, continues to attract devotion.

In their narratives, both act above the law to express their dissent to foreign rule. Both are embraced by the indigenous, largely agrarian/peasant community, who identify with their missions of rebellion. Both meet similar ends that mark the ambivalence of their respective careers. Jesse's legends may well draw, as a type, on Jesus (and, as we saw in Chapter 2, legends of David intertwine in both Jesus' messianism and Jesse's broader "American myth" of western genre literature and history). The differences normally cited between Jesus and Jesse are primarily rooted in arbitrary bifurcation between "high" and "low" culture, between "sacred" and "profane" history.

But what did Jesus or Jesse intend? What we have explored are the Jesus and Jesse of narrative; their narratives most certainly reflect the interests, needs, worries, expectations and hopes of subsequent communities of their followers. What could be known about the "historical" Jesus or Jesse James? In our next chapter—again focused on Jesus and Jesse—we will explore the mechanism of this legend itself, and will note similar ambivalence surrounding attempts to recover the "real" figures of history. We will find that, in each case, the "real" figure of history is largely erased by the very process of historical and popular narrative itself.

Chapter 4

10¢ GOSPELS: THE QUEST(S) FOR THE HISTORICAL
JESSE JAMES AND JESUS OF NAZARETH

Sinners and Saints

The citizens of St. Joseph, Missouri on the evening of April third likely retired to bed still abuzz with the morning's news; we may forgive them for thinking an era had passed when Jesse James was killed. For almost 20 years, Jesse James had ridden as guerrilla soldier, semi-political bandit and outlaw across more than half a dozen states disrupting interstate commerce, both by rail and by stage.[1] For the last year, Jesse and his family had been living in a rented house under the pseudonym Thomas Howard. As he lay dead from a gunshot to the head, small crowds first came to the commotion and then they swelled as news of the true identity of "Mr. Howard" spread. By late afternoon, Jesse's body, placed on ice at a local mortuary, had become a tourist attraction, the first of many Jesse-related tourist stops in northwest Missouri. As with all tourist attractions, Jesse came with a gift shop; his former possessions were almost immediately for sale.[2] The citizens of St. Joseph might have expected the next few days would certainly attract more crowds and reporters, but the end of Jesse James finally seemed at hand. But neither the bandit nor the drama would be buried anytime soon. Jesse, at his

---

1. In addition to the biographies surveyed below, see Robert J. Whybrow, "From the Pen of a Noble Robber: The Letters of Jesse Woodson James, 1847–1882." *Brand Book* 24, no. 2 (1987): 22–34; "'Ravenous Monsters of Society': The Early Exploits of the James Gang," *Brand Book* 27, no. 2 (1990): 1–24; Yeatman, *Frank and Jesse James*; and Cathy M. Jackson, "The Making of an American Outlaw Hero: Jesse James and Late 19th Century Print Media" (Ph.D. diss., University of Missouri-Columbia, 2004).

2. Jesse's mother got in on the action, as well, selling a photo of him to a visitor, saying, "I must have money now. They have killed him on whom I depended." Yeatman, *Frank and Jesse James*, 276. Yeatman speculates that support of his mother was a possible motive in Jesse's crimes.

death, was a cultural icon, a signifier for radical independence, for freedom, for an undaunted south. As a former criminal, he also had the lurid appeal of a captive or stuffed predator. As a dead man, he had grotesque attraction. It is difficult to think of what could provide greater spectacle.

And, of course, as all good carnival(esque) attractions, Jesse's death left plenty to think and talk about. Questions immediately circulated about whether or not Mr. Howard was indeed Jesse James. Until his death, not even his children knew his true identity or even their own real names.[3] Even during his lifetime, it was difficult to say for certain which crimes he had committed—the name "Jesse James" had circulated independently. Local bandits knew (or quickly learned) that announcing to a passenger car that it was being robbed by Jesse James inspired a compliant awe and fear among those being robbed in ways that declaring, say, "this here's Fred Smith" did not. No doubt many assumed Jesse's identity as they performed robberies. No doubt Jesse also knew that his reputation was his greatest weapon; allowing criminals to claim his name only increased the sense that he was both everywhere and nowhere at once. Jesse also used several aliases (John Davis "Dave" Howard was another common pseudonym). The accurate attachment of name with body was difficult to guarantee.

There are even questions about some of his most famous exploits. The James' may not have been as innovative about bank robbery as legend remembers. The first, peacetime, daylight bank robbery in America, the robbery of the bank in Liberty, Missouri, may not have been done by Frank or Jesse. Jesse was still convalescing from a severe gunshot wound to the chest. As a pilgrim center, Liberty, Missouri, particularly its jail, is far more important to pious Mormons.[4] Nevertheless, the historic old-town square of Liberty is home to the Jesse James Bank Robbery Museum, despite the real questions about the Jameses involvement, and in direct competition with the Liberty Jail.[5]

The Jesse James Bank Robbery Museum begs for analysis of its role in the "historical Jesse James." Which matters: the actual events of Jesse's life or the legends surrounding them? How do we recover the former, given a bandit's necessary subterfuge? And "matters" to whom?

---

3. Jesse Edwards James was named after his father and his father's most ardent defender—John Newman Edwards. He was given the alias Tim Howard. Mary retained her first name but also shared the Howard last name as an alias.
4. Brigham Young was incarcerated in Liberty, the result of religious persecution. In jail, he received visions.
5. Yeatman, *Frank and Jesse James*, 86; Settle, *Jesse James Was His Name*, 33–36.

In what way? Even as Liberty, Missouri celebrates Jesse's successful career as a robber (never mind that he was likely never a criminal in Liberty), to this day Northfield, Minnesota celebrates its annual weeklong "Jesse James Days" in which the James–Youngers' failure to rob is showcased. Unlike Missouri where nearly every county advertises some sort of Jesse James attraction (an array that spans caves, crime sites, wax figures and amateur archives), Minnesota revels in its triumph over James (never mind that Jesse escaped).[6] Which view of Jesse is more "historical?"

The larger question, debated by James' contemporaries, later biographers and historians, and in competing tourist attractions, is how to understand the character and career of Jesse James. In many ways, Jesse's career had long been intertwined with larger moments in the construction of American subjectivity. As we have seen, Jesse had begun, at the age of 16, to ride with "black flag" anti-abolitionist guerrilla gangs that formed in Missouri in response to "bloody Kansas" conflicts.[7] The James–Younger gang had a particularly effective partnership; they excelled in bold daylight bank robbery and ambitious highway and rail brigandage. Their robberies both were and were not social protests. They were, on the one hand, a form of local protests against foreign hegemony, a form of violent resistance, an ongoing program of terrorism. On the other hand, it was social protest and armed resistance that was also financially lucrative. Was Jesse a hero or was he just a cold-blooded criminal? The furor over Jesse James would, in no way, end with his death. A dead Jesse was a Jesse finally stable enough to serve as foundation for legend and tangible enough to initiate a quest for a life of Jesse James that cut through the legend to expose the flesh and bone of the "real Jesse."

To many, Jesse's career also represented rugged individualism and self-sufficiency of Western culture.[8] Newspaper founder and editor Robert Newman Edwards frequently wrote of Jesse's escapades. Edwards only vaguely (if at all) condemned Jesse's lawlessness. He wrote, more often, that Jesse was displaying everything noble about Missouri manliness:

> There are men...who learned to dare when there was no such word as quarter in the dictionary of the Border. Men who have carried their lives in their hands so long that they do not know how to commit them over

---

6. With re-enactments, parades, games and "food and fun for all ages" according to the official website of the festival: www.djjd.org.

7. See Goodrich, *War to the Knife*, for a remarkable survey of this era.

8. Eric J. Hobsbawm, "Social Bandits: A Reply," *Comparative Studies in Society and History* 14, no. 4 (1972): 494–505.

into the keeping of the laws and regulations that exist now, and these men sometimes rob. But it is always in the glare of day and in the teeth of the multitude. With them booty is but the second thought; the wild drama of the adventure first. These men never go upon the highway in lonesome places to plunder the pilgrim. That they leave to an ignobler pack of jackals. But they ride at midday... These men are bad citizens but they are bad because they live out of their time... [They] might have sat with Arthur at the Round Table... What they did we condemn. But the way they did it we cannot help admiring. It was as though three bandits had come to us from the storied Odenwald, with the halo of medieval chivalry upon their garments and shown us how things were done that poets sing of. No where else in the United States or in the civilized world, probably, could this thing have been done. It was done here, not because the protectors of person and property were less efficient but because the bandits were more dashing and skillful; not because honest Missourians have less nerve but because freebooting Missourians have more.[9]

Historians trained to be suspicious of received history and historical texts, particularly when in the presence of *tendenz* or ideological bias, must draw up a bit short when reading such essays. Edwards' rhetoric is, very literally, breathless and breath-taking. Edwards' rhetoric inhibits our ability to glimpse a "historical Jesse," yet it is Edwards who is also responsible for the very creation of "Jesse James." His remarks above were part of an editorial on a daylight robbery at the Kansas City Fair on September 26, 1872.[10] The James brothers are widely thought (then and now) to have been responsible. In broad daylight, the James brothers and one other rider, masked with bandannas over their face, simply rode horses through the crowds (estimated at 10,000 people) up to the booth selling admission tickets, drew guns and seized the cash box through an open window. After pocketing the cash, a scuffle ensued and a gunshot was fired. Edwards neglects to mention that, for paltry funds, the stray bullet wounded (and lamed for life) a little girl.[11] Edwards was a frequent celebrant of the James boys, particularly Jesse. His editorials first articulated the typical apology of the James gang's outlawry, a position he

---

9. As quoted in Settle, *Jesse James Was His Name*, 45–46.
10. See ibid., 44–45; Yeatman, *Frank and Jesse James*, 103.
11. The robbers collected just under $1000 which, admittedly, is a substantial amount for the era. Their timing, however, was off. They just missed, by moments, several thousand more dollars which had been taken from the cashbox to deposit in the bank. Sources differ as to whether or not the young girl was injured by a gunshot intended for Ben Wallace, the ticket booth manager, or was ridden over by one of the horsemen. In either case, it seems likely that the robbers both fired into the crowds and spurred their horses, recklessly, through these same crowds.

would reiterate in his *Noted Guerrillas*. Frank James and Robert Younger would, years later, explicitly invoke Edwards' arguments in their own legal defenses.

Over the course of Jesse James' career as a bandit, several letters under his name were sent to various newspapers, usually (but not exclusively) papers where Edwards worked. The letters were often denials of accusations, screeds against "Eastern" law and lawmakers, or manifesto-like calls for resistance; often they contain elements of all three. James' letters echo Edwards' sentiments and often sound suspiciously like Edwards' own prose.[12] Most modern, critical James biographers (Yeatman, Settle, Stiles, etc.) are very rightly suspicious of simply embracing the letters as James' own or using them uncritically to reconstruct a "historical Jesse." To begin, as a corpus, they are wildly uneven in language, vocabulary, style and rhetoric. No historian we read, however, suggests openly that Edwards was the author of some, though, to us, the possibility seems likely. Jesse James was a divisive symbol in the 1880s Missouri gubernatorial politics. Edwards—a staunch Democrat—combined his excoriation of Republicans and the Federal government with his open admiration of Jesse James. Edwards hated Crittenden and was among the first and most vicious to confront the new governor for his role in James' death.[13] In many ways, Edwards created "Jesse James"; in many ways, Edwards' antagonism of Crittenden also got James killed.

With Jesse's death, the vacuum formed by the absence of so notorious a hero-tyrant was quickly filled by multiple voices in support of and in opposition to Jesse. Even some who opposed Jesse's career of banditry found sympathy for him in his death.[14] His supporters asserted his essential manliness, courage and integrity; his detractors noted Jesse had slowed post-war development and expansion of Missouri.[15] The

---

12. For a collection and analysis of James' letters, see Whybrow, "From the Pen of a Noble Robber."

13. As one might imagine, "Major Edwards" was violently opposed to Reconstruction. To make matters even more volatile, he was, reportedly, also a serious alcoholic. See Settle, *Jesse James Was His Name*, 209 n. 11.

14. Stiles reports: "[Some] were not so quick to reconcile the ends with the means. 'It is revolting in the extreme,' Rabbi Elias Eppstein of Kansas City wrote in his diary, 'to contemplate upon the fact, that a mere boy lures himself into the friendship of a man to abide his time and opportunity to assassinate him for blood-money... The death of J.J. is a happy event in the annals of Missouri—but the manner of his going is a stroke into the face of morality and civilization'" (*Jesse James*, 378).

15. See Settle, *Jesse James Was His Name*, 118–28. Jackson, "Making of an American Outlaw Hero," 33–39, Thelen, *Paths of Resistance*, 72.

newspaper editorial pages were filled with lengthy articles, rebuttals, re-rebuttals. Ink from the editorial page, heated by strong opinions, often boiled over onto pages devoted to the news about verification (or not) of Jesse's body, summaries of Jesse's career and Bob and Charlie Ford's arrest and subsequent trial. The later trial of Frank James ratcheted the excitement up to an even higher pitch. Freed from the troublesome burden of an actual, physical, "real" living Jesse James, the character of Jesse was finally freed to grow. Ford's shot to the back of Mr. Howard's head (re)opened hundreds of psychological wounds in Reconstruction-era Missouri and set Jesse's spirit free to roam the wilds of the county unbound by mundane embodiment and flirting with a form of immortality in oral legend.

Unlike Ford, James fans were unable to imagine that Jesse was only in it for the money. Stories about his bandit largess began to circulate. In one popular story that has multiple variations associated with several different locations and dates, which is a common trait of oral transmission, the James–Younger gang is robbing a train (or a stage coach) and refuses to take the money of Confederate veterans. In another version, they return the money of a Baptist pastor, and even contribute additional funds (re-appropriated from other passengers) to his ministry needs. Catholic and Episcopal priests, however, faced a different fate. One priest on a train was robbed of his gold watch; Jesse asserted that, since Jesus had no need of riches, neither did the priest.[16]

Some stories (and biographers) flatly assert the James boys would not murder Clay County citizens; even those who "betray" Jesse to the authorities are either exiled or left to the vengeance of others. According to Triplett, even collaboration with the Pinkerton detectives—symbols of Eastern/Northern/urban life and a "policing" presence of hegemony—would only result in James' passive assault; he is present at the execution of the collaborators but does not act himself. Triplett, as we will see, even insists that, throughout his career, Jesse only resorted to violence in self-defense.

Jesse is often cast in stories after the fashion of Rob Roy or Robin Hood.[17] In one famous account (again with the tell-tale marks of oral circulation) a poor Clay County widow was being oppressed by her wicked (Eastern Bank) creditor. A collection agent arrived at her home and took her final dollars, promising that one more default would leave

---

16. Note, for example, Triplett, *The Life, Times and Treacherous Death of Jesse James*, 47, 68, 86–87, 115.

17. Apparently, not only did oral legend see the James gang as Robin Hood but they also frequently cast themselves as such. Stiles, *Jesse James*, 236, 238, 257.

her homeless. This same agent was beset by the James boys in the woods just away from the widow's farm. The James boys robbed the man of the widow's last savings as well as his own valuables. They then rode to the widow's house and returned her own money plus "interest" to her.[18]

Several stories of the James boys, even those beyond the obviously fictionalized accounts of the dime novels, even those often taken as "authentic" (if anecdotal) by James biographers, have all the elements of orality in their contents: variations of a single tale, variations on settings, reoccurring themes and wording, variations in character and dialog. Several have the characteristics of folkloric theme or *tendenz*. There are clear "apologetic" tendencies in Jesse's earliest biographies. Edwards stresses the super-imposition of bandit life. Triplett stresses the reticence to violence. The gist of these stories—as well as their obvious marks of oral development and popularity—is easy to see. Locals needed stories to clarify how the James brothers, a deadly hazard to "foreigners," were no harm at all to good, God-fearing, Protestant, Missouri-born Confederates. This connection both reassured sympathetic locals and warned any "strangers" found in their midst.

Jesse's exploits first circulated as oral legends. The stories about Jesse were tailored to fit various social, political and ideological needs and expectations. They were later written down and romantically expanded in popular books, even as Jesse became a romantic figure in popular fiction. During the early 1870s, the exploits of the James–Younger gang appeared in newspapers beyond Missouri, indeed, all over the country; they became heroes in pulp fiction novels, popularly called "dime" or "10 cent" novels, often written and published back East but always set in the "rugged West." These adventures are diverse. Jesse fights Mexicans and Indians, helps farmers and cattle men and, oddly, fights crime, even as he robs stagecoaches, banks and passing trains. Though a bandit, he is nearly always cast as the hero of his various adventures. Jesse was the rebel and outlaw many longed to suppress; he was the symbol and agent of resistance many others wanted; he was the free and independent man many longed to be.[19]

---

18. In other versions of this story, Jesse and Frank give the widow money to pay her mortgage and then rob the money back from the banker later. The anecdote, itself, not only bares signs of oral tradition, it has been resurrected in various songs and poems about Jesse, both eighteenth century and modern. See Arthur Winfield Knight, "Wanted," in *Jesse James: The Best Writings on the Notorious Outlaw and His Gang* (ed. Harold Dellinger; Guilford, Conn.: Globe Pequot, 2007), 63–64.

19. Hobsbawm, *Bandits*, 24, 55, 130, 153, 158. See, as well, his *Primitive Rebels: Studies in Archaic Forms of Social Movements in the 19th and 20th Centuries*

4. 10¢ Gospels

Contradictory views of Jesse align with contradictory biographies, and these biographies are extremely difficult to reconcile or refute. Only a few facts seem sure: Jesse James was involved in criminal activities punishable by the state; he was able to evade capture for almost 20 years; during this period, he had long stretches of non-bandit living.[20] Documenting the career of a criminal is, by its very nature, difficult. Criminals hide; criminals lie; their entire lives require subterfuge. What is at first surprising is that Jesse wrote (or was purported to have written) numerous press editorials, detailing his reasons for it or asserting his innocence, and left many tangible remains and verifiable evidence of his hideouts.[21] Yet, just like modern historians cannot rely on newspaper accounts as unbiased (when they are not plagiarizing one another, these accounts frequently differ in fact), Jesse's own letters and the memoirs of his associates and descendants are equally suspect.

What enables Jesse's popular attraction and defeats an accurate image of Jesse is the super-abundance of material about him, not the absence of data. The occasional killing of unarmed civilians can be ignored in favor of his support of the weak. Jesse's rampant racism can be ignored or "contextualized." His support of the simple frontier life, his humane resistance of mechanization and industrialization and his strong advocacy of state government and farmer's rights can be celebrated despite his chronic horse thievery, his absolute opposition to full suffrage and his affinity to the ideology of the Ku Klux Klan. The super-abundance of stories about Jesse, when conjoined to the relative "free floating," unverifiable quality of oral tradition, can readily support any biographical metanarrative. His fans may pick-and-choose from his legend to create whatever Jesse James they want or need.

Jesse's career was widely written about. Jesse and his exploits became, first, a reinforcement of popular prejudices against the "West" and the

---

(New York: Norton, 1965). Note, for counterpoint, Richard White, "Outlaw Gangs of the Middle Border: American Social Bandits," *Western Historical Quarterly* 12, no. 4 (1981): 387–408.

20. Bifurcated legends abound even about these more quiet periods of Jesse's life. While living under alias in Nashville, Tennessee and St. Joseph, Missouri, legend reports that he was highly religious—visiting local Baptist churches, preaching and leading singing. Legend also remembers him, simultaneously, as given to drink, poker and race horses.

21. Whybrow, "Pen." On some ventures, such as the robbery of the Gladstone Rail line, Jesse knowingly left the telegraph equipment intact so that the rail officials could contact authorities immediately on his departure. On this and other occasions of the same or similar action, see Yeatman, *Frank and Jesse James*, 101.

need for further Federal intervention and reconstruction.[22] Second, however, he became a romanticized notion of the "exotic" west, a living Wild West show that marked the "other within" the national identity. Even beyond his death, this trope—so celebrated in popular dime novels—became a cipher for an era of American innocence, rugged individuality, independence and a once-pure epoch before the spread of manufacturing, mechanization and industrialized cities.[23] A bandit and killer became a sign for a child-like celebration of innocence and adventure. There is too much data and too much context. It is not that a biography of Jesse James cannot be written. Too many can.

Writing the Biography of a Bandit

The actual Jesse James—what Jesse thought of his own career, where and how he lived, what crimes he personally committed, why he committed his crimes—is obscured by the legend of Jesse James, even as this legend is precisely the reason that Jesse, and not a host of other period-contemporary bandits, is remembered in popular fiction and film.[24] All this awakens a desire to locate the "historical Jesse James" and results in varied and complex ways of viewing the "real Jesse James." Three biographies—each presented as "definitive"—illustrate this point. In 1882, Frank Triplett published *The Life, Times and Treacherous Death of Jesse James.*[25] William A. Settle, Jr. wrote *Jesse James Was His Name* in 1966. Finally, T. J. Stiles followed with his own reconstruction of James and his career, proclaimed in the very title of his work, *Jesse James: Last Rebel of the Civil War* in 2002.

Attention to the ways in which history and legend are interwoven in Jesse's biography—the ways in which history gives rise to legend which, in turn, crafts the history—sheds light on the way another bandit figure's

---

22. Jackson, "Making of an American Outlaw Hero," 21.
23. On the appeal of dime novels, see Michael Denning, *Mechanic Accents* (New York: Verso, 1987).
24. For example, Frank James is nowhere near as popular as Jesse, despite being side-by-side with Jesse on their exploits. Frank was, very likely, the more debonair of the two, the more educated and literate (he frequently read and quoted Shakespeare and the Bible), the more experienced (he began riding with Quantrill years before Jesse) and perhaps the more instrumental in planning capers. Even the Younger brothers are scarcely known beyond historians and aficionados of the American West.
25. Triplett's biography was originally published in 1882; most of the first print run was "lost." Some suggest they were suppressed by anti-James sentiment.

biography has been shaped by the same. The actual Jesus of Nazareth—what Jesus thought of his own career, where and how he lived, what words he actually said and what deeds he personally did, and why he said and did them—is obscured by the legend of Jesus, even as this legend is precisely the reason that Jesus, and not a host of other period-contemporary bandits and messiahs, is remembered. As a young Albert Schweitzer so persuasively argued over a century ago, the root problem to the reconstruction of a historical Jesus is the complex and often contradictory nature of the evidence.[26]

The gospels, our primary source for the life of Jesus, are composed of oral traditions and legends. Scholarship on the canonical gospels, particularly on the Synoptics, has, for the last 150 years, continued to stress that the process of gospel composition—their sources, their redaction of sources, their alteration of narrative patterns, all driven by and reflective of their unique interests and theses—was a process laden with ideological/theological tendency on the part of the gospel writers. This tendency, we are discovering, was also located in the very sources of the gospels.[27] The message of Jesus and data regarding his life were handed down by oral transmission via a process that reflects the unique needs and interests of the various communities accepting Jesus of Nazareth as a messianic figure. Further, they were transmitted and collected by individuals who were believers and advocates. The stories were intended to be polemic and persuasive and were ordered into narratives that attempted to fix, once and for all, a stable narrative of the life of Jesus (John 20:30–31; 21:24–25; Luke 1:1–4; etc.). To add final complications, the gospels bear clear evidence of literary inter-dependence and reliance upon other written texts, now no longer extant. We know an abundance about how Jesus was perceived by followers in the first century. We can glimpse the historical Jesus only by hypothesis and reading behind the texts. We have even less evidence on which to construct any notion of how Jesus understood, for himself, his own mission.

In other words, the first biographers of Jesus (both oral and written) were telling stories perpetuated, selected and ordered by the bias of those interested in defining the career of Jesus via presentation of biography.

---

26. First released, in German, in 1901. Now in English translation as Schweitzer, *Quest for the Historical Jesus*.

27. Rudolf Bultmann, *History of the Synoptic Tradition* (trans. of *Die Geschichte der synoptischen Tradition*, 5th ed.; trans. John Marsh; Peabody, Mass.: Hendrickson, 1963); Christopher M. Tuckett, *Q and the History of Early Christianity: Studies on Q* (Edinburgh: T. & T. Clark, 1996); John S. Kloppenborg, *Excavating Q: The History and Setting of the Sayings Gospel* (Edinburgh: T. & T. Clark, 2000).

Biography in the gospels is not intended to be an account of the life of a given figure which would reflect the "lowest common denominator" of historical accuracy and certainty. Biography was a form of ideological argument. Scholarship on the gospels and the life of Jesus began, in the modern period, to understand that the process of historical recovery of the "real" Jesus of history would require the modern historian to engage in an analytic process of critical engagement of the historical datum, to strip away veneers of aggrandizement, apology, obscurity and elision which were, patina-like, laid atop our narratives by the bias of the ancient community. The clean image, unencumbered by bias, of the actual Jesus of history would remain. As we will see, the work of Schweitzer and others was largely a metahistorical argument examining the process of historical recovery itself and concluding that bias remains in the modern scholar who was himself attempting to strip away the bias of the ancient biographer. Scholarship sought to counter the bias of the biographer by critical reading of the text but the bias of the critical reader stymied any such hopes. The process of recovery seemed hopeless.

More contemporary studies of the historical Jesus, those of Crossan or Meier for example, attempt to find a neutral ground for inquiry via relentless attention to methodology.[28] Yet, even here, they fail to do much more than move the location of biased inquiry one step further back, from bias affecting one's reading (a bias controlled, they argue, by methodology) to bias that affects the selection of which methodology one adopts. For example, should Jesus be read within the larger Greco-Roman world's cultural norms and values, or via a distinctly (and exclusively) Palestinian Judaism? If the former, would Jesus not appear increasingly less Jewish, leaving one to wonder how or why he was described as a Messiah? If the latter, is this reflecting a form of cultural isolation and separation that betrays everything known about the ways altern and subaltern social groups interact (particularly in the context of colonial domination and the cultural hegemony that inevitably arises)? In other words, how would one decide if Palestinian Judaism was adopting itself to Greco-Roman norms, and, if it were instead forcibly and deliberately defiant of these norms, is the very emphasis on dissent, itself, a form of cultural modification? This systemic question, fraught as it is with methodological concern, does not even begin to address the far more intricate problem of how one prioritizes and evaluates the historical

---

28. See John P. Meier, *A Marginal Jew* (3 vols.; New York: Doubleday, 1991, 1994, 2001), 1:4–17, 21–39; John Dominic Crossan and Jonathan Reed, *Excavating Jesus: Beneath the Stones, Behind the Texts* (San Francisco: HarperSanFrancisco, 2001); Crossan, *Jesus: A Revolutionary Biography*.

reliability of the sources themselves (should, for example, Q, a very ancient but also hypothetical and reconstructed source, be given priority over John, a preserved document but also a much later and openly tendentious one?). The way a given scholar addresses these questions will almost certainly affect the outcome of that scholar's inquiry; the way a scholar addresses these questions will almost certainly arise from and reflect that scholar's biases; even modern scholarship that focuses on methodology is, nevertheless, affected by scholarly bias.

Three general movements seem to arise in the history of the history of Jesus. The first, represented by the gospels and by much subsequent, faith-community oriented, confessional scholarship on Jesus, was a scholarship of narrative selection, arrangement and explication driven by desires to articulate more clearly Jesus' identity and work within the frames of community ideological (theological, in this case) understanding, expectation and, frankly, need. Stories or readings that "distorted" the mission of Jesus were abandoned in favor of "more orderly accounts" leading to the "truth concerning the things" reported about Jesus, all so that readers and hearers "might believe" in Jesus as messiah.

The second, represented by Schweitzer and Bultmann (the so-called First and Second Quests for the historical Jesus), recognized the obvious circularity of former work (that it was a system practically designed to produce a biography of Jesus that cohered with pre-established beliefs and desires of the community) and attempted a corrective. Schweitzer argued that the modern historiographer could not simply counteract the forward push of biblical bias by a counter-push of scholarly incredulity. The problem is bias; scholars possess their own. Bultmann took this idea to its completion: the historical Jesus was unrecoverable.

A third movement (the so-called Third Quest) hopes to address the problem of scholarly bias by reliance on scholarly method. Again, however, this is proving less than successful, although a plethora of studies examining Jesus (most often via social-scientific methodologies) have arisen, attending to more and more nuanced aspects of Jesus' and the gospels' larger context. As even a cursory review of contemporary literature on the historical Jesus would reveal, such methodological emphasis most definitely allows the critical scholar to make positivist and specific statements about the Jesus of history. Yet as that same survey would reveal, the problem is the multiplicity of concurrent, often contradictory, positivist and specific accounts which can be described and, given appeal to the various methodological rules engaged by each, defended. So *many different* accounts of the historical Jesus can be composed that, once again, certainty is lost.

We would argue that these same three basic movements in historiography may be found in the biographies of Jesse James, represented in this study by the biographies of Triplett, Settle and Stiles, respectively. For many, the problem with recovering Jesus is the problem of confessional faith clouding both the original biographers and subsequent scholarship (in some cases of the latter, the resistance to confession). This explanation seems, to us, too quick and logically problematic. One could, of course, just as easily argue (indeed, many of the original gospel authors and confessional historians in fact *do* argue) that accurately understanding the historical Jesus produces faith. We will suggest that the problems of historical recovery of Jesse James—and by extension, Jesus of Nazareth—arise precisely because of the dual locus of bias in both the source material and in scholarship and that this bias arises because both figures were ideological ciphers and, themselves, signs (in the sense of semiotics) for a larger set of concerns and values held by both their original communities and by subsequent scholarship. In what follows, we will briefly sketch the development of Jesse James biography, interspersed with brief discussion of historical Jesus research in order to demonstrate this point more concretely.

Writing immediately after Jesse's death, Frank Triplett's work is largely composed of oral traditions and legends, dependent upon individuals who were believers and advocates. Triplett's biography was not the first full biography of James. Jesse was featured in Augustus C. Appler's *The Younger Brothers* and, of course, in John Newman Edwards' *Noted Guerillas, or the Warfare of the Border*.[29] Two more biographies specifically on Jesse James were written by Joseph Dacus and J. W. Buel before 1882.[30] Triplett's biography, while it appeared in print just seven weeks after James' death, was not even the first retrospective biography. A work by Jacob Spencer appeared within a week of Jesse's murder by Bob Ford.[31]

---

29. Augustus C. Appler, *The Younger Brothers: The Life, Character, and Daring Exploits of the Youngers the Notorious Bandits Who Rode with Jesse James and William Clarke Quantrill* (New York: Fell, 1955; originally St. Louis: Eureka, 1876).

30. James William Buel, *The Border Bandits* (Baltimore: I. & M. Ottenheimer, n.d.); Joseph A. Dacus, *Illustrated Lives and Adventures of Frank and Jesse James and the Younger Brothers, the Noted Western Outlaws* (St. Louis: N. D. Thompson & Co., 1882).

31. Joseph Snell, "Editor's Introduction," in Frank Triplett, *The Life, Times and Treacherous Death of Jesse James* (Stamford: Longmeadow, 1970), xi.

Triplett, however, was unique in his claims to have used Jesse's family, particularly his wife Zee and mother Zerelda, as sources.[32] Early editions were printed with an introduction reproducing the signatures of each woman affirming her participation.[33] Triplett, like the evangelist who wrote the Gospel of Luke, wrote to correct prior biographies. The full, original title of the work is *The Life, Times and Treacherous Death of Jesse James, The Only Correct and Authorized Edition. Giving Full Particulars of Each and Every Dark and Despicable Deed in the Career of this Most Noted Outlaw of Any Time or Nation.* Subtitled: *The Facts and Incidents Contained in This Volume, Were Dictated to Frank Triplett by Mrs. Jesse James, the Wife of the Bandit, and Mrs. Zerelda Samuels, His Mother. Consequently Every Secret Act—Every Hitherto Unknown Incident—Every Crime and Every Motive Is Herein Truthfully Disclosed.* What the title lacks in elegance, it makes up for in perspicuity of thesis. In its dedication, the book asserts "truth is more interesting than fiction." Triplett presses the matter further in the publisher's preface:

> When we concluded to issue a "Life" of the most remarkable outlaw that the world has ever seen, it was our intention to produce the best work of the kind extant—all of the matter we intended to be not only fresh, but well written, and in Lieu [sic] of the "blood and thunder" stories, usually found in works of this class, we determined to give only the facts.[34]

Reading the book (particularly in the editions which bear Snell's correcting notation), it is clear "facts" vary and no truly "dark and despicable" actions by Jesse will be revealed. To refer to Triplett as tendentious is understatement. Triplett's *Life* is hagiography. Triplett occasionally seems to have access to private materials (he describes things like the

---

32. Both Jesse's mother and wife had the same name because Zerelda (Zee) Mimms was named after Jesse's mother Zerelda. Zee's mother was Zerelda's sister; in other words, Jesse and Zee were first cousins. Oddly, no historian has probed the Freudian implications, particularly acute since Jesse met his wife as she was helping him convalesce from a chest wound. Biographies of Jesse James were written by his descendants, much later. See Jesse Edwards James, *Jesse James, My Father* (Independence, Mo.: Sentinel, 1899 and Stella F. James, *In the Shadow of Jesse James* (Thousand Oaks, Calif.: Dragon, 1990).

33. There is no record they ever received any compensation; to the contrary, both women later disavowed any acquaintance with the work's composition even as they sued for unpaid royalties. Their disavowals corresponded suspiciously with Frank James' subsequent surrender and trial. In the book, the James brothers together are said to have taken part in several robberies. Frank complained that the testimony of his own mother and sister-in-law was being quoted—via Triplett—against him.

34. Triplett, *The Life, Times and Treacherous Death of Jesse James*, xxii.

James–Samuels family Bible; he reports private conversations of Jesse). Yet, describing the work, Snell observes:

> [Triplett] is not known for his accuracy when it came to writing biography and one should keep that in mind when reading his *Jesse James*. Triplett must have been a diligent worker, for the production of the manuscript in only three weeks would be no small feat. There is indication, however, that much of it was not original nor dictated by the two Zereldas. He "borrowed" a considerable portion of his manuscript from newspaper and other authors. This is particularly noticeable in that portion of the book which deals with Jesse's death and the period immediately afterwards. Triplett apparently clipped articles from the Kansas City *Times* and perhaps other newspapers, edited the stories slightly, and inserted them into his manuscript. With careful comparison one can find page after page of text which agrees completely, except for minor word and punctuation changes, with news stories from the *Times* of April, 1882.[35]

Triplett is, again like the early gospel writers, copying, sometimes verbatim, from previous reports, claiming unverifiable eye-witness evidence, yet shaping the "facts" to fit his very clear agenda.

Triplett is a clear apologist. He asserts that "it is easy to carry out the parallel between the starving man and the James brothers and show that never, until forced by the utmost necessity, did they rob an individual or corporation."[36] Frank and Jesse's participation in a crime can be discerned primarily by the signs of both criminal boldness and restraint in violence. They are known for "no unnecessary brutality; no gratuitous murder. There was no reckless firing into streets and houses and everything was managed in a cool, systematic way."[37] Yet Jesse's robberies at Northfield, Minnesota and Blue Cut, Missouri (his last), his two most authentic and verifiable crimes, are unified in their gratuitousness, random violence, indiscriminate theft, lack of "unit cohesion" and general disorder. Triplett blames this on James' associates. He insists that Frank and Jesse James'

> plan in robbing seems to have been as little as possible to injure the individual, and to strike only wealthy corporations that themselves had the taint of monopoly or oppression about them… If the truth could be ascertained, it is extremely doubtful if the crime of deliberate murder could be fixed upon either of these men.[38]

---

35. Snell, "Editor's Introduction," xiv.
36. Triplett, *The Life, Times and Treacherous Death of Jesse James*, 57.
37. Ibid., 59. See also p. 66.
38. Ibid., 134.

In other words, the James boys hurt no one, individual or corporate, who didn't have it coming. Despite their violence, they are ultimately innocent because they were provoked.[39] This rhetoric is consistent with Missouri apologies for the Kansas–Missouri border wars and even for general Confederate protests of innocence and (compulsory) self-defense, many of which persist, despite the real fact that the first act of war—the firing on Fort Sumpter, South Carolina and secession from the Union—was conducted by Confederates.

It would take decades before more sober historical analysis revisited the life of Jesse James. William A. Settle, Jr.'s *Jesse James Was His Name* is the first scholarly biography of Jesse. Settle, a professor of American History at the University of Tulsa, chose James as the topic of both his masters thesis and doctoral dissertation (each at the University of Missouri-Columbia). In 1966, he adapted both into his first major academic monograph initially published by the University of Missouri. "The book was a critical and popular success, being praised as a well-documented, accurate account of the exploits of the James boys in the context of American cultural and social history. As a result, Settle achieved considerable notoriety as an authority on the James gang and other aspects of the history of the American West."[40] Settle wrote with Edwards and Triplett open in front of him. Snell, recognizing Settle's biography as "the finest biography of Jesse yet" suggests that Triplett and Settle should be read in tandem.[41] The expression "blood and thunder" biography occurs on the very first page of both Triplett's and Settle's work. Settle, however, clearly mistrusts his source(s).

Settle is highly suspicious of oral accounts and asks critical questions of sources and their origins. Settle is attempting to use a full arsenal of modern historical methodology to uncover the "real" Jesse. What emerges, however, is a monument to ambivalence. Settle cannot, with certainty, link Jesse to any authentic writings and rarely to any specific crimes even though Settle never allows for suggestions of Jesse's innocence. Triplett's James never did anything really wrong. Settle's James never really does anything at all (although, Settle would quickly add, what he cannot be said for sure to have done was definitely criminal). Settle notes the multiplicity of images of Jesse James and observes

---

39. The tendency toward idealization can also be seen in David's second "biography"—according to the Chronicler, David was a model of restraint in violence.

40. From the archives of Settle's papers at the University of Missouri. The catalog is available online at www.umsystem.edu/whmc/invent/3896.html.

41. Snell, "Editor's Introduction," xix.

that "fact and fiction are so entwined that it is difficult—at times impossible—to untangle them."[42] Further, "whichever form of the legend you favor, both are based on fact."[43] Both supporters and detractors of Jesse are exposed as biased and motivated to deception.[44] Even the physical wounds of Jesse are troublesome. Settle writes:

> [I]t is certain that Jesse [once] suffered a serious wound... [S]cars from this wound...in addition to the tipless middle finger on his left hand, were...identifying marks when he was killed. The finger tip probably was lost in June of 1864 in a battle in which two Clay Countians named Bigelow were killed by the Jameses and others... But Jesse's loss of a finger tip has also been credited variously to the marksmanship of soldiers of the Second Colorado Cavalry; to that of a prominent lawyer and Union soldier of Columbia, Missouri, named Carey H. Gordon; and to the accidental firing of Jesse's own gun.[45]

"Possibly," "likely," "reputedly" and "it would seem" pepper every page. Methodologically, Settle wants a catalog of purported facts about James and an evaluation of their critical worth to historians.

The modern attempt to discover the Jesus of history also began with a fundamental distrust of the sources—the gospel material and the traditions of the Church. The quest for the Historical Jesus is generally said to have begun with the posthumous publication in 1778 of an essay by Reimarus suggesting that Jesus actually claimed to be an eschatological messiah and led an open revolt against Rome which he promptly lost. As summarized by Schweitzer, the major turns of the debate traveled through D. Strauss and Wrede, both of whom also asserted that Jesus attempted to be an eschatological prophet who led a failed revolution. As an example of the historians' new suspicion of the gospels' accounts, Wrede suggested that the "Messianic secret" in Mark reflected the theological interest of the evangelist to cover up the historical flop of Jesus' career and was not an actual feature of Jesus' ministry. Schweitzer, himself, reconstructed a narrative where Jesus cast himself as an eschatological prophet who sought, by attacking the Temple, to force Rome to in turn attack him and thereby precipitate the Wrath of God and deliverance of Israel; he succeeded in the former, failed the latter.[46]

---

42. Settle, *Jesse James Was His Name*, 2.
43. Ibid.
44. Ibid., 55.
45. Ibid., 31.
46. Albert Schweitzer, *The Quest for the Historical Jesus* (trans. W. Montgomery from 1906 reprint of *Von Reimarus zu Wrede*; New York: MacMillan, 1968), 398–400. Schweitzer also argued that previous attempts to reconstruct the historical

These trends culminated in 1921 when Bultmann published his major work on the Synoptic Tradition. Bultmann, wedded to a form critical approach to the Gospels, was convinced that the early Church had so altered the oral narratives and traditions about Jesus to fit their contemporary setting, that recovery of the actual Jesus of history was impossible. Bultmann argued that the gospels were fundamentally theological works that incorporated data preserved and disseminated (orally, no less) by theologically interested parties. In short, then, it was impossible to reconstruct with certainty the Jewish Jesus with only the very Hellenistic and theologically loaded accounts of the Gospels. In many ways, Bultmann's work is a monument to ambivalence. Jesus clearly did something, but what that something was is now impossible to recover.[47]

Bultmann's student Ernst Käsemann disagreed. Käsemann insisted that there must be a Jesus who is recoverable by history. Taking the challenge, in 1959 another scholar named James Robinson published *The New Quest for the Historical Jesus*, which called for a renewed investigation, still suspicious of the sources but with even deeper attention to cultural context.[48] Much like the next stage in the search for the "historical Jesse," the third stage in the quest for the historical Jesus focuses on historical, social and cultural context, more seriously attending to the ways in which context shapes the individual, and even foregrounding the surrounding matrix of the legend itself.

---

narrative of Jesus (including the gospels) had been attempts to reconstruct Jesus according to the desires and ambitions of the given scholar. In other words, they found what they wanted to find. Contrary to popular convention, though, Schweitzer himself did not suggest that historical reconstruction of Jesus was impossible. See the treatment of Schweitzer's work in G. Aulen, *Jesus in Contemporary Historical Research* (Philadelphia: Fortress, 1976); A. E. McGrath, *The Making of Modern German Christology* (Oxford: Blackwell, 1986) and D. Pals, *The Victorian "Lives" of Jesus* (San Antonio, Tex.: Trinity University, 1982).

47. Just as one example, note Rudolf Bultmann, *Jesus and the Word* (New York: Scribner's 1934). For Bultmann, the historical Jesus was not only impossible, but unnecessary. Bultmann, with a theology firmly rooted in existential confession and practice, felt no need to unite the Jesus of faith with the Jesus of history. For the work of his student Käsemann, see *Essays on New Testament Themes* (London: SCM, 1964). For a (polemic) survey of this and related literature, see Ben Witherington III, *The Jesus Quest: The Third Search for the Jew of Nazareth* (2d ed.; Downer's Grove, Ill.: InterVarsity, 1997) and Craig Keener, *The Historical Jesus of the Gospels* (Grand Rapids: Eerdmans, 2009).

48. James M. Robinson, *The New Quest for the Historical Jesus* (New York: Macmillan, 1968).

We have, as it were, a modern "third quest" for the historical Jesse underway as well. T. J. Stiles, like Settle, is attempting to uncover the "real" Jesse James. His work, like Settle's, is suspicious of Jesse's legends. Clearly, Stiles knows he is undermining a popular figure and his revelations may spoil the party.[49] Stiles has read Settle's biography very carefully and describes it as "the only truly scholarly biography" of James, though it "suffers inevitably from age."[50] Stiles sees Settle's value in more than evaluation of sources; he observes that Settle "stumbles on a critical point where our subject and his context meet: to what extent was Jesse James a participant in his rise to legend, in his symbolic role in the public eye."[51] For Stiles, James must first be read in his larger historical context. No final understanding of James is possible without serious attention to the Civil War and Reconstruction. Having explored the surrounding matrix of legend itself, Stiles hopes to uncover the "true" Jesse James. The "true" James is no longer the one whose biographical data has the most verisimilitude; Stiles is searching for the real, operative and generative energies surrounding James' public identity. Giving credence to most of Jesse's writings,[52] Stiles nevertheless concludes, "Jesse James remains, in many ways, a hidden figure whose life will always be half known, at best."[53]

Stiles dismisses social scientific critiques (such as Hobsbawm's) of the social and vicarious nature of banditry, where the bandit is a popular cipher for social resistance and freedom.[54] Jesse's identity, Stiles argues, is rooted in and reducible to specific issues related to the American Civil War and its aftermath. Stiles observes, "cultural critics and social commentators have often explored what later generations have chosen to see in Jesse James. The unanswered question is what they have chosen *not* to see."[55] Summing up Jesse's real significance, Stiles concludes:

> Instead of an unreflective champion of apolitical small farmers, Jesse James was an intensely partisan and articulate hero of one specific segment of a politically sophisticated population. Certainly he took credit for some of the mythic qualities of the noble robber... But in his political consciousness and close alliance with a propagandist and power broker,

---

49. Stiles, *Jesse James*, 398.
50. Ibid., 5. Stile's critical eye has been developed from his own scholarly training; he holds an M.A. and M.Phil. in History from Columbia.
51. Ibid.
52. Ibid., 390.
53. Ibid., 393.
54. Ibid., 388.
55. Ibid., 394. Italics original.

in his efforts to win media attention with his crimes and his denunciations of his enemies, he resembles a character well known to our times. In many respects, Jesse James was a forerunner of the modern terrorist.[56]

Stiles also asks "to what extent was Jesse James a conscious agent in the making of his own public image?... [W]as he a self-aware actor on the political stage?"[57] Contra social theorists who might suggest James' identity was super-imposed by the community, Stiles argues James was an active participant. Still, James was also co-opted, in part, into his own myth. James' traitorous death cemented these tensions.

> If the death of Jesse James unveiled the small truths—his identity, his crimes, the names of his associates—it shrouded the larger truths about his life and significance. In a sense, this was because he died too late. He had outlived the issues that had brought him to public attention, so that his personal fame now eclipsed the causes he represented.[58]

James' apotheosis (Stiles' term) in popular culture creates his multiform identity.

The "Third Quest" for the historical Jesus began in earnest with the work of Robert Funk and John Dominic Crossan, who established the Westar Institute at Claremont University, and the latest quest has continued to be an infatuation largely to American New Testament scholarship. Funk and Crossan's work eventually led to the formation of the (now somewhat infamous) "Jesus Seminar." Although essentially still loyal to the assumptions and method of form-criticism, the seminar was established to see if there could be a consensus achieved among scholars as to whether or not some statements could be considered "probable," independently historical, and not modified by subsequent confessional communities. Far from establishing with certainty who Jesus might have been, the seminar struggled (and continues to struggle) to explore what, if anything, can be independently established as reliable historical evidence on Jesus' actual career.

Funk and Crossan are, perhaps, the two most recognizable figures associated with the seminar. In addition, Crossan has published independently on Jesus, suggesting that Jesus of Nazareth was an itinerant Jewish cynic peasant who practiced (and encouraged others to practice) commensality and challenged popular social values and Roman rule (although one is often hard pressed to discern from Crossan precisely

---

56. Ibid., 391.
57. Ibid., 389.
58. Ibid., 381.

why the *Romans* wanted to kill Jesus).[59] Several works have been published offering various competing hypotheses, but generally using the same methods. E. P. Sanders has argued (given the stress placed upon this theme by Reimarus, Strauss, Wrede or Schweitzer) that Jesus was a self-styled eschatological prophet who precipitated his own execution by an attack of the Temple.[60] J. Meier (who, according to the jacket of his first volume, *A Marginal Jew*, is "the premiere Biblical scholar of his generation") sees Jesus as a marginal Jewish figure convinced of his own role as Messiah and hence provocative to the elite of his day.[61]

In additional to the above, an entire body of literature designed to supplement the gospel accounts with socio-cultural data has emerged. Richard Horsley has commented on the situation of Jesus as a colonized Jew resisting Empire.[62] Elisabeth Schüssler-Fiorenza argues Jesus practiced an early egalitarianism.[63] Gerd Theissen has argued Jesus also challenged cultural norms, though he was much more Hellenistic than has previously been granted.[64] Ben Witherington and Craig Keener, however, have repeatedly argued against all approaches intending to "look behind" or supplement the Gospels.[65] It doesn't appear promising that we will ultimately reject Bultmann's challenge.

The details of Jesse's life are entangled with folk tale and oral structures. These oral and written traditions are inextricably tied with political and community identity issues. A variety of possible Jesses emerge; a

59. Crossan, *Jesus: A Revolutionary Biography* and the larger *The Historical Jesus: The Life of a Mediterranean Jewish Peasant* (San Francisco: HarperSanFrancisco, 1991).

60. Sanders, *Jesus and Judaism* and *Historical Figure of Jesus*. An argument similar to that of Sanders is also found in Paula Fredriksen, *From Jesus to Christ: The Origins of the New Testament Images of Jesus* (New Haven, Conn.: Yale University Press, 1988).

61. Meier, *A Marginal Jew*.

62. Richard Horsley, *Jesus in Context* and *Jesus and the Spiral of Violence: Popular Jewish Resistance in Roman Palestine* (Minneapolis: Fortress, 1987).

63. Elisabeth Schüssler-Fiorenza, *In Memory of Her: A Feminist Theological Reconstruction of Christian Origins* (New York: Crossroad, 1984).

64. Gerd Theissen, *The Gospels in Context: Social and Political History in the Synoptic Tradition* (Minneapolis: Fortress, 1987). On socio-scientific readings of the life of Jesus see Wolfgang Stegemann, Bruce J. Malina and Gerd Theissen, eds., *The Social Setting of Jesus and the Gospels* (Minneapolis: Fortress, 2002). Though, see Geza Vermes, *Jesus the Jew* (London: Collins, 1973) and *Jesus in His Jewish Context* (Minneapolis: Fortress, 2002).

65. Witherington, *Jesus Quest*; Keener, *Historical Jesus*. See, as well, Luke Timothy Johnson, *The Real Jesus: The Misguided Quest for the Historical Jesus and the Truth of the Traditional Gospels* (San Francisco: HarperSanFrancisco, 1996).

seemingly endless array of biographical metanarratives is enabled. The biographies we have surveyed move from "authentic" or "authorized" presentation of the legends about Jesse, to critical investigation of those legends which lead to historical ambivalence, to analysis of the cultural world from which Jesse's legends emerged. During the evening of April third, the citizens of St. Joseph could scarcely begin to dream how much longer Jesse James, or at least the story of Jesse James, would continue to live.

Within the literature on the quest for the historical Jesus, we can see (at least) three major stages. First, in their origins, the Gospels reflect oral traditions created, disseminated and collected by committed advocates. Each Gospel also has clear tendencies or ideologies which affected its organization and composition; these tendencies attempted to define Jesus' work and mission. The oral nature and tendentiousness of the Gospels awakened critique by later scholars. These "First" and "Second Quest" scholars investigated the Gospels to identify the most historically verifiable narrative of Jesus. As this work proceeded, many began to voice uncertainty that the project could ever succeed. The modern "new" or "Third Quest" has focused upon methodologies and directed its energy toward the socio-cultural context of Jesus. Traditions surrounding Jesus' Messiahship are set against larger political revolution, cultural hybridity and assimilation or resistance.

Compare these trends with the three major biographies of Jesse James surveyed above. First, Triplett's work resonates with late Synoptic and Johannine Gospel literature, particularly John and Luke. It draws from oral legends and redacts written texts. It claims exclusive authority. Settle, like Bultmann, cannot with certainty cut through the clouds of oral legend. He is unsure the "historical Jesse" can ever be recovered. Finally, notice Stiles' emphasis upon historical methodology and cultural context. Much like Crossan and Meier, Stiles is attuned to method and describes his subject vis-à-vis political revolution; Stiles is intent on critiquing the social theories surrounding and interpreting Jesse's historiography and is relentless in his attempt to define the function and focus of Jesse's legend. Surrounding (but oblivious to) all three is a popular celebration of a character steeped in literary romance and popular veneration. Despite any scholarly critique of their biography, millions of supporters continue to think about, tell stories about and celebrate their own reconstruction of Jesus and Jesse James.

Both Jesse and Jesus were culturally polarizing figures. Both have similar biographical and popular histories. Are there similar patterns because there is something similar in the careers (or the narration of the careers) of each, or because of similar methods and needs of modern biography? If we assume these structures are inherent to the figures and not scholarly impositions, comparisons of Jesse James' and Jesus of Nazareth's biographies reveal similar functions of the "outsider-hero" in oral narrative. At their origins, traditions surrounding both figures patch into pre-existing community needs for resistance and subjectivity. Both may exhibit characteristics of "social banditry" as outlined by Eric Hobsbawm. In both cases, we can never be finally sure we have reconstructed the "historical" Jesse or Jesus; the data are too elusive and too much a product of the location of the inquirer. Similarly, however, scholarly reconstructions of the "real" Jesse are just as likely to affect Jesse's continued hold on popular imagination and romance as a reconstructed historical Jesus will affect life in the average Christian congregation. Both transcend history; both embody the very limitations of history.

There are, of course, significant differences between the histories of the history of Jesus and Jesse James, yet we are attempting to note general trends that appear by the analogous comparison of each. The survey of their biographies could certainly be nuanced and expanded. We might also draw out, even deeper, our analogy to the extent that the springs of the metaphor strain under the weight and risk rupture. We might contrast the various fictional dime novels about Jesse with the second- and third-century non-canonical gospels. We could further engage in a parallel examination of canonical gospel source-criticism and contemporary inquiry into the various oral and written sources constructing Jesse's biography. Our survey of the historical Jesus research could most certainly benefit from expansion and nuance; the treatment of Jesse could be expanded, in turn, with a host of (at times incidental) treatments of Jesse ranging from scholarly exploration of Reconstruction-era Missouri to popular True West documentary. We could examine how rival claimants to Jesse's lineage (and tourist dollars) such as those represented by the supporters of the Jesse James Death House and the benefactors of the James Family Farm, resemble rival understandings of Jesus found in various Catholic, Orthodox and Protestant Christian communities.

The exploration of those broad trends reveals striking parallels in general historiographic arc. Like Jesus, the earliest accounts of Jesse reflect oral legend knit together by those supporting and those opposing his social banditry (even more, by those in essence constructing his status as a social bandit). Like Jesus, these accounts come under historical scrutiny that initially suggests sober historical analysis cannot possibly separate the legend from the reality. Like Jesus, this secondary scholarship is, in its turn, brought under examination that argues methodological controls will allow specific and positivist assertions about who Jesse "really" was; yet, again like Jesus, these assertions multiply to the extent that the "reality behind the legend" fragments into a plethora of shards, each still only reflecting a portion of the viewer.

We think it also important to note that the process of scholarship oriented toward the historical recovery of Jesse James is occurring roughly concurrent with the developing process of scholarship oriented toward the recovery of the historical Jesus. No doubt, scholarship on the biography of both Jesus and Jesse has been influenced by broader modernist and postmodernist intellectual development and debate. No doubt we could extend this analysis and find parallels in modern reconstruction of the biography of David (or, frankly, of a host of quasi-legendary/vaguely historical figures). The actual lives of Jesus and Jesse James are separated dramatically in cultural context, global location and in time, yet the scholarship of those lives is, largely, not. Certainly, as well, historiography of Jesse (both popular and scholarly, concurrent and subsequent) has been influenced by the prior historiography of Jesus, even if in the most indirect ways.

As we have argued earlier, both Jesse and Jesus are dissident, "outlaws" who engaged, willfully and knowingly, in forms of protest against hegemonic forces of the State. Both figures were popularly celebrated by their (subaltern) communities for this rebellion, and both figures were largely memorialized in anecdote, oral history, folk culture and legend. These multiple forces—the weight of status as cipher for communal identity, the agonistic context of both their careers and of the subaltern communities who revered them, the largely peasant status and oral culture of their initial followers, the way each embodied popular desires for independence—collude to compress their biography, their "history," into an indefinite mass of legend and ideology. Their prominence draws later scholarly critique, and later scholarly reconstruction, like moth to flame.

What links the two communities around Jesus and Jesse is a clear need for identity vis-à-vis hostile outside pressures and struggles with the malleability of hybrid subjectivity. Communities paradigmatically centralize Jesus or Jesse as exemplary figures who offer both a model of resistance and a vicarious means of transcending cultural forces that push for homogeneity and conformity. Later communities live out desires for resistance through these "bandits" and so resist alterity even while tacitly reinscribing its borders. The Jesse James of history is as elusive as the historical Jesus—but not because of cultural distance, language, time, documentation or even theology. Both figures remain elusive because of the fundamental energies invested in their initial memorialization. Ironically, these fundamental energies are also the fuel of that memorialization. Had either figure not so captured and embodied the needs and desires of their community, they would have been largely forgotten, two among millions of potential dissidents crushed into total historical disintegration by hegemonic forces. Yet precisely because they did so fully capture and embody the needs of their community, their very preservation carries within it the elements that prevent discovery of their "real" lives. Their legend and their history are inseparable. Their legend is their history; their history is perpetually legend.

The process is not the result of theology. Certainly, no one, no matter how enamored with Jesse James, believes he provides salvation or exclusive access to God. Jesus is not hidden by (just) theology or devotion. Further, the historical Jesse James remains hidden despite much physical evidence, personal writings and far greater historical and cultural proximity to his questers. Jesus is not hidden simply by lack of data or the patina of antiquity. In the case of each, we can only recover historical absence. We are left with signs and traces, empty tombs and empty cash boxes, and stories told by amazed-but-deeply-invested communities of "witnesses." We must be content as modern critics to identify the legend for each and to attempt to understand how and to whom that legend was relevant. In each case, we can recover only popular memory and legend not just because only popular memory and legend remain (more does), but because in each case, it is only the popular memory embodied in the legend that matters.

Exploring parallels in the history and historiography of Jesse James and Jesus of Nazareth is in part, an exploration of how forces of hero/outlaw construction function in terms of social deviance and how hero narratives can or cannot elude scholarship. We see, in comparison, similar problems awaken similar needs—both in the primary, orally driven community of nascent followers and in subsequent critical communities and scholarly groups. We also see the mechanisms both of hero construction and scholarly analysis. We can glimpse at the inner workings of hagiography and our own needs to either perpetuate or dismantle such systems. We see, in other words, that "history" and "memory" are fundamentally the same things.

What is revealed from the quests for either the historical Jesse or the historical Jesus is certainly not a definitive, final image of either figure. Certainly, as Schweitzer so aptly phrased it, the face glimpsed at the bottom of history's well—whether we are "questing" for Jesus or Jesse James—could well turn out to be our own. We are shooting at shadows, glimpsed only dimly. A comparative study of the processes of historiography and biography reveals, in the very comparison, the nature of these projects themselves. We may glimpse not only our familiar face, but the substance, nature and content of both the well of history and the reflective water that burbles up from its legendary depths. The work that remains, then, is an inquiry into legend, as legend.

Chapter 5

BANDITS BEYOND THE SUNSET

To Bury a Bandit

A crucified man was a warning. A crucified man was a message about the power the Empire wielded over life and death, and life beyond death. The body would remain on the cross, exposed to the elements, decomposing, fed upon by crows, vultures, rats and dogs, sometimes taken down and thrown into mass graves and disintegrated with lime. According to the gospels, Jesus' body did not hang on the cross long either before or after his death. His family and disciples petitioned the government for the release of his body. Joseph of Arimathea—rich, powerful, a member of the council—made the request to Pilate (Matt 27:57–61; Mark 15:42–47; Luke 23:50–56; John 19:38–42). In Mark, Pilate expresses surprise that Jesus is already dead (15:44), and indeed, a few hours were all it took to kill the man. He agrees to the request and gives the body to Joseph of Arimathea who buries Jesus in his own family's grave. In Matthew, a few Jewish leaders worry that the apostles will steal Jesus' body and proclaim him resurrected; therefore additional guards are posted at the tomb (27:62–65). Execution did not end the state's interest in the convicted criminal; in some ways death even compounded the concern.

Jesse James' assassination was an execution, orchestrated by the governing authorities. After death, James' body was subject to a wide array of government intrusions. Worried that his supporters would claim that the Fords had killed the wrong man, a parade of witnesses was brought in to identify the body and testify before the coroner's jury.[1]

---

1. In addition to the family members Zee James and Zerelda Samuel, the Ford brothers and Clay County sheriff James H. Timberlake, testimony was taken from William H. Wallace, Harrison Trow, one of Quantrill's men, James Wilkinson, J. Clay, Mattie Collins, T. W. Mimms, a cousin of James and C. D. Axman. Triplett,

Doubting Thomases could come and place their fingers on his wounded hands, could touch his scarred sides and see for themselves. The coroner conducted an autopsy to chronicle every scar, injury and distinguishing characteristic of the body. Multiple pictures were taken and circulated throughout the United States. The authorities also feared that members of his gang would steal his body and deny he had been killed; therefore police officers remained with the dead man all night long.[2] The local authorities then refused to release the body and its effects. Jesse's family and friends petitioned the government for the release of Jesse James' corpse. Thomas Crittenden—Governor of Missouri—issued the order to Sheriff Timberlake and Captain Craig of St. Joseph.[3]

Before the rock was rolled across the opening of the Jesus' tomb, before the first shovel-full of dirt hit Jesse's coffin, the two men had already begun to live second lives in glorified bodies. As his death was immediately compared to that of Jesus, the ways in which Jesse James has been memorialized also resonates with Christian modes of memory; their legendary afterlives cross through their own particular resurrection manifestations. Both inspire pilgrims to the place of their birth and the place of their death, the touch of both creates relics, both draw people from all over the world to their empty tombs. We will follow in the footsteps of these contemporary pilgrim-tourists to Kearney and St. Joseph, Missouri. Writers have continued to inscribe the identification between Jesus and Jesse James, especially evident in Ron Hansen's *The Assassination of Jesse James by the Coward Robert Ford*. We will explore such literary expressions of devotion. Both Jesus and Jesse James live on through pilgrimage sites and reliquaries, songs and legends, novels and poems. The books of their lives never closed; neither rode off into the sunset.

The Resurrection of a Bandit

Frank and Jesse James were more infamous than the Youngers because they had the support of John Edwards and became heroes in fiction; in other words, they were better known because they had already begun to live textual lives before their physical deaths. After his dramatic death, stories of Jesse's life certainly "resurrected" the bandit again and again.

The Life, Times and Treacherous Death of Jesse James, 232. See also Stiles, *Jesse James*, 376–77, and Settle, *Jesse James Was His Name*, 117–18.
  2. Triplett, *The Life, Times and Treacherous Death of Jesse James*, 230.
  3. Ibid., and Settle, *Jesse James Was His Name*, 118.

Echoing John 20:30, the historian William Settle, Jr. writes "the interest that attaches to the places of importance in the James history is reflected also in the continuing flow of news stories and feature articles... A compilation of these would fill many volumes."[4] Those who had opposed Jesse James (either for his lawless campaigns or for personal reasons) circulated stories about his involvement in numerous crimes and murders, some of which occurred on the same day in places more than one hundred miles apart; his supporters and friends denied these and other charges, the most extreme nearly suggesting that James had never been involved in any criminal activity at all or in any violence since his days in the Confederacy. Even death did not restrict Jesse's activity; stories circulated that the man shot for Jesse James was an imposter or that James had faked his death in order to finally avoid the authorities and leave his life of banditry.

In addition to his later manifestations in plays, Wild West shows, fiction and (later) film, James began to resurrect in legend and popular culture almost from the moment of his execution because many doubted he could be killed. People, supporters and non-supporters alike, believed James was too cagey simply to be shot, especially by a member of his own gang. Jesse James would never have trusted someone as untrustworthy as Bob Ford; he would have never turned his back to him. Adding to the reluctance to admit that he was as vulnerable and as mortal as he, like any human being, was, there had been earlier reports of his demise which were later shown to be untrue.

It took less than a year before a farmer in Clay County, Missouri claimed to have seen Jesse James.[5] One tradition, from 1939, claimed the James boys had snuck off to Nebraska where they married Native American women, set up a trading post and raised families. Never mind that Frank James very publicly surrendered to authorities and trial after Jesse's death. Jesse was also reported to have gone to Mexico. Years later a man would announce to the world that he was Jesse (DNA comparisons with known relatives and descendents has not supported his claim). Reports circulated later that Frank and Jesse (again, oddly, both Jameses) had faked their deaths.[6] Henry Ford of Brownsville, Texas said he was Jesse in the 1880s. A man in Wayton County, Arkansas named

---

4. Settle, *Jesse James Was His Name*, 165.
5. Ibid., 169.
6. Ibid., 168–69. Frank died in 1915. Settle also notes the number of people claiming to be illegitimate children of Frank and Jesse—immortality through progeny.

5. Bandits Beyond the Sunset 117

Joe Vaughan was identified as Jesse James in 1926. James Sears of Wetmore, Colorado claimed in 1931 to be Jesse. Another "Jesse" emerged in 1932 and petitioned the Missouri Government for a pardon (he was refused). Despite being, literally, unable to fit into Jesse's boots and being publically discredited by Jesse's surviving family, he led a successful Wild West show in 1937; he died in a mental hospital in Little Rock, Arkansas in 1947, claiming to the end to be the bandit.[7]

Settle reports that at least twenty-six claimants have arisen. Yeatman dedicates an entire chapter to the "resurrection of Jesse James."[8] Yeatman's chapter includes the 1938 road tour of Jesse's skeleton (by all evidence, a fraud). Dressed and armed with a six shooter, the skeleton, with a mechanized mouth, told anecdotes, spoke witticisms and made predictions. Skeletal Jesse went on a carnival tour; his highest fame came with his appearance at the 1974 Kentucky State Fair.[9] Jesse's most recent resurrection was embodied by Frank Dalton, a Lawton, Oklahoma resident who claimed to be Jesse in the late 1940s. Dalton died in August 1951, five months after the death of Jesse Edwards James (Jesse's only undisputed son). Dalton was buried in Granbury, Texas under a tombstone reading "Jesse James," yet another grave for the outlaw.[10]

As we saw in the introduction, the body of Jesse was disinterred and subjected to DNA testing (comparing mitochondrial DNA from Jesse's teeth and known descendents) which still has not quieted the conspiracy theories and claims of a faked death. Aptly, Jesse's final interment had a service of Christian burial which "centered on a reading from the book of Job: 'if a man die, shall he live again?'"[11] In the case of Jesse James, this seems a legitimate question.

It is very hard to let such a figure actually die. On one level, he simply cannot. Jesse had long before become a character of legend and fiction. As such, his "death" would always feel as the climax in crises expected for each hero story. Images of Jesse laying in seeming defeat made his "audience" lean forward wondering what he would do now, how could

---

7. On these, see ibid., 169–70. Even these resurrection stories begin to diverge in detail. Compare Settle's version of this last imposter with Yeatman's (*Frank and Jesse James*, 323–24).
8. Yeatman, *Frank and Jesse James*, 323–40.
9. Ibid., 325.
10. Ibid., 333.
11. Ibid., 338. Yeatman also discusses the DNA testing of Jesse. He notes, wryly, that when the body was exhumed, it was found laying face downward. Local wags suggested that the things subsequently said about Jesse James had, indeed, led James to turn over in his grave.

he manage to get out of *this*. Jesse's resurrection was prefigured in early comparisons of his executioner to Judas Iscariot. At least twice before, Jesse had attempted to assume a new identity and go underground as a private citizen prompting rumors of his death.[12] Even after his body was identified and buried in 1882, rumors and debate persisted. Indeed, as we have seen, Jesse's body seems to have a regular aversion to burial. Buried three times and exhumed twice (the last time, found turned in his grave), roughly every three or four decades, Jesse, physically, pops back up in the news and popular imagination, letting each subsequent generation get a good look at him. So hard to find and define in life, Jesse in death seems amazingly amenable to examination and popular use.

The resurrection stories of Jesus are hardly more diverse and divergent. The claim that approximately thirty-six hours ("three days") after he was buried, Jesus stood up and walked out of the tomb, is central to Christian confession. In fact, without the stories of the resurrection, Christianity may have never developed into the world-wide religion it is today. Yet, in the (at least) five stories about this resurrection recorded in the New Testament, not a single detail is the same. Paul's account is the first: "he appeared to Cephas, then to the twelve. Then he appeared to more than five hundred brothers [the NRSV adds to the Greek 'and sisters'] at one time, most of whom are still alive, though some have died. Then he appeared to James, then to all the apostles. Last of all, as to one untimely born, he appeared also to me" (1 Cor 15:5–8). Next, Mark's account is written. Whereas Mark records that three disciples—Mary Magdalene, Mary the mother of James and Salome—found the tomb empty, he writes of no resurrection appearances. They find the stone already rolled from the tomb, filled only by an unidentified young man (Mark 16:4–5). Later scribes add two different stories, one that simply notes that "Jesus himself sent out through them [the apostles], from east to west, the sacred and imperishable proclamation of eternal salvation" (Mark 16:8b). The second is significantly more elaborate, recounting that Jesus first appeared to Mary Magdalene, and then to two unnamed disciples, and finally to the eleven (unlike in Paul's account, Jesus presumably skips visiting Judas; an understandable choice), after which, he ascends to heaven (Mark 16:9–20).

Matthew agrees with Mark's editors that Mary Magdalene was among the first to see the risen Jesus, but he thinks that "the other Mary" was

---

12. In 1878 there was a widely circulated report that Jesse had been shot down by a local bounty hunter, though the body had mysteriously vanished when confirming agents were dispatched to investigate. Jesse and Frank James, both in fiction and in "reality," had arch-enemies in the Pinkerton Detective Agency.

with her too (Salome gets deleted all together from Matthew's account). They experience an earthquake and then see an angel descend to frighten away the guards and roll back the stone on an already empty tomb (Matt 28:2–5). Jesus meets up with the eleven disciples in Galilee and commissions them (Matt 28:9–10, 16–19). Luke multiplies the women at the empty tomb, again forgetting poor Salome, but specifically naming Mary Magdalene, Joanna and Mary the mother of James (Luke 24:10). This time the women discover the tomb already opened (no earthquake) and find two men dressed in white who explain it all (Luke 24:1–6). Peter also gets an early look at the empty tomb (Luke 24:12). Jesus does not appear to the women at all; rather, he makes his first appearance to a couple of disciples walking on the road to Emmaus and later to the eleven disciples all together in Jerusalem before ascending to heaven (again giving a snub to Judas; Luke 24:13–53).

John focuses on Mary Magdalene to a greater degree than the three gospels that precede him. She alone finds Jesus' tomb empty. There is no young man, angel from heaven or duo in white to explain things. Understandably confused and afraid, she runs to tell Peter and the unnamed "beloved disciple" what she saw, and they run to confirm her report—the unnamed "beloved disciple" out-racing Peter to the tomb. Strangely, these two men simply go back home, leaving Mary Magdalene to see the risen Jesus first (John 20:1–18). He later appears to the ten in Jerusalem, then Thomas who was not there initially, then he goes to the Sea of Tiberias and hangs out with six (John 20:19–29, 21:1–24—this last story probably added by an editor of John).

All of the accounts agree that there was an empty tomb—but who found it—Salome (and who is she anyway?), Mary Magdalene, Peter? Who saw the risen Jesus first—Cephas (and is Cephas another name for Peter or a different person altogether?), Mary Magdalene or an unnamed disciple? Did they find the tomb already opened or was there an earthquake? What strange men (or angels) were there? How old? How many? Dressed? Did James get an appearance at all? Judas? In Galilee or Jerusalem? Vast crowds or an intimate group? Once, twice, five times before his ascension? In every case, how and when did Jesus get out of the grave? A bit of a wanderer before death, not even the tomb could curtail Jesus' activities; instead of a single account of a resurrection (or even several accounts that have some measure of agreement), the stories multiply with abandon. The most substantial point of agreement is the emptiness of the tomb. Although decidedly less famous than Jesse James at the time of his death, we can still imagine segments of the Jerusalem population abuzz on the 14th or 15th of Nisan, debating the career and character of this most recent messianic pretender, some confident of his almost supernatural powers and therefore suspicious that he could be killed so simply and quickly, especially with the participation of one of his very own. It is very hard to let such a figure actually die. On one level, he simply cannot.

The legendary afterlives of Jesus of Nazareth are so well known, there is no need to document them here. Not only Jesus, but key members of his family (especially his mother Mary) appear regularly throughout the Christian world. He has inspired devotion, both religious and secular; he has informed art, literature, music and (more recently) television programs and film, both high and low. The development of the Internet has provided another world for Jesus to inhabit as Son of God and pop culture icon. Textual and virtual Jesses are doing well, too. On the frontiers of popular culture and cyberspace, he is alive and well:

> Jesse James is one of the best known bandits in America. It would be safe to say that more has been written about him than any other desperado, gunfighter, or outlaw in all the United States. His life has been the subject of more than half a hundred books, countless articles, several motion pictures, and at least one television series.[13]

The situation has not changed with the advent of modern media and the Internet. Indeed, it is even more pronounced, and the last five years show no signs of Jesse slowing down. He stars in both documentary and dramatic film—in 2006 Jesse James was the subject of a PBS / American Experience documentary,[14] and the film *The Assassination of Jesse James by the Coward Robert Ford* opened in 2007 directed by Andrew Dominik and starring Brad Pitt, based on a novel by Ron Hansen.[15] A casual search of the Internet discovers not only historical society pages[16] but also an invitation from the new James–Younger gang ("organized in 1866; reorganized 1993") to "Come Ride With Us." "You too can become a member of the Gang!" they announce, and so presumably both collect and disseminate information via numerous web links and an annual convention.[17] The Jesse James Museum of Sedalia, Missouri, has

---

13. Snell, "Editor's Introduction," ix.
14. Online: www.frontline.org.
15. To learn more, visit www.imbd.com/title/tt04436801.
16. Such as the one for the "Friends of the James Farm" in Kearny, Missouri. Online, one may visit the bookstore and gift shop which features *The Essential Handbook of Victorian Etiquette*, *The Jesse James Cookbook* and "a variety of T-shirts, ball caps, bonnets and Civil War kepi hats in many styles." See www.jessejames.org.
17. Online: www.islandnet.com/~thegang/. Romantic, in some ways, but decidedly un-bandit like.

a website that offers a link to the nearby Merimac Caverns (Jesse and company often hid in the bowels of "America's Cave").[18] The St. Joseph "Jesse James Death House" has an address on the web.[19] Several genealogical websites vet assertions of direct ancestry from Jesse, separating pretenders from the real.[20]

What had become "Jesse James" was much larger than any one person could embody. Generations after Jesse would argue and bicker over whether or how closely they were related to the James brothers. The family would produce "official" genealogies, keeping painstaking record of all known descendants, cousins, grand-nieces and nephews, all kin.[21] The premier Jesse James attraction, the James Family Farm, is run and supported by Jesse's descendants; it uses this linkage to establish its own "authentic" and premiere status and offers various lectures and study tours through the course of a year to educate properly the public about Jesse James. We were told by a docent on our visit that a major role of the Family Farm is to "separate fact from fiction" surrounding Jesse.

The vast number of sites both real and virtual demonstrate how many people engage in pilgrimage to James-related locations, desire to "join the Gang" (admittedly, metaphorically) or feign ancestry from Jesse James. Jesse was a serial robber and murderer who routinely endangered the lives of innocents, killing children and the elderly; yet, even in his afterlives, he has his supporters. The "Crime Library" database of the website for Court TV has certainly not forgotten the sinister aspects of Jesse's career.[22] Neither has the town of Northfield, Minnesota, which celebrates the town's defeat of the James–Younger gang on the first

18. Online: www.roadsideamerica.com/attract/MOSTAjesse.html and www.americascave.com.
19. Online: www.ci.ct-joseph.mo.us/history/jessejames.cfm.
20. See, for example, www.rootswebb.com.
21. See, for example Phillip W. Steele, *Jesse and Frank James: The Family History* (Gretna, Calif.: Pelican, 1987). The book reads like the rather more boring portions of 1and 2 Chronicles. Steele outlines the genealogy (in both tabular and narrative formats) of all the major characters in the post-1880 James saga including the West and Howard families (the family of Jesse's brother-in-law Tillman Howard West, the inspiration for Jesse's pseudonym), the Hite family and even Bob Ford, but, oddly, excluding the Youngers. The book also contains several photographs. It is difficult to imagine anyone really reading this text; it is more likely used as defense or rebuttal. Even so, the book has gone through more than six printings. It has sold more copies than this, our manuscript, probably will.
22. Online: www.crimelibrary.com. See, also www.hiwaay.net/~dbennett/places.html, which catalogs pilgrim sites for the Jesse-faithful but with a sober view of what went on at each location.

weekend after Labor Day. But the world cannot seem to stop talking about a social bandit, lauded by some and condemned by others, who tapped into something deep and essential about his particular political moment, complex enough in personality to allow for a wide range of interpretations of his life, betrayed in death in ways that have fired the imagination of generations.

In Jesse's Steps

Quite by happenstance, Oscar Wilde was visiting St. Joseph, Missouri in the days that followed Jesse James' murder:

> Outside my window about a quarter mile to the west stands a little yellow house, with green paling, and a crowd of people are pulling it all down. It is the house of the great train robber and murderer, Jesse James, who was shot by his pal last week, and the people are relic hunters. They sold his dust-bin and foot scraper yesterday by public auction, his door knocker is to be offered for sale this afternoon, the reserve price being about the income of an English bishop. The citizens of Kansas have telegraphed to an agent here to secure his coal-scuttle at all hazards and at any cost, and his favourite chromo-lithograph was disposed of at a price which in Europe only an authentic Titian can command, or an undoubted Mantegna. The Americans are certainly great hero worshippers, and always take their heroes from the criminal classes.[23]

From the moment of his death to the present day, the hero worship and relic hunting continues, as thousands make the pilgrimage, every year, from all over the world to the homes where Jesse James was born and where he died.

Pilgrimage to sacred sites is a universal religious phenomenon, but Christian pilgrimage developed to address specific historical circumstances. Christianity eschewed attaching holiness to particular places in its earliest centuries. Sacred place was a characteristic of pagan religiosity and in a circumstance where Christians were out-numbered by pagans, certain lines of demarcation were carefully constructed and maintained. Biblical support was also marshaled against the construction of holy sites. Paul in Acts says, "The God who made the world and everything in it, he who is the Lord of heaven and earth, does not live in shrines made by human hands" (Acts 17:24). Church fathers understood Paul's statement as a warning against the idea of holy space; Christianity was a spiritual religion and did not invest physical objects or places with

---

23. From a letter written by Oscar Wilde to Norman Forbes-Robertson, April 19, 1882. As quoted in Dellinger, ed., *Jesse James*, v.

sacredness. But in the fourth century, a remarkable transformation took place in Christianity—a religion that had once been staunchly opposed to sacred sites became a religion replete with holy places and holy items, a religion of pilgrimage and relics.

According to a seminal essay by R. A. Markus, such a revolution happened because of "new feelings" associated with "venerating and visiting the burial places of martyrs."[24] Before the conversion of Constantine, a core aspect of Christian identity was rooted in suffering. Once Christianity was adopted by the Emperor and the Empire, no longer were Christians vulnerable to persecution and harassment: "the new conditions of a Christianity favoured by emperors, fashionable, prestigious and likely to confer worldly advantage, required a huge spiritual adjustment from its adherents. They needed to be able to see themselves as the true descendants of the persecuted Church and the rightful heirs of the martyrs."[25] Consequently, Markus argues, new rituals developed around the burial sites and the relics of the martyrs. These new rituals abolished the gulf between the present and the past, allowing Christians to reclaim the past of the martyrs in their radically different present.[26] Not only did these new rituals establish continuity between past and present, but they allowed the newly triumphant Church to identify still as the persecuted Church. "The new importance of the martyrs was crucial"[27] in the development of sacred place and therefore pilgrimage in Christianity.

The place of martyrdom becomes the locus for the collapse between past and present. Such a conflation of time allows the pilgrim to commune with the past and to incorporate aspects of past identity and ideology into the pilgrim's current sense of self. The fact that James was an internationally known criminal already drew the curious to his modest home in St. Joseph, Missouri. The fact that Jesse James was murdered, and that this murder was immediately perceived as unjust, a betrayal, a type of martyrdom, guaranteed that such natural curiosity would be transformed into something more, that James would become a powerful symbol that would continue to fascinate.

People travel for a wide array of reasons and the line between tourism and pilgrimage is not absolute. The holy attracts the simply inquisitive; the secular inspires the spiritually motivated. Reviewing the scholarship, anthropologist Katharina Schramm notes that "The recent literature on

---

24. R. A. Markus, "How on Earth Could Places Become Holy? Origins of the Christian Idea of Holy Places," *Journal of Early Christian Studies* 2 (1994): 257–71.
25. Ibid., 268.
26. Ibid., 269.
27. Ibid.

pilgrimage has shown that the framing of pilgrimage within the discourse and practice of the tourism industry is far from unusual. Rigid distinctions between (serious) pilgrims—always on a journey to a sacred site—and (playful) tourists—always on a trip to places of secular pleasure—have become blurred."[28] The blurred boundaries are a result of the difficulties in defining all of the relevant terms: the sacred, pilgrim, tourist. Focusing on the motivation of the traveler, rather than fixed definitions, recent studies suggest that a pilgrimage is "the pursuit of the ideal,"[29] a trip "deliberately shaped for expressive and communicative, rather than simply instrumental, purposes."[30] Just like issues of identity were fundamental to the development of Christian pilgrimage, issues of identity are also key to understanding the distinctions in motivation between the tourist seeking pleasure and the pilgrim seeking some kind of transformation.[31]

A pilgrimage is an "act of memory." There is something powerful about standing in the very space where a significant event happened or where a hero also stood. Time moves on and we can never inhabit the same time twice; yet space, while not static, is stable enough to allow us to return. By inhabiting the same space, we can use our imaginative and empathetic capacities to collapse the differences in time. We can connect and commune. Christianity is now replete with pilgrimage sites and Judaism has also given rise to a few. In Israel ("the Holy Land"), the conventional pilgrimage sites include the Western Wall, the path of Jesus as he carried his cross, and the tombs of Hannah and her seven sons. Some of these sites are real—the Western Wall is really the last remaining vestige of the Second Temple, although it is just a retaining wall built by Herod the Great. Other sites are imaginary—we really have no idea the route Jesus took from his prison to the place of his execution and the evidence suggests that the Via Dolorosa has been altered several times.[32] Despite having a place of burial outside the Israeli city of Safad, Hannah and her sons are literary not historical figures (2 Macc 7). Yet, the path is made real by its reenactment; the martyrs live through their mourning.

---

28. Katharina Schramm, "Coming Home to the Motherland: Pilgrimage Tourism in Ghana," in *Reframing Pilgrimage: Cultures in Motion* (ed. Simon Coleman and John Eade; New York: Routledge, 2004), 134.
29. Morinis's definition of "the holy" as quoted in Coleman and Eade, eds., *Reframing Pilgrimage*, 13.
30. Adler, as quoted in ibid., 10.
31. Schramm, "Coming Home," 134–35.
32. Yoram Tsafrir, "Byzantine Jerusalem: The Configuration of a Christian City," in *Jerusalem: Its Sanctity and Centrality to Judaism, Christianity, and Islam* (ed. Lee I. Levine; New York: Continuum, 1999), 140.

The pilgrimage sites associated with Jesse James share in these observations. James is certainly an historical figure, yet much of his life is obfuscated by legends, legends that arose and circulated even before his demise. Questions of historical accuracy haunt many of the sites. Yet, the authenticity of any given site relies less on historicity and more on the meaning infused into the place. In making the journey to the places of his birth and death, Jesse's "pilgrims" are not learning a history lesson; rather, Jesse's pilgrims are reconstructing identity. In particular, they are participating in a conversation about what it means to be an American. Catrien Notermans observes:

> Challenging the narrow definition of pilgrimage as a journey to venerate a particular saint in a specific sacred place, scholars of pilgrimage have recently argued that sites of journeys become sacred when pilgrimage fulfils the need to construct and reconstruct particularly painful periods of (inter)national and personal history and thus heals pilgrims' physical and emotional wounds.[33]

In the case of Jesse James, these wounds are not personal but part of the cultural memory of the United States. Not only does James represent rugged frontier life but he is also seen as "the last rebel of the Civil War."

Pilgrimage to Jesse's numerous attractions allows the people of the United States to connect with certain core aspects of their (in many ways fictive) identity—life on the frontier cultivated tough, self-sufficient, industrious, resilient and independent characters; the Civil War from the Confederate perspective was a just struggle against the tyranny of the federal government. Americans, in general, are haunted by the realization that they have achieved their home, history and identity by the seizure and erasure of someone else's (the vast and various Native American peoples who possessed the land before the European conquest). White southerners, in particular, are confronted with the knowledge that even though they fought for freedom, that freedom was primarily the freedom to own other human beings. Jesse James allows his pilgrims to re-frame the Civil War so that it was not primarily a racist struggle about the enslavement of people of African descent; the Civil War was about state rights and individual freedom. Men fought to defend their families and communities.

---

33. Catrien Notermans, "The Power of the Less Powerful: Making Memory on a Pilgrimage to Lourdes," in *Powers: Religion as a Social and Spiritual Force* (ed. Meerten B. ter Borg and Jan Willem van Henten; New York: Fordham University Press, 2010), 182.

All of the encroaching conditions fought against by the James–Younger gang—the Union, the railroad, the banks, the federal system of law enforcement—won. As they were winning, some of the people of the United States sought a way to maintain connection with elements thought to be core components of American identity; hence James becomes a hero, his place of death and burial a pilgrimage site and the objects of his life relics. Just like Christians who moved from being hunted by the Empire to being the Empire, the people of Missouri were ultimately integrated into the economies of the East and woven into the fabric of the federal government. The murder now martyrdom of Jesse James allows his pilgrims to connect with an identity that is still opposed to such "infringements" of their freedom.

The first step Jesse James took on the path to his own legendary life was his participation in the massacre in Centralia, Missouri. This event signals many of the contradictions and tensions that Jesse would embody throughout his violent career. On September 27, 1864, under the leadership of William T. "Bloody Bill" Anderson, between two and four hundred Confederate guerrillas, including both Frank and Jesse James, marched into this small town. Ostensibly, their mission was to gather information about the position and movement of federal troops in the area. Their actions, however, belie such a routine task and suggest that the guerrillas' true purpose was to spread terror and mayhem. They broke into houses and stores, waved their pistols, stole cash and plundered goods. At the train depot, barrels of whiskey were discovered and the band of marauding soldiers soon became a drunken mob. The violence increased accordingly. When the train came in, forced to a stop by a pile of wooden railway ties on the tracks and a flurry of bullets from the guerrillas, all of their fury was focused on the unsuspecting passengers. Thousands of dollars were looted from the baggage cars, passengers were robbed and some killed. When it was discovered that there were furloughed federal soldiers on board, Anderson ordered them separated from the civilian passengers and stripped down to their underwear. Taking one sergeant as a hostage for a prisoner exchange, Anderson then ordered his men to open fire on the unarmed, half-naked men. Twenty-two soldiers were massacred on that day. Under the auspices of war, a seventeen year old Jesse James had begun his career of theft and murder.[34] The bifurcated identity of Missouri itself—a place through which furloughed Union soldiers felt safe to travel and Confederate soldiers went on recognizance missions, a place where the line blurred

---

34. Stiles, *Jesse James*, 119–27.

5. Bandits Beyond the Sunset

between legal war-time violence and cold-blooded murder—is the ground in which Jesse's career took root and his legend sprung forth.

Centralia is an attraction for both Civil War and Jesse James pilgrims alike. However, the primary sites of Jesse's devotion are the places of his birth and death. On September 5, 1847, Jesse James was born to Zerelda Cole James and Robert James, their second surviving son (Frank was born in 1843 and Robert was born and then died in 1845). Even after her husband, seized by missionary zeal (and perhaps a desire to take a break from his expanding family), left for California and died soon after arriving (1850), Zerelda continued to live on the homestead. She married Benjamin Simms in 1852 but he died from a fall off a horse (hence, reportedly, dodging an imminent divorce). Reuben Samuel was Zerelda's third and final husband whom she married in 1855. Together, they had four more children and raised them all in the home built by her first husband.

Several notable events in Jesse James' life happened in the house as he visited his mother and step-father frequently throughout his career. For example, the home was the site of the disastrous raid by Pinkerton detectives on January 26, 1875. Attempting to apprehend both Jesse and Frank who were reported to be at the family home, the Pinkertons surrounded the house and threw a smoke bomb through the window. When members of the family tried to remove the smoke bomb, it rolled into the fireplace and exploded. Jesse and Frank's nine year old brother Archie Samuel was killed, Zerelda lost part of her arm, and one of their servants was also injured. Opinion is divided about whether the James brothers were present in the house during the raid. Some evidence suggests that they were—the intelligence obtained by the Pinkerton detectives clearly indicated that the brothers were home, and when neighbors began to arrive to help, Zerelda asked everyone to leave her alone in the main room for a brief interval, and a local doctor's horse disappeared from the Samuels' barn only to turn up days later and miles away.[35] Others rely more on their belief in Frank and Jesse's honorable character and aver that the James brothers would have never crept away after the murder and maiming of their family members. Had they been there, they would have stood and fought.[36]

---

35. Settle, *Jesse James Was His Name*, 77.
36. For example, when we toured the house, our docent was adamant that the James brothers could not have been in the house that night and argued with us forcefully (and sincerely) that the James boys would certainly have killed "every last Pinkerton on the lot" had they been home.

The botched raid by the Pinkerton detectives that resulted in the death of the young Archie and the maiming of Zerelda fueled the public debate around Jesse James, the legitimacy of government power and the encroachment of economic interests from the East. It was an embarrassing episode for the government that helped further to cast James as a hero who stood against the powers that intruded from outside of Missouri. After his death, he could be memorialized as a martyr to individual freedom and Jesse James' mother capitalized on her son's popularity by opening up the house to the curious even while she still lived in it. Frank took over the Kearney farm after Zerelda died on February 10, 1911. Under Frank's direction, the farm was turned into a full-fledged tourist attraction.[37] Even though Archie, not Jesse, died at the family farm, even though the house is miles away from where Jesse actually was assassinated, even though his Kearney grave stone marks an empty tomb, he is memorialized nevertheless throughout the property with particular attention to the way he died and with a funerary obelisk marking the space where his body was once interred.

Dramatic deaths draw crowds. The highest honors for Christian relic hunters have always been associated with Jesus' death and burial. Enough pieces of the "true cross" of Jesus surfaced in the fourth and fifth centuries that, if they were collected, they would outweigh Jesse James' entire Death House. The spear that pierced Jesus' side, as well as the cup of the Last Supper, were singular relics whose existence fueled centuries of imagination. Many faithful followers insist to this day, despite quantifiable and documented evidence to the contrary, that his burial shroud is in Church possession. One of the earliest and most notorious ancient relic hunters was Helena, the mother of Constantine I. Helena was also a devout pilgrim; her visits to the "Holy Land" were largely searches for key cities in Christian sacred history. She was particularly obsessed with Jesus' birthplace, Golgotha, and Jesus' tomb. Many of Christianity's holy sites today are based upon Helena's identifications rather than any archaeological or historical investigation.

During a pilgrimage to Jerusalem around 326 C.E., Helena "discovered" the grave of Jesus. The complex of buildings and atria (chapel, baptistery, a large rotunda over the site of the tomb) called collectively the Church of the Holy Sepulcher was then built by her son Constantine

---

37. He even made a failed attempt to franchise the farm by sending one of the property's cabins to Hot Springs, Arkansas with the intention of setting up a Jesse James display. The site was never established and the dismantled cabin has been lost. Yeatman, *Frank and Jesse James*, 317.

and dedicated in 335.[38] Under Constantine's rule, Jerusalem became a pilgrimage site for Christians and the city was built up to both attract and accommodate the travelers. Constantine's conversion to Christianity, an act which included the baptism of his entire army, effectively ended Christianity's role as a countercultural movement opposed to state power. Regardless of any sincere spiritual transformation, Constantine's embracing of Christianity was also a shrewd political move that co-opted a rebellious element and helped him forge his vast Empire together through the cohesive power of shared religious commitment. The Church of the Holy Sepulcher occupied the center of Christian Jerusalem in the sacred imagination—for example, it is prominently positioned in the middle of the Madaba map despite the geographical inaccuracy.[39] As Christians were being integrated into the government (including the army), as the forces of Empire that Christianity had previously opposed were winning, Constantine simultaneously transformed the Holy Land into a network of pilgrimage sites, sites that allowed Christian pilgrims to connect with an identity still opposed to such power. Under Constantine, the sites of state-sponsored slaughter were transformed into state-controlled tourist attractions.

Dramatic deaths draw crowds, and Jesse James' status as a martyr of state-sponsored murder is particularly evident in his last home in St. Joseph, Missouri. As witnessed by Oscar Wilde, the relic hunters were out in full force from the moment his murder was known. People have a remarkable ability to invest material objects with significance and power. Even trivial objects—a dustbin, for example—become weighty with the import of a life. Even mundane spaces—an unremarkable street corner in a small Missouri town—take on a luminescence if inhabited by a remarkable life. One hundred and thirty years later, people still flock to the home where Robert Ford killed Jesse James. The bullet hole in the wall, the blood stains on the floor and the various and sundry relics that fill the small rooms of the old house draw both the curious and the reverent.

The first focal point for the visitor is the hole in the wall, purportedly made by the bullet after it passed through Jesse's head. Visitors used to be allowed to touch the hole and the experience of touching the plaster and paper that touched the hot metal that passed through the brain and bone of James was so compelling that the small hole is now the size of a large fist and covered with clear plastic to prevent any further

38. Tsafrir, "Byzantine Jerusalem," 135–36.
39. Ibid., 142–43.

communion. As discussed in the Introduction, this hole is contested like so many other aspects of James' story. A bullet was removed from James' skull in a later autopsy—a fact noted in the museum but not a fact that deters either the curators or the tourists from still regarding the hole as significant. Even James' biographer Frank Triplett, known for his radical support for Jesse and a less than critical eye toward the data, assures us that the bullet never left the head. Triplett would, however, assert that the autopsy found "the brain was a most remarkable one, and showed the great power, earnestness and determination of the man. It also showed the thought and courage, and in most men would have accomplished wonderful things."[40] Neither this autopsy, near mystical in its insight, nor the later autopsy, meticulous in its empiricism, could quell public rumor or the enthusiasm of the pilgrim.

A similar drama of authenticity is played out on the floorboards below the "bullet" hole. On the floor, blood from Jesse's fatal wound soaked into the wood and left large stains. Today, this discolored wood bears the marks of having been gouged and splintered. A reproduction of a newspaper notice from April 6, 1882 informs the visitor that unknown persons broke into the house and chipped away at the floor in order to carry off small pieces of the blood-soaked wood, "jubilant in the conviction of possessing even so paltry a curiosity commemorative of the taking-off the dreaded Jesse James." The newspaper article is illustrated by a drawing that captures the dramatic scene—James lies dead on the floor, while his wife and children cry at his side, his blood pooling around him. However, historical research reveals another story underneath the boards. In his biography, Ted Yeatman notes, "The boards on the spot where Jesse hit the floor were pulled up and replaced, and the new boards were said to have been doused with chicken blood. Splinters from these new additions were sold to hapless tourists for a quarter a piece."[41] The museum is silent about the continuing history of the house's floor boards giving the impression to today's tourists that they are looking at the real blood of the outlaw.

The next rooms in the Death House are full of various relics. There are castings of Jesse's skull on a rotating pedestal, ringed by his teeth. Shards of glass from the lid of his first coffin are on display, as is a piece of the "Original Chair," as labeled by the museum curators. This otherwise unremarkable splinter of wood is said to be a part of the chair upon which Jesse was standing when the fatal bullet hit, a type of "true cross."

---

40. Triplett, *The Life, Times and Treacherous Death of Jesse James*, 293.
41. Yeatman, *Frank and Jesse James*, 276.

5. Bandits Beyond the Sunset

Other relics include the bullet taken from his lungs (an earlier injury), and a collection of "petrified walnuts and acorns" collected and donated by one Mrs. Carol Fisher. These nuts had the distinction of washing down the hill upon which the Death House originally stood.

The museum, so concerned with creating a certain experience of immediacy and authenticity, is full of recreations, reproductions, replicas and obfuscations of truth. In fact, the house itself gestures toward authenticity while simultaneously obscuring history. The house may be the very place where Jesse and Zee lived with their two children, the very place were Bob Ford shot Jesse James in the back of the head, but the house no longer inhabits the plot of ground it did when all of these events took place. As we chronicled in the Introduction, it was moved down the street and set up next to the Patte House, thereby connecting Jesse James more explicitly to the romance of the Wild West and the freedom of the frontier, as well as making the experience more convenient for the tourist. Moving from the Patte House to 1318 Lafayette Street entails a walk of several blocks through a quiet street with small houses and unkempt lawns. We expected the lot where the house originally stood, the place where the James family had actually lived, to be marked in some way but it was not. It looked like so many other vacant lots in disintegrating urban contexts—wild grasses and weeds, the remains of an illegal fire, broken bottles, a dead snake.

We had one last destination and that was Jesse James' final resting place. James was originally buried on his family's farm but the gravestone was stolen in bits and pieces by relic hunters. Zerelda erected another monument, closer to the house so that she could guard the grave more effectively. Eventually, it was considered prudent to move the grave to Mount Olivet Cemetery. Although Jesse's body moved, the second marker still stands next to the small farm house, a large obelisk that practically shouts in outrage that Jesse James was "murdered by a coward whose name is unworthy to appear here." The current grave site is more modest and unassuming. When we arrived, we expected to find some kind of sign or marker directing visitors to Jesse James' grave. But like the plot of earth where his house originally stood, there was nothing here directing the pilgrim. We parked the car near the center of the cemetery, and fanned out to find the grave of Jesse James.

Two stones now mark the tomb. There is what appears to be an older stone simply inscribed with the Confederate "military regiment" in which he served, followed by his birth and death dates. In front of the older stone is a newer marker that memorializes both James and his wife Zee. Jesse's inscription reads:

JESSE W.
BORN SEPT. 5, 1847
ASSASSINATED
APRIL 3, 1882

Jesse and Zee's grave is flanked by the graves of Jesse's mother Zerelda and his step-father Rueben Samuels. On the other side of his mother's grave is a small marker, flush with the earth, for Archie who was "killed by a bomb" in 1875. Someone had stuck a small American flag in the ground at Archie's grave, the burial place of a boy killed by people acting on behalf of the United States government while they were searching for his older brothers, avowed enemies of that government. As the state takes over, it co-opts defiance and neutralizes it by rebranding it as patriotism; Archie lies under the enemy's flag.

The cemetery is quiet and unkempt. It had not always been so. When the grave was first moved from the Kearney family farm to Mount Olivet Cemetery in 1902, James' daughter Mary lived near-by in order to watch her father's grave, as her grandmother had when it was on the farm. After she died in 1935, the marker was again chipped to pieces.[42] But now, the grass is long and messy with clover, a yellow flowering plant had peaked weeks ago and was poised between lush glory and bare demise. We were surprised that we were the only people there. More pilgrims, apparently, haunt the sites of birth and death, view the original marker, now an empty tomb, with its loud protests against Jesse's killer, than seek out this more modest repose. In many ways, such restraint was welcome after days touring the more grandiose pilgrimage sites and reliquaries, which veered dangerously into kitsch (sometimes, alas, going completely through). It was another way that the man is separate from his legend; the criminal quietly decomposes while the bandit lives on the other side of town.

Literary Afterlives

Despite the fate of Jesse's body, which came into the world in the typical way and quietly decomposed in a grave as all others do, his name has lived an incredibly complex and variegated life as it has circulated in

---

42. Ibid., 321. Seeing the public response to his brother's dead body, Frank took precautions to prevent his corpse from becoming the object of relic hunters: "Possibly fearing that his bones might be stolen and put on display or sold to morbid souvenir hunters, Frank's remains were cremated, and, ironically, kept in a bank vault in Kansas City for later interment beside his widow" (p. 319).

word and text, song, poem and story, intoned by advocates and detractors alike. In fact, in the analysis of at least one biographer, his name may hold the key to his grip upon the American imagination:

> Jesse James! The magical words are pregnant with romance. Their terse, alliterative compactness was of heroic stuff... In truth, it seems possible that the name may account, as much as anything, for his reputation; so far as one can see, he was not essentially greater than the others in his gang, except in this one point. His brother, Frank, appears to have equaled him in almost every way; but—*Frank* James! No, it wouldn't do; it sounded altogether too prosy and common to fit a demi-god and demi-devil.[43]

Even before his death, his name had severed itself from his immediate control to accumulate both crimes and noble deeds. James himself even acknowledged the unruliness of his name (or used it as a cover for his own crimes) in an interview with John Newman Edwards. When asked about the bank robberies of which he had been accused, James responds: "The first robbery with which our names have been connected was the robbery of the bank at Russellville, Kentucky, which took place on March 20th, 1868... Should occasion ever require proof on this point, we could bring two hundred respectable people to swear that on the day of the robbery we were fifty miles from the town of Russellville."[44] The conduct of his name could not be vouched, even though his own conduct could be easily verified as innocent.

After his death, his name continued to accumulate deeds, as did his corpse. MacKinlay Kantor, in his memoir *Missouri Bittersweet*, describes a traveling museum that came to his town when he was just a boy, a museum that boasted of the body of Jesse James. "In that glorious pink-painted van he reposed in an absolutely terrifying coffin, clad in the exact costume which Jesse wore the day when the Dirty Little Coward shot him (so said the proprietor)."[45] The price for admission was ten cents. He took his $1.00, earned through a paper route, gave the requisite $.25 to his mother, and spent sixty cents "worshiping beside Jesse James' bier."[46]

The proprietor would open James' shirt to show the crowd his autopsy scars and stitches; he could set up his glass eyes to open and close. How

---

43. R. F. Dibble, *Strenuous Americans*, as quoted in Dellinger, ed., *Jesse James*. See also Sam Sacket, "Jesse James as Robin Hood," in ibid., 210.
44. As quoted in ibid., 31–32; see also p. 33—James makes repeated claims to this effect.
45. *Missouri Bittersweet* by MacKinlay Kantor, as quoted in ibid., 232.
46. Kantor as quoted in ibid., 232.

did the man obtain the body of the notorious gunman? He claimed that a tramp killed in a knife fight really lay beneath the ground on the Kearney farm.

> Some friends of Jesse's—my own brother Claiborne was one of em—was fearful that maybe the enemies of Jesse James would dig up his corpse in the dark of the moon, and cut it up, and sell the pieces for souvenirs. So they carried his body to a place of safety, and nobody else knew any different. That's how come that I am now enabled to exhibit before your very eyes the positively genuine body of the one and only Jesse Woodson James, treacherously slain by Robert Judas Iscariot Ford for the sake of thirty pieces of silver.[47]

As Robert Ford becomes Judas Iscariot, Jesse moves toward identification with Jesus not only in their shared identity as bandits but also through resurrection, the language of worship and the multiplication of burial sites empty of their corpses.

The identification of Jesus with Jesse continues to have a life of its own in various works of fiction. Most recently, Ron Hansen's *The Assassination of Jesse James by the Coward Robert Ford* (1983), made into an Academy Award-nominated movie in 2007,[48] foregrounds Jesse's religiosity from the opening paragraph: "He would flop open the limp Holy Bible that had belonged to his father, the late Reverend Robert S. James, and would contemplate whichever verses he chanced upon, getting privileged messages from each. The pages were scribbled over with penciled comments and interpretations; the cover was cool to his cheek as a shovel."[49] It is a relationship physical and intimate but not wholly orthodox. The Bible is "limp"—from age or overuse or lack of strength? Certainly the biblical prohibitions against theft and murder held no power over Jesse. Jesse flops open his Bible, engages in lively conversations with the verses, talking back, albeit in pencil, to what they proclaim in ink, listening beneath and behind their plain meaning to their secrets meant only for him. Such engagement is not necessarily uncommon—many people of faith read their Bibles more like seers read the innards of a sacrificed animal. But it is a type of reading that has more to do with spiritualism (in James' case, nineteenth-century spiritualism) than *lecto divinitas*.

---

47. Kantor as quoted in ibid., 233.
48. Even though Andrew Dominik's rendition of the novel is remarkably faithful, the religious framework is more obvious in Hansen's book because the prose is laden with biblical reference and allusion in a way impossible to capture in film.
49. Hansen, *Assassination of Jesse James*, 3–4.

According to Hansen, Jesse is more than just a man with a relationship to scripture. In the first chapter, he is identified with both David and Jesus. On the day Bob Ford meets Jesse James, he is giddy with a schoolboy's excitement; he has just met his hero. He endeavors to ingratiate himself to both Frank and Jesse, hoping to earn an honored place in the gang. Later that evening, after a successful train robbery, Jesse and Bob retire together to Jesse's home for tea, cigars and further conversation. While there, Zee calls Jesse "Dave."[50] When Bob questions the name, Jesse explains, "'You know your Good Book? David is the begotten of Jesse.' He winked for reasons that Bob couldn't intuit. 'You might call it my alias...'"[51] Bob seems confused by this biblical allusion, but he is an expert on other scriptural Jesses—he has been an avid reader of the dime store novels about the James–Younger gang. James attempts to tamp down his enthusiasm for the stories by first noting that those books are full of lies.[52] After Ford reads from a passage that he had torn out of a book and carried with him always, a passage that describes Jesse James in quite romantic terms, James replies: "I'm a no good, Bob. I ain't Jesus."[53] And thus ends the interview.

In a scene that begins with a reference to David and ends with a reference to Jesus, Hansen plays with various identifications, messianic and otherwise. James takes his biblical namesake—Jesse, father of David—and slides from father to son. By embracing the connection between Jesse James and the biblical David, Hansen suggests that the biblical David may be "a no good" like James himself. As described in Chapter 2, both Jesse and David are bandits, both hide out in the wilderness and gather around them a group of disaffected locals willing to do their bidding in theft and murder. Jesus has much the same profile—hence his inclusion in the play of identifications around Jesse James. He too hid out in the wilderness and assembled around him a group of disaffected locals. He too used his charisma to lead his men into criminal activity. Hansen has James reject the divinization of Ford's ardor with a succinct rebuke—"I ain't Jesus." But it is a rejection that is also an identification—otherwise, why even mention Jesus in this context? The interplay between is/is not mirrors the biblical interplay between messiah and bandit, savior and criminal that we have chronicled throughout our study.

50. Before he was "Thomas Howard," Jesse James sometimes used the alias "John Davis Howard" or "Dave."
51. Hansen, *Assassination of Jesse James*, 31.
52. Ibid., 32
53. Ibid., 34.

According to Hansen's story, James sees even deeper affinities between David and himself. They both have a special relationship with God, one that confers both blessing and curse. After the deaths of his twin infant sons, Jesse "thought of himself as the cause of their miseries and Zee would awake at night to see him sitting on the edge of the mattress, his blue nightshirt rucked and screwed about him, a white buttock windowed by the gather at his waist, his papa's pencil-marked Holy Bible open in his hands."[54] As David's misdeeds were responsible for the death of his first born son, James saw God's hand in the deaths of his first born sons, killed by God on account of the sins of the father. Consequently, he returns to his childhood nickname of "Dave."

Other biblical identifications continue to flirt with Jesse James. Hansen recounts the injuries James sustained toward the end of the Civil War and his long period of rest and recuperation after being returned to his family. His first cousin Zee is his primary nursemaid: "'And you were here,' Jesse said with no little melodrama, 'and you anointed me with ointments like the sisters of Lazarus, and I have come forth from the tomb.'"[55] James avoids comparing himself directly with Jesus in this scene, but he does position himself as another dead one brought back to life. The raising of Lazarus does foreshadow Jesus' own resurrection. As the last and greatest "sign" in the Gospel of John (John 11), Jesus demonstrates his power over death while he points forward to his own triumph over the tomb. The particular language Jesse uses to describe the actions of the sisters (anointing with ointments) also calls Jesus to mind—John's account makes no mention of Lazarus' sisters anointing him but the women who discover Jesus' empty tomb in two of the gospels are there because of their intention to anoint Jesus with spices and ointments (Mark 16:1, Luke 23:56–24:1). Hansen again plays with an identification that "is/is not" since Jesus is implied in several ways but is actually absent from James' comparison.

Jesse never completely healed from the injuries sustained during the war; his precarious physical health mirrors a mental instability. Hansen portrays Jesse as frequently on the edge of sanity. He hears voices, has premonitions and uses the Bible like an occult object. It is as if the words on the page speak directly to him. In January of 1874, for example, "Jesse shook Zee awake and read the verses in the Gospel of Matthew pertaining to the Holy Family's flight from Herod into Egypt, saying he'd been getting premonitions and that they ought to fly from

---

54. Ibid., 66.
55. Ibid., 38–39.

Missouri."⁵⁶ Here, James identifies himself explicitly with Jesus. Like Jesus and his family, the James family was being pursued by hostile government forces. Jesse and Zee were in Nashville by the end of the week.

The associations between Jesus and Jesse become more acute as Jesse's death draws near. Hansen deliberately highlights the interconnections between Jesse's assassination and Christianity's construction of sacred time; from Bob Ford's meeting with the Missouri governor to hatch the plot against James' life through the assassination itself, Jesse James is undergoing his own Passion. Bob Ford's meeting with Governor Thomas Theodore Crittenden takes place during the night of Ash Wednesday. As Ford waits for the Governor, he reads the newspaper out loud to his partner in betrayal—Dick Liddil. First, he reads an article about the conviction and execution of Charles Guiteau, the man who assassinated President James Garfield: "a jury decided that Charles J. Guiteau was governed not by God or insanity but by his own wickedness."[57] When the verdict was read, Guiteau screamed, "'I am here as God's man! God Almighty will curse every man who has anything to do with this case!'"[58] Hansen uses this news item to highlight the tensions that can emerge between "the laws of God" and the "laws of men" as people feel called by God to engage in criminal behavior. Such men stand at the intersection of holiness, insanity and evilness; they will be regarded differently by different communities and the executed are always convinced of their own righteousness despite the judgment of the governing authorities.

Next, Ford reads a second news item:

> The newspaper reminded its readers that it was Ash Wednesday, and that the following forty days were "a time for penitential retirement from the world and abstinence from the festivities of ordinary life in order to afford an opportunity for reflections, undistracted by secular pursuits, on sins committed and preparations to do battle in the future against temptations and fleshly lusts."[59]

The newspaper piece on Ash Wednesday is read without further comment, but Hansen goes on to describe the festivities in which the Governor is partaking while the would-be assassins wait for him upstairs. Crittenden was attending a gala event in the ballroom of the St. James

---

56. Ibid., 53.
57. Ibid., 162.
58. Ibid.
59. Ibid., 162–63.

Hotel, the Craig Rifles Ball, honoring Henry Craig and his men for their help in tracking down members of the James gang. The night also happened to correspond to the birthday of George Washington. Everyone who attended the dinner and celebration was wealthy and/or politically powerful, their wives all "sumptuously ornamented."[60] The food was rich and the wine freely flowed. The Governor later meets Ford and Liddil in his suite—the men walk down a corridor carpeted in purple, with white fleur-de-lis on the ceiling to enter the governor's receiving room. He is clothed in a red silk robe—the effect is both rich and royal, a man above and beyond the religious rituals of the people he reigns over.[61] Hansen juxtaposes the austerity of Ash Wednesday with the state's display of wealth and power. The governor proceeds to paint a black picture of James and his crimes, dismissing the argument that he is some kind of hero who is striking back at the government for what his family suffered during the Civil War: "'I'm saying his sins will soon find him out. His cup of iniquity is full. I'm saying Jesse James is a desperate case and may require a desperate remedy.'"[62] Liddil and Ford are prepared to act as Crittenden's "desperate remedy."

Despite the analysis of Crittenden, James did not regard himself as an unrepentant criminal. Once when James and the Fords spent the night in a Lutheran Church outside St. Joseph, Jesse picked up one of the Bibles and read from the Psalms (23 and 41—both Psalms of David). Bob asked him if he ever thought of his past actions or regretted what he had done. Jesse does not at first understand the question and the reader has the impression that Jesse really does not reflect much about his past. Bob continues to probe and Jesse finally responds: "Jesse shut the book [the Bible] and rubbed a thumb across the two gold words on the black leather cover. Rainfall was the only noise. He said, 'I've been forgiven for all that.'"[63] When Bob still persists in his line of questioning, Jesse again repeats that he has been forgiven.

Jesse James is portrayed as having preternatural abilities, as if he were something more than human. As the Passion Week nears, Bob buys himself an Easter suit and then composes a telegram to Police Commissioner Craig about his progress. It was difficult, he muses, to kill Jesse because of his hyper-vigilance born of paranoia. But even more, Ford ascribes all sorts of powers to James:

60. Ibid., 163.
61. Ibid., 165.
62. Ibid., 167.
63. Ibid., 181.

He once numbered the spades on a playing card that skittered across the street a city block away; he licked his daughter's cut finger and there wasn't even a scar the next day; he wrestled with his son and the two Fords at once one afternoon and rarely even tilted—it was like grappling with a tree. When Jesse predicted rain, it rained; when he encouraged plants, they grew; when he scorned animals, they retreated; whomever he wanted to stir, he astonished.[64]

What manner of man is this? As the fateful day of his assassination nears, Charlie Ford and Jesse are out riding when they encounter a fire ball rolling down the road then disappearing. Ford was surprised and mystified. James, however, reacted calmly to the strange phenomenon. He told Ford that it was an omen, "that fire had come to him many times in the past in various manifestations and each visitation was followed by an affliction."[65] Jesse continues: "'I've seen visions that would make Daniel swoon; I've been warned as often as Israel.'"[66] James' own megalomania is religiously constituted as he considers himself worthy of warning by God, akin to the great prophets of biblical times.

Jesse's own Passion Week nears its climax on Palm Sunday. The family attends the 10:00 Palm Sunday service at the Second Presbyterian Church in St. Joseph, Missouri. Bob Ford declined to attend with the family citing a history of forced church services with his father, another preacher. Late that night, both unable to sleep, James and Ford find themselves outside on the porch in a kind of replay of Gethsemane. James reproaches Ford for his absenteeism and recites another Psalm of David (Ps 55:12–14) about a friend who betrays:

> For it was not an enemy that reproached me; then I could have borne it: neither was it he that hated me that did magnify himself against me; then I would have hid myself from him. But it was thou, a man my equal, my guide, and mine acquaintance. We took sweet counsel together, and walked unto the house of God in company.[67]

James recommends pairing this passage with Matt 26—the chapter that tells of Judas' agreement with the authorities and his taking of 30 pieces of silver. David, Jesus and Jesse come together and all impute Ford. Jesse's conversation grows increasingly esoteric and Ford becomes increasingly more agitated and confused. Jesse remarks, "His voice is like a waterfall"[68] alluding to the description of the Christ in Rev 1:15.

64. Ibid., 193–94.
65. Ibid., 196.
66. Ibid., 198.
67. Ibid., 204.
68. Ibid., 205.

And then declares, "If I could stand in it for a second or two, all my sins would be washed away."[69] The next morning, Bob shoots Jesse in the back of the head as he straightens a picture on the wall.

In Hansen's book, as well as in the popular lore surrounding this fateful moment, there is the suggestion that the Fords did not take Jesse unaware—for who could take the man by surprise?[70] Rather, Jesse offered himself up, consenting to be killed by his friend. This too shares in the theology around Jesus' own betrayal and crucifixion. The Son of God could not have chosen a disciple who would turn him over to the authorities unless that was, somehow, part of the divine plan. The Christ would certainly not invite a viper into his company without at least awareness if not intention. Standard Christian theology avers that Jesus was incarnated in order to die, that he knew his purpose from the beginning, that the Romans only arrested him because he assented, killed him because he had chosen to die.

The Ford brothers immediately run out of the house and to the sheriff's, but the city marshal had already been dispatched to the house on Lafayette Street on report of a gun battle. Bob and Charlie return to the scene of their crime and Zee screams at them, calling them cowards and snakes, accusing them of killing their friend.[71] The police reporter questions the Fords, asking them why they did it. Bob at first speaks of ridding the country of a "vicious and bloodthirsty outlaw" but then Charlie chimes in about the reward money. The reporter queries: "You shot him for the money?" and Charlie responds enthusiastically, "Only ten thousand dollars!"[72] As the tradition speculates on Judas' motivations, the Ford brothers are questioned, the role of money highlighted for each.

Hansen's novel chronicles the explosion of interest in the dead body of Jesse James as pilgrim-tourists came from all over the country:

> Railway companies had by then rather gleefully scheduled special coaches that would carry the inquisitive to the city at greatly reduced rates; thus a thousand strangers were making spellbound pilgrimages to the cottage or were venerating the iced remains in Seidenfaden's cooling room. Reporters roamed the city, gathering anecdotes and apocrypha, garnering interviews with the principles, relentlessly repeating themselves, inaccurately recording information, even inventing some stories in order to please a publisher.[73]

69. Ibid.
70. Ibid., 211, 224.
71. Ibid., 217.
72. Ibid., 218.
73. Ibid., 225.

Armed men had to be stationed at the house, and the authorities worried that the dead man was not Jesse so multiple people came to identify the body. Secretly, in the middle of the night, the doctors performed an autopsy, noting especially the wounds the body had endured—the scar on his right side; the wound in his leg; the fractured ankle bone. His mother arrived the next day and mourned over his body like an American Pieta. As she caressed him, she cried out, "O, Jesse! Jesse! Why have they taken you from me? O, the miserable traitors!'"[74] Zerelda continues to feed the legend that James knew of his imminent demise: "She said, 'You know, he must've had a foreshadowing that this was about to happen. One of the last things he said to me was "Mother, if I never see you on earth again, we're sure to meet in Heaven."'"[75] Later, when she sees Dick Liddil, she berates him, calling him a coward and a traitor, and swearing God's vengeance upon him for the part he played in the death of her boy.[76]

Rumors flew. One rumor circulated that James' body was going to be stolen and enshrined; that the Fords were going to be lynched. Crowds continued to gather and his body was put on display. His funeral was on Holy Thursday in the Chapel of William Jewell.[77] When Jesse James was finally lowered into the ground, his wife and mother gave full expression of their grief: "they cast themselves upon the casket, screaming for God to avenge the man slain by a coward for money."[78] His mother insisted the men reopen the casket to make sure that no parts of his body had been stolen, but was calmed by the minister before they could do so. The Governor himself had to demand proper burial for Jesse James. James' funeral costs were extravagant—"more than ten times the price of a standard funeral."[79] At first, the men who buried James remained anonymous, but later it turned out that James R. Timberlake and Henry H. Craig had made the arrangements and paid the bill. Like Jesus, rich men of standing in the community gave the criminal more of a burial than others in his position got or deserved.

The Fords were tried, convicted, sentenced to die by hanging and then unconditionally pardoned by the governor. Within the year, they had put together a play entitled *How I Killed Jesse James* which enacted the

74. Ibid., 228.
75. Ibid.
76. Ibid., 228–29.
77. Ibid., 236–37.
78. Ibid., 237.
79. Ibid., 226.

events leading up to that fateful day, as well as the assassination itself.[80] Bob himself muses that never before had anyone repeated his act of betrayal as many times as he did in his play. But the repeated reenactment was not just about continuing profit; the Ford brothers were haunted by their crime. The guilt and fear began to manifest in their bodies. Like the legends of Judas, whose death gets progressively more and more gruesome as the tales accrue, whose body becomes more and more grotesque as it moves through time and legend, the Fords suffered for what they had done.[81] In fact, after one of their performances, Bob receives an anonymous note that

> conveyed an account of Judas that was never accepted into the gospels. It said the disciple lived on after his attempt to hang himself, providing an example of impiety in this world. He grew huge and grotesque, his face became like a goatskin swollen with wine, his eyes could not be perceived even by an examining physician, to such a depth had they retreated from the sunlight, and his penis grew large, gruesome, a cause for loathing, yellow pus and worms coming out of it along with such a stink that he could stay in no village for long before he was chased away. After much pain and many punishments, Judas died in the place he belonged and, according to the account, the region still permitted no approach, so great was the stench that progressed from the apostate's body to the ground.[82]

Bob thought that he might have committed suicide after he shot James or accepted the verdict of the court and hung. Even if he had, he concludes, the public would still pronounce him guilty and refuse their forgiveness, just like Judas remains unforgiven.[83] Charley Ford finally breaks under the psychological strain as well as the pain of his physical deterioration (he contracts tuberculosis and is addicted to morphine); he commits suicide just two years after his betrayal of Jesse James.

Bob Ford, in Hansen's portrayal, continues on after the suicide of his brother like one under a curse. He gives up the play, secretly visits the grave of James, and wanders out west without a map. Once he chops off the head of a rattlesnake, putting his body in a sack for later consumption. When he opened the bag later that night, the body "slashed out and socked Bob's neck, striking hard as a strong man's fist."[84] In the Christian understanding, the serpent in the Garden of Eden (Gen 3) is

---

80. Ibid., 247–53.
81. Ibid., 254.
82. Ibid., 262. This account of Judas is found in Papias.
83. Ibid., 263.
84. Ibid., 263–64.

Satan, the arch-betrayer. God promises the snake's descendents will be entwined in a perpetual conflict with the descendents of the woman, who will bruise its head as it bruises his heal (Gen 3:15). Bob, both snake and snake-struck, is finally murdered himself by a stranger avenging the name of Jesse James.

Hundreds of dime store novels and perhaps thousands of newspaper articles (most of which are no longer extant) were written about Jesse James while he still lived. After Jesse James died, his name went on to garner even more fame through countless books of fiction, biography and academic study.[85] Poems, songs and plays have also proliferated, and (in the twentieth and twenty-first centuries) at least 44 movies and television shows showcase Jesse James.[86] The impulse to reposition James as a hero and a martyr, someone known more for his religiosity than his criminality, is common to these representations.

Such rehabilitation and re-sanctification was present from the beginning. In the *Gazette* on April 6, 1882, under a heading "Worthy of Notice," it is reported that "It is positively known that Jesse James attended the Sunday services at the Presbyterian church, opposite the World's Hotel, repeatedly..."[87] Immediately following this note, the newspaper also includes a description of the day that Zerelda and Zee moved the property out of the house on Lafayette Street. Among the items was a well-worn Bible. When Zee was asked by the reporter if her husband read that Bible, she responded: "Yes, he read it very often."[88] By placing these two observations together, the newspaper reporter is trying to create the impression that James was a religious man, not just a notorious bandit, a thief and a murderer. The Bible-reading, church-going son of a minister only turned to crime through circumstance not core identity.

Such re-sanctification inscribes James into a particular set of narratives and his story is almost entirely composed of common legendary motifs. Even more enduring in the American context, Jesse James' life resonates with Christian legendary motifs, in particular the motifs of betrayal and sacrifice. As the folklorist Sam Sackett writes,

---

85. Dellinger counts 500 books where James is the primary subject, over one thousand where he is the secondary subject.

86. Film count from Dellinger, ed., *Jesse James*, 249–50.

87. From *The Rise and Fall of Jesse James* by Robertus Love, as cited in ibid., 200.

88. Love, in ibid.

>More germane to an explanation of this survival is the fact that Jesse was assassinated. As a leader cut down in his prime, he obviously joins the ranks of martyred heroes with whom he has nothing else in common... As the case of James A. Garfield makes clear, assassination is not enough to ensure apotheosis; but when it is combined with other elements, it can give legend a powerful impetus. Moreover, there is an inherent structural irony in the story: Jesse was assassinated by one of his own band, who betrayed him for a reward. If I were forced to put my finger on one single factor which, more than any other one, contributed to the endurance of the James legend, I would select the dramatic irony of the fact that it was one of his own confederates and comrades who killed him. The analogue to this is too well known to need specifying; one suspects that it was for a good, through subliminal, reason that Woody Guthrie chose the tune of the Jesse James song for his "Ballad of Jesus Christ."[89]

The moment of betrayal plays out again and again, like Jesse James' own Passion Play, in historical writings, academic journals, Hollywood film and popular song. In a poem like a prayer, Harold Hersey intones

>*Ford followed Jesse James to thuh place where he wuz hid,*
>*Like Judas sellin' out hiz God he wuz bought for thuh highest bid;*
>*And he shot him in the back, leavin' a widder and a kid.*

>*Up there in thuh starry heaven*
>*Before thuh mighty Lord*
>*I'd rather be in Jesse's shoes*
>*Than in those of Robert Ford.*[90]

From that fateful day in April to the present day, Jesse and Jesus live on, due in part to the fact that their young lives were cut short by the betrayal of a friend, a betrayal seen as more treacherous than any other act they may or may not have committed during their own legendary lives.

---

89. Sackett, as quoted in ibid., 211.
90. Harold Hersey, *Singing Rawhide: A Book of Western Ballads* as cited in ibid., 196.

Conclusion:
On Death and Birth and Jesse's Lineage

On Genealogy

[13]So Boaz took Ruth, and she was his wife: and when he went in unto her, the LORD gave her conception, and she bare a son...[17]And the women her neighbours...called his name Obed: he *is* the father of Jesse, the father of David. [18]Now these *are* the generations of Pharez: Pharez begat Hezron, [19]And Hezron begat Ram, and Ram begat Amminadab, [20]And Amminadab begat Nahshon, and Nahshon begat Salmon, [21]And Salmon begat Boaz, and Boaz begat Obed, [22]And Obed begat Jesse, and Jesse begat David. (Ruth 4:13, 17–22)

[1]These *are* the sons of Israel; Reuben, Simeon, Levi, and Judah, Issachar, and Zebulun, [2]Dan, Joseph, and Benjamin, Naphtali, Gad, and Asher. [3]The sons of Judah; Er, and Onan, and Shelah: *which* three were born unto him of the daughter of Shua the Canaanitess. And Er, the firstborn of Judah, was evil in the sight of the LORD; and he slew him. [4]And Tamar his daughter-in-law bare him Pharez and Zerah. All the sons of Judah *were* five. [5]The sons of Pharez; Hezron, and Hamul. [6]And the sons of Zerah; Zimri, and Ethan, and Heman, and Calcol, and Dara: five of them in all. [7]And the sons of Carmi; Achar, the troubler of Israel, who transgressed in the thing accursed. [8]And the sons of Ethan; Azariah. [9]The sons also of Hezron, that were born unto him; Jerahmeel, and Ram, and Chelubai. [10]And Ram begat Amminadab; and Amminadab begat Nahshon, prince of the children of Judah; [11]And Nahshon begat Salma, and Salma begat Boaz, [12]And Boaz begat Obed, and Obed begat Jesse, [13]And Jesse begat his firstborn Eliab, and Abinadab the second, and Shimma the third, [14]Nethaneel the fourth, Raddai the fifth, [15]Ozem the sixth, David the seventh: [16]Whose sisters *were* Zeruiah, and Abigail. (1 Chr 2:1–16)

At some point, a book titled *Jesse's Lineage* must address genealogy. As literature, genealogies seem to obscure as much as they reveal. The Tolstoy-esque complexity of any human life is reduced to a few salient facts of birth and death. Compared to biblical genealogy, modern genealogies, with their tendency to include birth date, death date, marriage, places of residence, children and occasionally occupation or profession, are positively verbose. In both biblical and modern cases, however, genealogies function as ciphers for narratives that are the ideological constructions of identity. Genealogies tell us, at the most basic level, who we are; they are records that locate our loyalties and identities in historical epoch. They are cryptic incantations of names, dates, places that conjure up images of our family's location in history, our family loyalties, our family status, our ethnicity, our religion. They are annotations of our connection to history. They are schematics of the influences on our lives and extending outward from our lives. They speak, they "mean," by their associations and potential influence.

Genealogies burst from biblical text at somewhat regular moments, rooted deeply within books that nostalgically and retrospectively tell stories of the past to undergird arguments describing and interpreting the present. In nearly every case, they are located within moments of biblical narrative where identity and continuity are critical to the thesis at hand. David's genealogy (or, better, genealogies) makes a fine example. Except for the naming of his father Jesse, David has no genealogy in the books of Samuel–Kings. In Chronicles, the concern with genealogy is so acute that the opening nine chapters are little more than lists of fathers and sons. The entire book of Chronicles is a nostalgic retrospective on the kingship of Israel and Judah, focused on the glorious reign of David. Struggling with the trauma of the actual broken promises of God—the loss of nationhood, priesthood, possession of the land and Davidic kingship—Chronicles manufactures continuity through genealogy.

Names of mothers, narratives, are all omitted.[1] Repetitions and gaps abound. The focus of these genealogies is not the accurate relation of individual lives; it is the rhetoric of relation, of influence, of descending ethnicity and unbroken connection. The importance of these genealogies is not the narratives of the aggregate, but the sweep of the whole. In the final chapter of Ruth, the opposite dynamic occurs. Ruth is tied to David, tied to legends of kingship, via the genealogy of Ruth 4. Redeemed from destitution by marriage to Boaz, she is saved from obscurity by mothering Obed.

Jesus' genealogy (or, better, genealogies) is famously complex, as well. Each advances the ideology of the gospel writer, as is evident in the rather troublesome fact that the two genealogies given for Jesus (Matt 1 and Luke 3) do not match. Matthew, arguing for a Jesus as Jewish Messiah and King, focuses his genealogy on Abraham and traces the line through David's royal sons. Luke, looking for a Jewish Messiah

---

1. There are a number of remarkable exceptions to this statement. See, for example, Julie Kelso, *O Mother, Where Art Thou? An Irigarayan Reading of the Book of Chronicles* (London: Equinox, 2008).

as Universal Human Savior, traces his genealogical arc back to Adam through the sons of David who did not sit upon the throne. In both cases, the themes of God's redemptive action in history and Jesus' role in that plan are integral. In both cases, as well, the direct and explicit linkage of Jesus to David is critical. Ironically, it is exactly in Jesus' connection to David where the two genealogies diverge the most sharply.

Genealogies seem specific in their content even if aggregate in focus. They are, in substance, the personal and intimate names of individuals. They record our most intimate and personal moments—birth, death, sexual partnerships, childbirth. Yet, in the end, they are really not about the lives they relate but are instead about narrative arcs, about large scale stories, narratives of another, amalgamated Subjectivity. David must be redeemed from banditry by a genealogy that demonstrates his venerable connections to his tribe. The fiction of a nation of 12 tribes, all descended from Jacob, himself the descendent of Abraham, must be maintained. David's genealogies accomplish this. Early followers of Jesus needed to reinforce claims about his messianic status. They needed to argue that Jesus could fulfill the promise made to David; they needed to demonstrate Jesus' Jewishness, humanity and kinship to David. Each and every necessary name in those genealogies becomes an element within a larger, political and ideological argument, a moment of history-become-memory.

Jesse's ancestry and lineage are themselves complex, and their collection constructs a necessary story arc, as well. In his case, the problems arise from false claimants. As Phillip W. Steele, the James family's official genealogist, explains:

> Legend and folklore have generated within American families a desire for reflected glory, and today it has become quite popular to claim a relationship to the James brothers. The James family home near Kearney, Missouri, has been completely restored and is operated as a major Missouri tourist attraction... Each year hundreds of visitors seek to prove a family connection with the James brothers. Most claims are based on a hapless comment by "grandmother" to the effect that the family is "kin" to Jesse and Frank James. Usually, these grandmothers have conveniently died before elaborating on this claim to their descendents... [O]n at least two occasions, families have even resorted to alleging illegitimacy to validate their claims... It is the desire by so many to establish a family connection with the James that has prompted this writer to pursue their family history.[2]

Jesse's ancestry and lineage are claimed. The hunger for historical authenticity challenges all claims.

---

2. Steele, *Jesse and Frank James*, 16, 19.

Yet these genealogies also betray an agenda. For example, among James aficionados there is a common tendency to disregard for claims of "illegitimate" ancestry, as if Frank and Jesse would murder and steal, drink and carouse, lie and dissemble, but would never, never, never commit adultery or rape. There is a desire to root Jesse within a particular place in history and within a particular set of peoples, but also to assert a "pure" ancestry. This longing for purity betrays a sublimated desire to see Jesse in light of ideology. These connections establish Jesse's political, religious and personal loyalties; they serve as the ground for interpreting his actions.

There are also concerns about "authenticity," as we have seen, that surround the James legend. These concerns arose within James' own lifetime; he and his brother were plagued by the "lies" told about them in fiction and in the news of the day. These concerns, the hunger to "separate fact from fiction," survive Jesse's death. More critically and commercially, there is a financial benefit to being a relative of Jesse James. The family inheritance is the name and its legend, and the value of this name must be maintained by the regular policing of counterfeit claims. Without any sense of irony whatsoever, the family has worked to prevent others from usurping the rights to the name of a known murderer and thief. Like claimants to Jesse's resurrected body, claims to Jesse's lineage must be investigated and controlled. Jesse, like David and Jesus before him, is beset with the problems of a resurrected identity glorified in legend and giving birth to a problematized genealogy.

Genealogy is the construction of narratives of Self, knit patchwork from the lives of the dead. These themes of trauma, legend, resurrection, generation and the construction of new life from the bodies of the dead crystallize in perhaps the most absurd of Jesse James movies, a movie that trades on his name and legend and is steeped in fearful generation.

Resurrection of the Dead, Messianic and Monstrous

[1]The book of the generation of Jesus Christ, the son of David, the son of Abraham. [2]Abraham begat Isaac; and Isaac begat Jacob; and Jacob begat Judas and his brethren; [3]And Judas begat Phares and Zara of Thamar; and Phares begat Esrom; and Esrom begat Aram; [4]And Aram begat Aminadab; and Aminadab begat Naasson; and Naasson begat Salmon; [5]And Salmon begat Booz of Rachab; and Booz begat Obed of Ruth; and Obed begat Jesse; [6]And Jesse begat David the king; and David the king begat Solomon of her *that had been the wife* of Urias; [7]And Solomon begat Roboam; and Roboam begat Abia; and Abia begat Asa; [8]And Asa begat Josaphat; and Josaphat begat Joram; and Joram begat Ozias; [9]And Ozias begat Joatham;

and Joatham begat Achaz; and Achaz begat Ezekias; [10]And Ezekias begat Manasses; and Manasses begat Amon; and Amon begat Josias; [11]And Josias begat Jechonias and his brethren, about the time they were carried away to Babylon: [12]And after they were brought to Babylon, Jechonias begat Salathiel; and Salathiel begat Zorobabel; [13]And Zorobabel begat Abiud; and Abiud begat Eliakim; and Eliakim begat Azor; [14]And Azor begat Sadoc; and Sadoc begat Achim; and Achim begat Eliud; [15]And Eliud begat Eleazar; and Eleazar begat Matthan; and Matthan begat Jacob; [16]And Jacob begat Joseph the husband of Mary, of whom was born Jesus, who is called Christ. [17]So all the generations from Abraham to David *are* fourteen generations; and from David until the carrying away into Babylon *are* fourteen generations; and from the carrying away into Babylon unto Christ *are* fourteen generations. (Matt 1:1–17)

[23]And Jesus himself began to be about thirty years of age, being (as was supposed) the son of Joseph, which was *the son* of Heli, [24]Which was *the son* of Matthat, which was *the son* of Levi, which was *the son* of Melchi, which was *the son* of Janna, which was *the son* of Joseph, [25]Which was *the son* of Mattathias, which was *the son* of Amos, which was *the son* of Naum, which was *the son* of Esli, which was *the son* of Nagge, [26]Which was *the son* of Maath, which was *the son* of Mattathias, which was *the son* of Semei, which was *the son* of Joseph, which was *the son* of Juda, [27]Which was *the son* of Joanna, which was *the son* of Rhesa, which was *the son* of Zorobabel, which was *the son* of Salathiel, which was *the son* of Neri, [28]Which was *the son* of Melchi, which was *the son* of Addi, which was *the son* of Cosam, which was *the son* of Elmodam, which was *the son* of Er, [29]Which was *the son* of Jose, which was *the son* of Eliezer, which was *the son* of Jorim, which was *the son* of Matthat, which was *the son* of Levi, [30]Which was *the son* of Simeon, which was *the son* of Juda, which was *the son* of Joseph, which was *the son* of Jonan, which was *the son* of Eliakim, [31]Which was *the son* of Melea, which was *the son* of Menan, which was *the son* of Mattatha, which was *the son* of Nathan, which was *the son* of David, [32]Which was *the son* of Jesse, which was *the son* of Obed, which was *the son* of Booz, which was *the son* of Salmon, which was *the son* of Naasson, [33]Which was *the son* of Aminadab, which was *the son* of Aram, which was *the son* of Esrom, which was *the son* of Phares, which was *the son* of Juda, [34]Which was *the son* of Jacob, which was *the son* of Isaac, which was *the son* of Abraham, which was *the son* of Thara, which was *the son* of Nachor, [35]Which was *the son* of Saruch, which was *the son* of Ragau, which was *the son* of Phalec, which was *the son* of Heber, which was *the son* of Sala, [36]Which was *the son* of Cainan, which was *the son* of Arphaxad, which was *the son* of Sem, which was *the son* of Noe, which was *the son* of Lamech, [37]Which was *the son* of Mathusala, which was *the son* of Enoch, which was *the son* of Jared, which was *the son* of Maleleel, which was *the son* of Cainan, [38]Which was *the son* of Enos, which was *the son* of Seth, which was *the son* of Adam, which was *the son* of God. (Luke 3:23–38)

Narratives of David, Jesus and Jesse James are narratives that reanimate, resurrect the dead to construct a new narrative, an Agency that teeters on the edges of our control. Of course, the reanimation of the dead in narrative and legend is a moment that can be both hopeful and horrific. These themes mix in the 1966 film *Jesse James Meets Frankenstein's Daughter*. At a time when both the Western and the horror movie genres were waning, *Jesse James Meets Frankenstein's Daughter* had a modest success. In drive-in theaters throughout the country, it was commonly paired with another amalgamation of genres also directed by William Beaudine—*Billy the Kid Versus Dracula*. These two movies anticipate, perhaps, our own strange pairings of Jesus and David with Jesse James.

Jesse James Meets Frankenstein's Daughter is a strange mixture in many ways. The movie opens with villagers loading their possessions into carts during a dark and stormy night. A castle looms above them on a hill. Visually, the movie gestures toward the Europe of the Frankenstein or even the Dracula movie. The villagers, however, are dark-skinned and speak in Spanish-inflected English. Perhaps the movie is set in Mexico or along the Mexican–American border. The mix of locative cues and genre markers leaves the viewer unmoored. Out of the dark and stormy night, a young woman named Juanita runs into one of the houses and her conversation with her parents is the exposition of the plot. Children have gone up to the mansion on the hill to work with a female scientist (another strange combination) and her brother. While there, they have been struck by a terrible fatal and highly contagious disease (or so the villagers have been told…). Juanita's brother is among the dead. Seized by a fear of the disease and some suspicion that all is not as it seems on the hill, the villagers, including Juanita and her family, are evacuating the town.

Juanita is played by a popular Cuban actress—Esterlita Rodriguez, the Cuban Spitfire. As Beaudine tries to breathe new life into tired genres, Rodriguez joined the cast in an attempt to revive her fading career. Rather than the vehicle of her resurrection, however, the movie was her final performance. She died of influenza soon after the film was completed. The movie was the final production of many of its actors. Narda Onyx who plays the mad woman scientist (Frankenstein's granddaughter), Nestor Pieta who plays her brother and Cal Boulder who has the role of Jesse James' sidekick Hank Tracy all never made another film. Even the director William Beaudine, one of the most prolific B-movie directors of all time (350 films), made his last film with *Jesse James Meets Frankenstein's Daughter*. As noted by the DVD commentator Joe Bob Briggs, this is the movie where careers came to die.

The film is shot through with various themes of death and resurrection. Like her grandfather before her, Frankenstein's grand-daughter Maria is intent on bringing the dead back to life. The children who go into the mansion and die are actually the subjects of her experimentations—she kills them and then attempts to animate them once again. Unlike her grandfather who was compelled by the very human desire to unlock the mysteries of life and help people to live forever, the reason for the second Dr. Frankenstein's experiments is so that she can create slaves who are entirely intent on carrying out her will.

Into this unfolding horror scenario steps Jesse James (John Lupton). The film cuts to a dusty street, outside of a bar, where two muscular men are fighting. They are the instruments of a wager between two other men who stand among the on-lookers cheering the fighters on. When one rises victorious, his friend tries to collect the money they won. When the other fellow resists, making excuses about why he should not have to honor the bet, the man in black reveals that he is Jesse James. The name inspires fear—the other turns over the money. The scene reveals that Jesse James and his sidekick Hank Tracy are low on cash. After this incident, they ride to Arizona to join forces with another bandit gang in order to rob a stagecoach. Arizona, it turns out, is the strange Transylvanian–Mexican–American locale of the terrorized village. The two stories are moving toward collision.

For several inexplicable reasons, the stagecoach robbery goes awry. Hank is shot and Jesse escapes with him. Meanwhile, Juanita and her parents have fled their village and are camping in the woods. An Indian ambushes Juanita and tries to kill her, apparently because that is just what Indians do. Jesse James happens to be nearby and runs to Juanita's rescue. Jesse and the injured Hank join Juanita and her family at their camp. Juanita decides that the only doctor who can save Hank is the mad scientist in the castle on the hill. So she returns with the two outlaws to her village and Jesse James knocks on the door of Maria Frankenstein.

All sorts of entanglements ensue: Hank falls in love with Juanita who has already fallen in love with Jesse who loves Juanita but is pursued by Maria who wants to marry him too; Hank is killed by Maria and then brought back to life then almost killed again by Maria's brother who has misgivings about his mad sister's meddling. Hank then becomes Maria's first successful zombie-slave and his first task is to capture Jesse because he rebuffed Maria's advances. In the climactic scene, Hank hits Jesse on the head and knocks him unconscious. Meanwhile, the Marshall who has been pursuing the outlaws ever since the failed robbery enters the castle and finds Jesse unconscious and restrained. Hank attacks the Marshall which gets him temporarily out of the scene. Juanita tries to save Jesse, Maria orders Hank to stop her but he cannot harm Juanita because somewhere in that addled brain of his, he remembers that he loves her. Hank turns on Maria and kills her instead. Hank then still tries to kill Jesse so now Juanita has to come to his rescue, which she does by shooting Hank and killing him. Why no one—not even the famous bandit—had yet thought of simply shooting the monster is still another plot point never made clear. Jesse then inexplicably (a theme in this film) turns himself in to the Marshall and they ride off into the sunset with Juanita waving good-bye to her now incarcerated man.

Jesse James Meets Frankenstein's Daughter may capitalize on the notorious name of the bandit in order to drive up ticket sales, but the character of Jesse James is strangely ineffectual. He is broke and engaging in various gambling wagers to make a little money. Lipton is too old for the part; Jesse seems tired and haggard. The one robbery he attempts is a bust that results in the shooting of his friend. He does trounce the Indian who was threatening Juanita, but otherwise, he is incapable of protecting anyone, including himself. He cannot protect Hank from Maria or Juanita from Hank. Even in terms of his interactions with women, he is more the object of pursuit than the active pursuer. In the end, he is captured by the mad lady-scientist, nearly killed by his side-kick, and saved by his would-be girlfriend. In the Western, the outlaw is often the hero; in the horror movie, the hero kills the monster. In *Jesse James Meets Frankenstein's Daughter*, Jesse James merely looks on while others act on him and around him. Rather than ending in triumph—killing the monster, escaping the law, getting the girl—he turns himself in to the Marshall and ends the movie by meekly riding off to jail. Perhaps the aging, tired, friendless, impotent Jesse of this film, now well-schooled on the potential terrors of resurrection, knows it is time to retire.

Frankenstein's monster is always already a parody of resurrection and a cautionary tale that our thirst for gnosis and power can become hubric. The monster, the only begotten offspring of the would-be-divine Frankenstein, is a hybrid mixture of living and dead. Jesus of Nazareth as Messiah is in many ways the reanimated body of David. Jesus regenerates, reanimates David. Jesse regenerates, reanimates Jesus. Their legends, their oral histories, reanimate and resurrect their mundane "history" as memory. The processes of their various birth-after-death experiences are similar because the tensions, always present in their "histories" are similar.

Conclusion 153

Birth and life after death merge in our fascination and fear of Frankenstein. They are present in our stories of Jesse James, Jesus of Nazareth and David. The spiritual and sacred merge in our fascination and fear of Jesse James, even as the secular and political intrude into the sacred (and literary) biblical world. We have in David, Jesus and Jesse the hunger to maintain our legends—legends provoked by hunger to associate, to connect, to resurrect, to give birth to new manifestations of our hopes. These legends overwhelm our "history." Jesse's lineage is the memory-soaked legend, ever living, fearful, grotesquely alluring, and constant in its cautions that our descriptions of history and reality are, in the end, only a series of names, dates, figures. Living monsters, reanimations of the remains of the dead knit into a new form, these narratives seek their own agency, their own survival and destiny. They lurch beyond our control, risking an almost inevitable moment of harm when their interests conflict with those of others.

Narratives of Lineage

William James, believed to have been born in 1754 in Pembrokeshire, Wales, came to America with his family at an early age. Originally settling lands in Montgomery County, Pennsylvania, he later moved to Virginia... It was there he was married, on July 15, 1774, to Mary Hines... William and Mary had the following children: John James (Born: 1775; Died: 1827; Married: Mary "Polly" Poor, March 26, 1807), Nancy Ann James (Born: February 24, 1777; Married: David Hodges, December 21, 1799), Mary James (Married: Edward Lee, December 22, 1796), William James, Jr. (Born: April 27, 1782; Died: 1807), Richard James (Married: Mary G. Poor, December 18, 1813), Thomas James (Born: December 14, 1783; Married: Mary B. Davis, September 3, 1834), Martin James (Born: 1789; Died: 1867; Married: Elizabeth Key, November 21, 1825).

The lineage of Jesse and Frank James continues with John and Polly Poor James, paternal grandparents to the famous brothers...John James was a farmer and minister.

John and Polly James left Virginia in 1811 and settled lands in Logan County, Kentucky... Their first child was born in Virginia and the rest, as follows, were born in Kentucky: Mary James (Born: September 28, 1809; Died: July 23, 1877; Married: John Mimms, a cousin, 1827), William James (Born: September 11, 1811; Died: November 14, 1895; Married: Mary Ann Varble, December 2, 1843, Mary Ann Gibson Marsh, April 24, 1865), John R. James (Born: February 15, 1815; Died: October 25, 1887; Married: Amanda Polly Williams, September 1, 1836, Emily Bradley, 1872), Elizabeth James (Born: November 25, 1816; Died: November 2, 1904; Married: Tillman Howard West, 1837), Robert Sallee James (Born: July 17, 1818; Died: August 18, 1850, California; Married: Zerelda Cole, Kentucky, December 28, 1841), Nancy Gardner James (Born: September

13, 1821; Died: 1875; Married: George B. Hite, May 7, 1841), Thomas Martin James (Born: April 8, 1823; Died: December 25, 1903; Married: Susan S. Woodward, Goochland County, Virginia), Drury Woodson James (Born: November 14, 1826; Died: July 1, 1910, California; Married: Mary Louisa Dunn, September 15, 1861).

Robert Sallee James married Zerelda Cole in Kentucky on December 18, 1841 and moved to Missouri in 1842. The following children were born to them in Clay County: Alexander Franklin James, 1843; Robert R. James, 1845; Jesse Woodson James, 1847; and Susan Lavenia James (Parmer), 1849. Their son Robert lived only thirty-three days.

On April 24, 1874, Jesse married his first cousin, Zerelda (Zee) Amanda Mimms, at the home of Zee's sister, Lucy Mimms Browder, in Kearney, Missouri. Because Jesse was already a highly sought-after outlaw, the Reverend William James, brother of Jesse's father, tried to discourage the union, but he failed to do so and finally performed the ceremony. A "wanted man," Jesse took Zee to Nashville, Tennessee around 1875, where he hoped they would live in peace under his alias John Davis Howard.[3]

In Chapter 1, we outlined our major concepts for this study, focusing in part on establishing that David, Jesus and Jesse James are all Hobsbawmian Social Bandits. The context and subsequent "afterlives" of each show broad patterns of agreement. We argued that social bandits, martyrs, and messiahs alike participate in various forms of social memory and communal subjectivity. These observations provided the structure for our comparison of David, Jesus and Jesse James. The substance of that comparison—our real reason and intent behind the parallel study of these three figures in triptych—lies in our reading of cultural studies as foundation for the study of communal identity construction and articulation of history.

By engaging Jesse James alongside Jesus and David, we are constructing a comparative study that bridges biblical studies and cultural studies. Cultural Studies is not so much method as it is a deliberate set of inquires (and often juxtapositions) that foreground questions of communal production of "culture," noting how cultural programs, values and artifacts both construct and reflect a community's values, needs and types. It also challenges the reality of binary division between "high" and "low" art and culture, between "scholarly" and "popular" analysis and meaning, between communal and individual experience of culture and all its products. We would continue that it also offers a moment to reflect on

---

3. Taken from Steele, *Jesse and Frank James*, 23–24, 26–29, 31. Close readers of this genealogy of James will note his own discrepancies of record. For example, note the differing dates of marriage for Robert James and Zerelda Cole in this quoted block. December 18 or 28?

and problematize the separation of culture into "profane" or "secular" and "sacred" or "religious" categories. Cultural studies questions these binaries while simultaneously revealing that their initial construction participates in moments of a broader hegemonic struggle, often one that simultaneously arises from both within and without a particular community's boundaries.

In Chapter 2 we explored the figure of David as social bandit and the ways in which this category intertwines with subsequent notions of messiah. The ambivalence surrounding David's complicated persona drove later communities who venerated David (communities derived from David's protest) to gloss over his bandit career. Chronicles is the earliest example of the reshaping of David's character. David is the ideological forerunner of the messianic identity that surrounds Jesus of Nazareth. "Messiah" in the canonical New Testament is unintelligible without a rooting in promises and expectations surrounding David; to understand the canonical Gospels' claims about Jesus as Messiah, one must understand the intervening veneration and idealization of David. And yet, the undercurrent of outlawry is never completely absent. It reemerges in the ways in which David provides a significant foundational "type" for heroic figures found in the modern mythology of the American West. David is ideological forerunner to both the construction of Jesus' messianic status and to various American cultural ideologies, both of which are the ground out of which the legends of Jesse James have grown.

In Chapter 3 we began to explore in more detail the intersection of Jesus and Jesse James. We opted to focus more closely on Jesse James in this chapter (and in Chapter 4) because of our awareness that our audience is largely composed of biblical scholars who will have more training in the narratives and scholarship on Jesus of Nazareth than on Reconstruction-era Missouri or Jesse James. Jesus and Jesse share broad and fundamental elements in their discrete narrative arcs. These broad arcs exist because each figure shares a great deal of geo-social-political context and thus draws from elements of the social bandit type. Each was a popular protest figure, living on the margins of accepted society, supported by locals, betrayed by intimates and executed by the state. There are multiple moments of popular "veneration" surrounding Jesse; there are multiple moments of "criminality" surrounding Jesus. Not only does such comparison then destabilize the categories of legal and illegal, but also the separation between official and popular history, religious and secular spheres. Indeed, both men may have been acting in ways dissident to state authority for motives both ideological and personal.

Chapter 4 explored our need to use the word "may" in the last sentence. To put the matter simply, we really have no idea what either Jesus or Jesse thought or intended. Both Jesus and Jesse have complex biographical narratives that make the actual figures of history difficult to extract. This problem is famously central to scholarship on Jesus of Nazareth, a history of inquiry that we, again, assume our audience of biblical scholars will have encountered (and, so, again focus much of our attention on Jesse James). There are similar broad trends in the quests for the historical Jesus and the historical Jesse James. We explore these trends via analysis of Jesse's subsequent biography. Like Jesus, the reconstruction of any historical Jesse is obscured by the needs and desires of the scholarly and popular communities that engage him. It is critical to note that this does not arise from the antiquity, transmission or obscurity of the data. It also does not arise from the intrusion of devotional or "religious" celebration of Jesus. It arises from the similar intertwining of ideology, memory and communal narrative that forms the substance of the history and biography of each figure. This messy porridge of authenticity, memory, ideology, record, bias and oral history is brewed from the messy motivations of both social bandits and messiahs. History is, we argue, really (dis)utopian etiological myth—it is a story, a narrative that must function to construct communal subjectivity.

In giving up on historical reconstruction we turned in Chapter 5 to examination of cultural and popular celebration. If history is social memory, then how figures are remembered reveals the various needs and desires at play, unveiling the agendas, fears, hopes and desires of the memorial community. In this chapter we return to David and Jesus as they manifest in the stories of Jesse James. Again the foregrounding of Jesse demonstrates that the binary of sacred and profane does not function to designate some objectively real segregation, much like the binaries between history and legend, popular and scholarly are also not objectively "real" but mark instead the location of the observer. Finally, we see that popular culture simultaneously reflects and constructs communal values.

Our inquiry has led us to some general observations. First, messianic figures are also bandits. Bandits, in turn, are both able to be "religious" (better: ideological) figures and, in a way, dynastic. Second, scholarly process and popular reception are equally problematic and potentially fertile. Third and most importantly, all three—David, Jesus and Jesse James—are constructions born of mythic tradition. If the three figures arise from the same crucible, address the same concerns, exhibit the same qualities, encounter the same problems, and function in the same way in later communities, where and how do they, ultimately, differ? The implications of this argument are manifold. To begin, we are left to conclude that history (like myth) is (dis)utopian etiology—an explanation of the current moment with an eye toward the potential inherent in the future. The refinement of history is a process of social memory. This process blends the sacred and the profane, the high and the low, the popular and the professional, the real and the legendary in ways that (re)create figures and narratives to meet communal needs. History lurches forward like a Frankenstein's monster, stitched together from various pieces and parts of texts, narratives, artifacts whose genealogies form complex webs of meaning across cultures, across times.

The problem of Frankenstein's monster is not that humans seek to create life. People frequently make more people via childbirth. The problem is also not a desire to transcend death. Medical science prolongs life and temporarily cheats death every day. And once dead, we memorialize, commemorate, rename, reread and reanimate the essence of the dead in multiple venues of cultural memory and production. The paramount concern, then, is not the monster himself nor is it the hope he might represent. The monster's threat is his ability to elude control, to obtain agency, to seek his own good and define his own self, perhaps at the loss of others. The problem, as well, is the ethical violation of the dead, the desire to reanimate those who may not wish to become the patchwork form of another Agent.

In a similar way, we regard history. The central problem is not that history is composed of bits and pieces of legend, that it is social memory, that it grows in ways that seem to suggest its own agency. The problem is the potential of our patchwork history-monster, reanimated memories and bodies of the dead, acting in ways that distort ethics and bring harm, violating the agency of the dead even as it is unleashing new life that will, in time, seek out its own ends and needs.

BIBLIOGRAPHY

Adam, A. K. M. *What Is Postmodern Biblical Criticism?* Minneapolis: Fortress, 1995.
Adorno, T. W. *The Culture Industry: Selected Essays on Mass Culture*. New York: Routledge, 1991.
Aichele, George. *The Control of Biblical Meaning: Canon as Semiotic Mechanism*. Harrisburg, Pa.: Trinity Press, 2001.
———, ed. *Culture, Entertainment and the Bible*. Journal for the Study of the Old Testament: Supplement Series 309. Sheffield: Sheffield Academic, 2000.
———. *Jesus Framed*. Biblical Limits. New York: Routledge, 1996.
———. *The Limits of Story*. Society of Biblical Literature, Semeia Studies. Chico, Calif.: Scholars Press, 1985.
Aichele, George, and Richard Walsh, eds. *Screening the Scriptures: Intertextual Connections Between Scripture and Film*. Harrisburg, Pa.: Trinity Press International, 2002.
Alter, Robert. *The David Story: A Translation with Commentary of 1 and 2 Samuel*. New York: Norton, 1999.
American Bar Association Presidential Showcase Program. *The Trial of Jesse James—High Tech Meets the Wild West*. Chicago: ABA, 1996.
Appler, Augustus C. *The Younger Brothers*. New York: Fell, 1955. Originally published St. Louis: Eureka, 1876.
Aulen, G. *Jesus in Contemporary Historical Research*. Philadelphia: Fortress, 1976.
Ayers, Edward L. *The Promise of the New South: Life After Reconstruction*. New York: Oxford University Press, 1992.
Bar-Efrat, Shimon. "From History to Story: The Development of the Figure of David in Biblical and Post-Biblical Literature." Pages 47–56 in *For and Against David: Story and History in the Books of Samuel*. Edited by A. Graeme Auld and Erik Eynikel. Leuven: Uitgeverij Peeters, 2010.
Barthes, Roland. *Image–Music–Text*. Trans. Stephen Heath. New York: Hill & Wang, 1977.
Baudrillard, J. *Le Système des objets*. Paris: Gallimard, 1968.
Bauer, Walter. *A Greek–English Lexicon of the New Testament and Other Early Christian Literature*. Edited by W. F. Arndt and F. W. Gingrich. 3d ed. Revised and edited by Frederick William Danker. Chicago: University of Chicago Press, 2000.
Beal, Timothy, and Tod Linafelt, eds. *Mel Gibson's Bible: Religion, Popular Culture, and "The Passion of the Christ."* Chicago: University of Chicago Press, 2006.
Bernal, Misty. *She Said Yes: The Unlikely Martyrdom of Cassie Bernall*. New York: Pocket, 2000.
Bible and Culture Collective. *Postmodern Bible*. New Haven: Yale University Press, 1995.

Biran, Avraham, and Joseph Naveh. "An Aramaic Stele Fragment from Tel Dan." *Israel Exploration Journal* 43, no. 2–3 (1993): 81–98.
———. "The Tel Dan Inscription: A New Fragment." *Israel Exploration Journal* 45, no. 1 (1995): 1–18.
Blok, Alan. *Mafia of a Sicilian Village: A Study of Violent Peasant Entrepreneurs 1860–1960.* Oxford: Blackwell, 1974.
———. "The Peasant and the Brigand: Social Banditry Reconsidered." *Comparative Studies in Society and History* 14 (1972): 495–504
Bloom, Harold, and David Rosenberg. *The Book of J.* New York: Grove Weidenfeld, 1990.
Boer, Roland. *Knockin' on Heaven's Door: The Bible and Popular Culture.* New York: Routledge, 1999.
Bourdieu, Pierre. *The Field of Cultural Production: Essays on Art and Literature.* Cambridge: Polity, 1992.
Bowen, Don R. "Guerrilla War in Western Missouri, 1862–65." *Comparative Studies in History and Society* 19 (1977): 30–51.
Breihan, Carl W. *The Day Jesse James Was Killed.* New York: Fell, 1961.
Britton, Wiley. *The Civil War on the Border.* New York: G. P. Putnam's Sons, 1899.
Brophy, Patrick, ed. *Bushwackers of the Border: The Civil War Period in Western Missouri.* Nevada, Mo.: Vernon County Historical Society, 1980.
Brownlee, Richard S. *Grey Ghosts of the Confederacy: Guerilla Warfare in the West, 1861–1863.* Baton Rouge: Louisiana State University Press, 1958.
Buel, James William. *The Border Bandits.* Baltimore: I. & M. Ottenheimer, n.d.
Bultmann, Rudolf. *History of the Synoptic Tradition.* Translated by John Marsh. Trans. of 5th ed. of *Die Geschichte der synoptischen Tradition.* Peabody, Mass.: Hendrickson, 1963.
———. *Jesus and the Word.* New York: Scribner's, 1934.
Castel, Albert E. *William Clarke Quantrill: His Life and Times.* New York: Fell, 1962.
Castelli, Elizabeth A. *Martyrdom and Memory: Early Christian Culture Making.* Gender, Theory and Religion. New York: Columbia University Press, 2004.
Coleman, Simon, and John Eade, eds. *Reframing Pilgrimage: Cultures in Motion.* New York: Routledge, 2004.
Connelley, William Elsey. *Quantrill and the Border Wars.* New York: Putnam, 1910. Repr. New York: Pageant, 1956.
Crossan, John Dominic. *The Historical Jesus; The Life of a Mediterranean Jewish Peasant.* San Francisco: HarperSanFrancisco, 1991.
———. *Jesus: A Revolutionary Biography.* San Francisco: HarperSanFrancisco, 1993.
Crossan, John Dominic, and Jonathan Reed. *Excavating Jesus: Beneath the Stones, Behind the Texts.* San Francisco: HarperSanFrancisco, 2001.
Culbertson, Philip, and Elaine M. Wainwright, eds. *The Bible in/and Popular Culture: A Creative Encounter.* Semeia 65. Atlanta: Society of Biblical Literature, 2010.
Dacus, Joseph A. *Illustrated Lives and Adventures of Frank and Jesse James and the Younger Brothers, the Noted Western Outlaws.* St. Louis: Thompson & Co., 1882.
Davies, Philip R. "'House of David' Built on Sand: The Sins of the Biblical Maximizers." *Biblical Archaeological Review* 20 (July/August 1994): 54–55.
———. *In Search of "Ancient Israel."* Sheffield: Sheffield Academic, 1992.
Dellinger, Harold, ed. *Jesse James: The Best Writings on the Notorious Outlaw and His Gang.* Guilford, Ct.: Globe Pequot, 2007.

Denning, Michael. *Mechanic Accents*. New York: Verso, 1987.
During, Simon, ed. *The Cultural Studies Reader*. 2d ed. New York: Routledge, 1993.
Edwards, John Newman. *Noted Guerillas, or the Warfare of the Border*. St Louis: Brand & Co., 1877.
———. *Shelby and His Men*. Cincinnati: Miami Printing & Publishing, 1867.
———. *Shelby's Expedition to Mexico*. Kansas City: Kansas City Times, 1872.
Ehrman, Bart D. *The New Testament: An Historical Introduction to the Early Christian Writings*. 3d ed. Oxford: Oxford University Press, 2004.
Exum, J. Cheryl, and Stephen D. Moore, eds. *Biblical Studies/Cultural Studies*. Sheffield: Sheffield Academic, 1998.
Fellman, Michel. *Inside War: The Guerrilla Conflict in Missouri During the Civil War*. New York: Oxford University Press, 1989.
Finkelstein, Israel, and Amihai Mazar. *The Quest for the Historical Israel: Debating Archaeology and the History of Early Israel*. Atlanta: Society of Biblical Literature, 2007.
Finkelstein, Israel, and Neil Asher Silberman. *David and Solomon: In Search of the Bible's Sacred Kings and the Roots of the Western Tradition*. New York: Free Press, 2006.
Fiske, J. *Understanding Popular Culture*. Boston: Unwin Hyman, 1989.
Fredriksen, Paula. *From Jesus to Christ: The Origins of the New Testament Images of Jesus*. New Haven: Yale University Press, 1988.
Freedman, David Noel, and Jeffrey C. Geoghegan. "'House of David' Is There!" *Biblical Archaeology Review* 21 (March/April 1995): 78–79.
Friedman, Richard Elliott. *The Hidden Book in the Bible*. San Francisco: HarperSanFrancisco, 1998.
Frieson, Steven. *Twice Neokoros: Ephesos, Asia and the Cult of the Flavian Imperial Family*. Religions in the Greco-Roman World 116. Leiden: Brill, 1993.
Frow, J. *Cultural Studies and Cultural Value*. Oxford: Clarendon, 1995.
Gilmour, Michael J. *Gods and Guitars: Seeking the Sacred in Post-1960s Popular Music*. New York: Continuum, 2009.
Goodrich, Thomas. *War to the Knife: Bleeding Kansas 1854–1861*. Mechanicsburg, Pa.: Stackpole, 1998.
The Greek New Testament. Edited by Kurt Aland, Matthew Black, Carlo Martini, Bruce M. Metzger and Allen Wikgren. 4th ed. London: United Bible Societies, 1992.
Grey, Zane. *Riders of the Purple Sage*. San Francisco: HarperCollins, 1992.
———. *The Vanishing American*. New York: Pocket, 1982.
Grossberg, L., C. Nelson and P. Treichler, eds. *Cultural Studies*. New York: Routledge, 1992.
Halbwach, Maurice. *Les cadres sociaux de la mémoire*. Paris: Libráirie Félix Alcan, 1925.
———. *La mémoire collective*. 2d ed. Paris: Presses Universitaires de France, 1968.
———. *La topographie légendaire des évangiles en terne sainte: Étude de mémoire collective*. Paris: Presses Universitaires de France, 1941.
Halpern, Baruch. *David's Secret Demons: Messiah, Murderer, Traitor, King*. Grand Rapids: Eerdmans, 2001.
———. "Erasing History: The Minimalist Assault on Ancient Israel." *Bible Review* 11, no. 6 (1995): 26–47.

Bibliography

Hansen, Ron. *The Assassination of Jesse James by the Coward Robert Howard.* New York: Knopf, 1983. Repr. New York: Norton, 1990. Repr. New York: Harper Perennial, 1997. Reissued 2007.

Hengel, Marin. *Crucifixion.* Grand Rapids: Eerdmans, 1977.

Hobsbawm, Eric J. *Bandits.* New York: Harmondsworth, 1985. Rev. New York: New Press, 2000.

———. *Primitive Rebels: Studies in Archaic Forms of Social Movements in the 19th and 20th Centuries.* New York: Norton, 1965.

———. "Social Bandits: A Reply." *Comparative Studies in Society and History* 14, no. 4 (1972): 494–505.

Hoggart, Richard. *The Uses of Literacy.* San Francisco: Penguin, 1957.

Horsley, Richard A. *Archaeology, History and Society in Galilee: The Social Context of Jesus and the Rabbis.* Harrisburg, Pa.: Trinity Press, 1996.

———. *Galilee: History, Politics, People.* Valley Forge, Pa.: Trinity Press International, 1995.

———. *Hearing the Whole Story: The Politics of Plot in Mark's Gospel.* Louisville: Westminster John Knox, 2001.

———. *Jesus and the Spiral of Violence: Popular Jewish Resistance in Roman Palestine.* Minneapolis: Fortress, 1987.

———. *Jesus in Context. Power, People and Performance.* Minneapolis: Fortress, 2008.

Horsley, Richard A., and John S. Hanson. *Bandits, Prophets, and Messiahs: Popular Movements in the Time of Jesus.* New Voices in Biblical Studies. New York: Winston, 1985.

Jackson, Cathy M. "The Making of an American Outlaw Hero: Jesse James and the late 19th Century Print Media." Ph.D. diss. University of Missouri, Columbia, 2004.

James, Jesse Edwards. *Jesse James, My Father.* Independence, Mo.: Sentinel, 1899.

James, Stella F. *In the Shadow of Jesse James.* Thousand Oaks, Calif.: Dragon, 1990.

Johnson, Luke Timothy. *The Real Jesus: The Misguided Quest for the Historical Jesus and the Truth of the Traditional Gospels.* San Francisco: HarperSanFrancisco, 1996.

Käsemann, Ernst. *Essays on New Testament Themes.* London: SCM, 1964.

Keener, Craig. *The Historical Jesus of the Gospels.* Grand Rapids: Eerdmans, 2009.

Kelso, Julie. *O Mother, Where Art Thou? An Irigarayan Reading of the Book of Chronicles.* London: Equinox, 2008.

Kirsch, Jonathan. *King David: The Real Life of the Man Who Ruled Israel.* New York: Ballantine, 2000.

Kloppenborg, John S. *Excavating Q: The History and Setting of the Sayings Gospel.* Edinburgh: T. & T. Clark, 2000.

Knight, Arthur Winfield. "Wanted," Pages 63–64 in Dellinger, ed., *Jesse James.*

Koosed, Jennifer L. *Gleaning Ruth: A Biblical Heroine and Her Afterlives.* Studies on Personalities of the Old Testament. Columbia: University of South Carolina Press, 2011.

———. "Nine Reflections on the Book: Poststructuralism and the Hebrew Bible." *Religion Compass* 2 (2008): 499–512. Online: http://religion-compass.com/.

Lemche, Niels Peter. "Habiru, Hapiru." Pages 3:6–10 in *The Anchor Bible Dictionary.* Edited by David N. Freedman et al. 6 vols. New York: Doubleday, 1992.

Leslie, Edward E. *The Devil Knows How to Ride: The True Story of William Clarke Quantrill and His Confederate Raiders.* New York: Random House, 1996.

Markus, R. A. "How on Earth Could Places Become Holy? Origins of the Christian Idea of Holy Places." *Journal of Early Christian Studies* 2 (1994): 257–71.

McCarter, P. Kyle. "The Apology of David." *Journal of Biblical Literature* 99 (1980): 489–504.

McGrath, A. E. *The Making of Modern German Christology*. Oxford: Blackwell, 1986.

McKenzie, Steven L. *King David: A Biography*. New York: Oxford University Press, 2000.

Meier, John P. *A Marginal Jew*. 3 vols. New York: Doubleday, 1991, 1994, 2001.

Monaghan, Jay. *The Civil War on the Western Border*. Boston: Little & Brown, 1958.

Moore, Stephen D. *Poststructuralism and the New Testament: Derrida and Foucault at the Foot of the Cross*. Minneapolis: Fortress, 1994.

Moore, Stephen D., and Yvonne Sherwood. *The Invention of the Biblical Scholar: A Critical Manifesto*. Minneapolis: Fortress, 2011.

Myers, Ched. *Binding the Strong Man: A Political Reading of Mark's Story of Jesus*. Maryknoll, N.Y.: Orbis Books, 1997.

Notermans, Catrien. "The Power of the Less Powerful: Making Memory on a Pilgrimage to Lourdes." Pages 181–93 in *Powers: Religion as a Social and Spiritual Force*. Edited by Meerten B. ter Borg and Jan Willem van Henten. New York: Fordham University Press, 2010.

O'Malley, Pat. "The Suppression of Banditry: Train Robbers in the US Border States and Bushrangers in Australia." *Crime and Social Justice* 16 (1981): 32–39.

Pals, D. *The Victorian "Lives" of Jesus*. San Antonio, Tex.: Trinity University, 1982.

Parrish, William E. *Missouri Under Radical Rule, 1865–1870*. Columbia: University of Missouri Press, 1965.

Pinsky, Robert. *The Life of David*. New York: Schocken, 2005.

Price, S. R. F. *Rituals and Power: The Roman Imperial Cult in Asia Minor*. Cambridge: Cambridge University Press, 1987.

Read, Opie. *Mark Twain and I*. Chicago: Reilly & Lee, 1940.

Reinhartz, Adele. *Jesus of Hollywood*. New York: Oxford University Press, 2007.

Robinson, James M. *The New Quest for the Historical Jesus*. New York: Macmillan, 1968.

Runions, Erin. *How Hysterical: Identification and Resistance in the Bible and Film*. New York: Palgrave, 2003.

Sanders, E. P. *The Historical Figure of Jesus*. London: Allen Lane/Penguin, 1993.

———. *Jesus and Judaism*. Philadelphia: Fortress, 1985.

Sawyer, John F. A., ed. *The Blackwell Companion to the Bible and Culture*. New York: Blackwell, 2006.

Schramm, Kathrina. "Coming Home to the Motherland: Pilgrimage Tourism in Ghana." Pages 133–49 in *Reframing Pilgrimage: Cultures in Motion*. Edited by Simon Coleman and John Eade. New York: Routledge, 2004.

Schüssler-Fiorenza, Elisabeth. *In Memory of Her: A Feminist Theological Reconstruction of Christian Origins*. New York: Crossroad, 1984.

Schweitzer, Albert. *The Quest for the Historical Jesus*. New York: Macmillan, 1973.

Seesengood, Robert Paul, and Jennifer L. Koosed. "Crossing Outlaws: The Lives and Legends of Jesus of Nazareth and Jesse James." Pages 361–71 in *Sacred Tropes: Tanach, New Testament and Qur'an as Literary Works*. Edited by Roberta Sterman Sabbath. New York: Brill, 2009.

Settle, William A., Jr. "The James Boys and Missouri Politics." *Missouri Historical Review* 36 (July 1942): 412–29.

———. *Jesse James was his Name: Or, Fact and Fiction Concerning the Careers of the Notorious James Brothers of Missouri*. Lincoln: University of Nebraska Press, 1966.

Shaw, Brent. "Bandits in the Roman Empire." *Past and Present* 105 (1984): 3–52.

Sherwood, Yvonne, and Kevin Hart, eds. *Derrida and Religion: Other Testaments (Reading a Page of Scripture with a Little Help from Derrida)*. New York: Palgrave Macmillan, 2004.

Snell, Joseph. "Editor's Introduction." Pages ix–xix of *The Life, Times and Treacherous Death of Jesse James*. By Frank Triplett. Stamford, Ct.: Longmeadow, 1970.

Steckmesser, Kent L. "Robin Hood and the American Outlaw." *Journal of American Folklore* 79 (1966): 348–55.

Steele, Philip W. *Jesse and Frank James: The Family History*. Gretna, Calif.: Pelican, 1987.

Stegemann, Wolfgang, Bruce J. Malina and Gerd Theissen, eds. *The Social Setting of Jesus and the Gospels*. Minneapolis: Fortress, 2002.

Stiles, J. T. *Jesse James: Last Rebel of the Civil War*. New York: Knopf, 2002.

Stone, Anne C., James E. Starrs and Mark Stoneking. "Mitochondrial DNA Analysis of the Presumptive Remains of Jesse James." *Journal of Forensic Sciences* 46, no. 1 (2001): 173–76.

Theissen, Gerd. *The Gospels in Context: Social and Political History in the Synoptic Tradition*. Minneapolis: Fortress, 1987.

Thelen, David. *Paths of Resistance: Tradition & Dignity in Industrializing Missouri*. New York: Oxford University Press, 1986.

Thompson, Thomas. *The Bible in History: How Writers Create a Past*. London: Cape, 1999.

———. *The Messiah Myth: The Near Eastern Roots of Jesus and David*. New York: Basic, 2005.

———. *The Mythic Past: Biblical Archaeology and the Myth of Israel*. New York: Basic, 2000.

Thurman, Eric. "Looking for a Few Good Men: Mark and Masculinity." Pages 137–61 in *New Testament Masculinities*. Edited by Stephen D. Moore and Janice Capel Anderson. Semeia Studies 45. Atlanta: Society of Biblical Literature Press, 2004.

Tompkins, Jane. *West of Everything: The Inner Life of Westerns*. New York: Oxford University Press, 1992.

Triplett, Frank. *The Life, Times and Treacherous Death of Jesse James*. Repr. 1970. Stamford, Ct.: Longmeadow, 1882.

Tsafrir, Yoram. "Byzantine Jerusalem: The Configuration of a Christian City." Pages 133–50 in *Jerusalem: Its Sanctity and Centrality to Judaism, Christianity, and Islam*. Edited by Lee I. Levine. New York: Continuum, 1999.

Tuckett, Christopher M. *Q and the History of Early Christianity: Studies on Q*. Edinburgh: T. & T. Clark, 1996.

Vermes, Geza. *Jesus in His Jewish Context*. Minneapolis: Fortress, 2002.

———. *Jesus the Jew*. London: Collins, 1973.

White, Richard. "Outlaw Gangs of the Middle American Border: American social Bandits." *Western Historical Quarterly* 12, no. 4 (1981): 387–408.

Whybrow, Robert J. "From the Pen of a Noble Robber: The Letters of Jesse Woodson James, 1847–1882." *Brand Book* 24, no. 2 (1987): 22–34.

———. "'Ravenous Monsters of Society': The Early Exploits of the James Gang." *Brand Book* 27, no. 2 (1990): 1–24

Witherington III, Ben. *The Jesus Quest: The Third Search for the Jew of Nazareth.* 2d ed. Downer's Grove, Ill.: InterVarsity, 1997.

Yeatman, Ted P. *Frank and Jesse James: The Story Behind the Legend.* Naperville, Ill.: Cumberland House, 2000.

Younger, Thomas Coleman. "Real Facts About the Northfield, Minnesota, Bank Robbery." Pages 125–47 in *Convict Life at the Minnesota State Prison, Stillwater, Minnesota.* Edited by William Caspar Heilbron. 2d ed. St Paul, Minn.: Heilbron, 1909.

Webography

Patee House Museum: www.ponyexpressjessejames.com
St. Joseph Missouri: www.stjomo.com
www.americascave.org
www.ci.ct-josept.mo.us/history/jessejames.cfm
www.crimelibrary.com
www.frontline.org
www.hiwaay.net/~dbennett/places.html
www.imbd.com/title/tt04436801
www.islandnet.com/~thegang/
www.jessejames.org
www.jessejamesintexas.com
www.roadsideamerica.com/attract/MOSTAjesse.html
www.rootswebb.com
www.theoutlaws.com
www.umsystem.edu/whmc/invent/3896.html

INDEXES

INDEX OF REFERENCES

HEBREW BIBLE/		
OLD TESTAMENT		
Genesis		
3		142
3.15		143
Leviticus		
19.18		56
19.34		56
Ruth		
4.13		145
4.17–22		145
1 Samuel		
9		22
10		22
11		22
16.14–23		22
17		22
19.1		46
19.11		46
19.12		22
21.3		46
21.7		46
21.10		46
21.14		46
22.1–2		46
23		48
23.5–6		48
23.12		48
23.14		47
23.24		47
24.1		47
25		48
25.7–8		48
25.23–31		48
25.23–24		48
25.40–42		48
27.2		48
27.9–11		49
28.1–2		49
29		49
29.33		49
31		22
2 Samuel		
2.4		22
5.1–5		22
7.11–16		43
8.3		43
11		44
1 Chronicles		
2.1–16		145
Psalms		
23		57, 58, 138
23.6		57
41		138
55.12–24		139
121		55, 58
Isaiah		
11.1–5		43
11.4		57
11.5		58
NEW TESTAMENT		
Matthew		
1		146
1.1–19		149
1.6		43
2.16–18		76
19.19		56
21		78
21.12–16		79
21.12–13		77
22.39		56
26.14–16		76
26.54		78
26.55		80
27.11		80
27.29		80
27.37		80
27.57–61		114
27.62–65		114
28.2–5		119
28.9–10		119
28.16–19		119
Mark		
3.22–27		83
4.14		78
4.41		78
5.1–20		77
6.6		78
6.51–52		78
8.17–21		78
8.27–32		78
9.17–29		78
9.32–34		78
10.24		78
10.37–45		78
11.15–19		79
11.15–17		77
11.27–32		78
12.31		56
13.3		78
14.41–46		76
14.47		78
14.48		80
15.2		80

166   *Index of References*

Mark (cont.)
15.9	80
15.12	80
15.18	80
15.26	80
15.42–47	114
15.44	114
16.1	136
16.4–5	118
16.8	118
16.9–20	118

Luke
1.1–4	97
3	146
3.23–38	149
3.31	43
6.15	78
7.16	77
9.54	78
10.27	56
19.45–58	79
20	78
22	78
22.3–6	76
22.50	78
22.52	80
23.3	80
23.37–38	80
23.50–56	114
23.56-n–24.1	136
24.1–6	119
24.10	119
24.12	119
24.13–53	119

John
2.13–16	77, 79
4	55
4.10	55
6.14–15	83
6.15	78
11	136
13.2	76
18.10	78
19.3	80
19.19–21	80
19.38–42	114
20.1–18	119
20.19–29	119
20.30–31	97
21.1–24	119
21.24–25	97

Acts
| 1.16–19 | 76 |
| 17.24 | 122 |

1 Corinthians
| 15.5–8 | 118 |

Revelation
| 1.15 | 139 |
| 6:8 | 58 |

INDEX OF AUTHORS

Adam, A. K. M. 14
Adorno, T. W. 16
Aichele, G. 14, 17, 19, 83
Alter, R. 46
Appler, A. C. 100
Aulen, G. 105
Ayers, E. L. 27

Bar-Efrat, S. 45, 46
Barthes, R. 59
Baudrillard, J. 16
Bauer, W. 80
Beal, T. 17
Bernal, M. 38
Biran, A. 45
Blok, A. 30
Bloom, H. 43
Boer, R. 17
Bourdieu, P. 16
Bowen, D. R. 27
Britton, W. 26
Brophy, P. 26
Brownlee, R. S. 27
Buel, J. W. 100
Bultmann, R. 97, 105

Castel, A. E. 27
Castelli, E. A. 36, 37
Coleman, S. 124
Connelley, W. E. 27
Crossan, J. D. 80, 98, 108
Culbertson, P. 14, 17

Dacus, J. A. 100
Davies, P. R. 42, 45
Dellinger, H. 122, 133, 134, 143, 144
Denning, M. 96
During, S. 16

Eade, J. 124
Edwards, J. N. 64

Ehrman, B. D. 80
Exum, J. C. 14

Fellman, M. 27
Finkelstein, I. 22, 23, 44, 45, 47, 50, 51, 59
Fiske, J. 16
Fredriksen, P. 108
Freedman, D. N. 45
Friedman, R. E. 43
Frieson, S. 77
Frow, J. 16

Geoghegan, J. C. 45
Gilmour, M. J. 17
Goodrich, T. 25, 26, 90
Grey, Z. 54, 55, 57–59
Grossberg, L. 16

Halbwach, M. 36
Halpern, B. 44, 45, 49, 51–53
Hansen, R. 10, 134–42
Hart, K. 14
Hengel, M. 80
Hobsbawm, E. J. 29–34, 39, 46–49, 53, 67, 90, 94, 95
Hoggart, R. 16
Horsley, R. A. 23, 24, 29, 79–83, 108

Jackson, C. M. 88, 92, 96
James, J. E. 101
James, S. F. 101
Johnson, L. T. 108

Käsemann, E. 105
Keener, C. 105
Kelso, J. 146
Kirsch, J. 43, 46, 48
Kloppenborg, J. S. 97
Knight, A. W. 94
Koosed, J. L. 14, 61

Lemche, N. P. 50
Leslie, E. E. 27
Linafelt, T. 17

Malina, B. J. 108
Markus, R. A. 123
Mazar, A. 45
McCarter, P. K. 52
McGrath, A. E. 105
McKenzie, S. L. 48
Meier, J. P. 98, 108
Monaghan, J. 26
Moore, S. D. 14, 44
Myers, C.

Naveh, J. 45
Nelson, C. 16
Notermans, C. 125

O'Malley, P. 29, 30

Pals, D. 105
Parrish, W. E. 27
Price, S. R. F. 77

Read, O. 3
Reed, J. 98
Reinhartz, A. 17
Robinson, J. M. 105
Rosenberg, D. 43
Runions, E. 17

Sanders, E. P. 80, 108
Sawyer, J. F. A. 17
Schramm, K. 124
Schüssler-Fiorenza, E. 108
Schweitzer, A. 80, 97, 104
Seesengood, R. P. 61

Settle, W. A., Jr. 71, 84–86, 89, 91, 92, 104, 115–17, 127
Shaw, B. 29
Sherwood, Y. 14, 44
Silberman, N. A. 22, 23, 44, 45, 47, 50, 51, 59
Snell, J. 100, 102, 103, 120
Starrs, J. E. 4
Steckmesser, K. L. 30
Steele, P. W. 121, 147, 154
Stegemann, W. 108
Stiles, J. T. 30, 92, 93, 106, 107, 115, 126
Stone, A. C. 4
Stoneking, M. 4

Theissen, G. 108
Thelen, D. 66, 67, 92
Thompson, T. 43, 53
Thurman, E. 29, 77, 83, 84
Tompkins, J. 16, 54–56, 59, 60
Treichler, P. 16
Triplett, F. 5, 6, 61, 62, 70–72, 93, 100–102, 115, 130
Tsafrir, Y. 124, 129
Tuckett, C. M. 97

Vermes, G. 108

Wainwright, E. M. 14, 17
Walsh, R. 14
White, R. 30, 95
Whybrow, R. J. 88, 92, 95
Witherington, B. 105, 108

Yeatman, T. P. 3, 5, 6, 27, 65, 69, 70, 72, 88, 89, 91, 95, 117, 128, 130, 132
Younger, T. C. 65